CANADA

Alert Bay ⑬
Vancouver Island

UNITED STATES

Los Angeles ⑭

MEXICO

# Being Ourselves for You:
## the global
## display of cultures

① Jakarta: *Taman Mini Indonesia Indah*

② Agats, Irian Jaya: *Asmat Museum and Cultural Centre*

③ Damai Beach, Sarawak: *Sarawak Cultural Village*

④ Shenzhen Bay, China: *Splendid China, China Folk Culture Villages and Window of the World*

⑤ Ping Tung, Taiwan: *Taiwan Aboriginal Cultural Park*

⑥ Central Taiwan: *Formosan Aboriginal Cultural Village (Nantou County); Taiwan Folk Village (Changhua)*

⑦ Nagasaki: *Huis ten Bosch*

⑧ Honiara, Solomon Islands: *Solomon Island National Museum and Cultural Centre*

⑨ Port Vila, Vanuatu: *Vanuatu Cultural Centre and Museum*

⑩ Tanna Island, Vanuatu: *Port Resolution and Yakel Village*

⑪ Viti Levu, Fiji: *Orchid Island; Pacific Harbour Culture Centre*

⑫ Laie, Oahu, Hawaii: *Polynesian Cultural Center*

⑬ Alert Bay, British Columbia: *U'mista Cultural Centre*

⑭ Buena Park, Los Angeles: *Knott's Berry Farm*

FRENCH
POLYNESIA

PITCAIRN
ISLANDS

*South Pacific Ocean*

## SCHOOL OF
## MANAGEMENT STUDIES

### University of Surrey

Nick Stanley

MATERIAL CULTURE SERIES

# Being Ourselves for You:
## the global display of cultures

Middlesex University Press

Published in 1998 by
Middlesex University Press

Middlesex University Press is an
imprint of Middlesex University
Services Limited, Bounds Green
Road, London N11 2NQ

A CIP catalogue record for this book
is available from The British Library

ISBN 1 898253 16 1

Design and production by
Eugenie Dodd Typographics, London

Series produced in association with
Book Production Consultants plc,
25–27 High Street, Chesterton,
Cambridge CB4 1ND, UK

Photographs by Nick Stanley

Map by Sally Moore

Typeset in Photina and Frutiger

Printed in Great Britain by
Bell & Bain Limited, Glasgow

# Contents

# Acknowledgements

I owe a myriad of intellectual debts and deep personal gratitude for the kindness and friendship extended me throughout the period of researching, writing and revising this book. Many individuals have put aside large amounts of time and made numerous arrangements to provide me with the best possible conditions to pursue my study. For this assistance I am most grateful. This should not, of course, be taken as implying that my hosts are in any manner implicated in the errors that occur in this text. These are mine alone. Nor are those cited necessarily in agreement with my analyses or conclusions. In certain cases I am aware that my opinion is not shared, although I have discussed our differing stances whenever I have been able.

I should also like to thank especially those who have read through and commented on drafts of my complete text: Tim Putnam, my editor at Middlesex University Press, Mike Hitchcock, Helga Loeb and Sarat Maharaj. I am also grateful to Jenny Hewings for her constant assistance in organising travel, and maintaining my correspondence in good order.

I thank for their advice on Chapter 1, Gunnar Elfström of Gamla Linköping, Lee Harvey at University of Central England and Jane Kuenz of Georgia State University.

For Chapter 2 on tourism in Fiji, Michael Quinnell, Department of Anthropology, Queensland Museum, Brisbane. At the University of Hawai'i, Manoa, Robert Kiste, Director of the Center for Pacific Islands Studies (and for his generous hospitality), Mara Rosenthal, East–West Center (Pacific Islands Development Program), Murray Chapman, Department of Geography, Deborah B. Waite, Department of Art (and for her comments on my draft) and Geoff White, East–West Center (and for his comments on my draft). At Brigham Young University-Hawai'i, Jon Jonassen, School of Social Science (and for his comments on my draft), I. Rene Yang, Management Information, Dale Robertson, Editor of Pacific Studies, Vernice Wineera, Director of Institute of Polynesian Studies, Max Stanton, Department of Anthropology, and at the Polynesian Cultural Center, John Muaina, Senior Vice

President, Human Resources, Longo Apolo-Leilua, Director of Cultural Training, Roger Epping, Costume Designer.

On Taman Mini Indonesia Indah, Jakarta, Mike Hitchcock, Centre for Leisure and Tourism Studies, University of North London, Kaes van den Meiracker, Museum voor Volkenkunde, Rotterdam, E. Gunawi Sp, Jogjakarta, M. Winarko, Taman Mini.

On Chinese style tourism at the Shenzhen Parks, Siu King Chung, School of Design, Hong Kong Polytechnic University, Wong Shiu-Wah, School of Design, Hong Kong Polytechnic University, Ma Chi Man, former Director, Chinese Folk Culture Villages, Shenzhen, Jigang Bao, Centre for Urban and Regional Studies, Zhongshan University, Guangzhou.

In Taiwan, Chiung-Huei Chang, Taipei, Eric H. Y. Yu, Secretary General, Shung Ye Museum of Formosan Aborigines, Peter L. M. Pan, Manager, Shung Ye Group, Perng-Juh Shyong, Curator, Shung Ye Museum, Allen Chun (and for his comments on my draft), Bien Chiang, Hu Tai-Li, Ho Tsui-ping, Hsu Cheng-kuang, Ch'en Mau-thai, all of the Institute of Ethnology, Academia Sinica, and elsewhere, Margaret Byrne Swain, Dept of Anthropology, University of California, Davis, Steve Smith, Dept of History, University of Essex, and Matthew Turner, Department of Design, Napier University, Edinburgh.

For Chapter 3: Romain Batick, former Minister of Education, Vanuatu, Port Vila, Lissant Bolton, Australian National University, Canberra (and for her comments on my draft), Peter Burns, University of Luton (and for his comments on my draft), Don Boykin, Pacific Architects, Honiara, Lawrence Foanaota (Director) (and for his comments on my draft), and Castro Teahanu (National Cultural Centre) at Solomon Islands National Museum, Honiara, Kirk Huffman, former director of Vanuatu Cultural Centre, Port Vila (and for his comments on my draft), Mrs F. Kona, War Museum, Vilu, Guadalcanal, Chief Noel Mariasua, President of the Malvatumauri, Port Vila, Grace Mera Molisa, Port Vila, Ralph Regenvanu, Director, (and for his comments on my draft), Jean Tarisesei and Jacob Sam at Vanuatu Museum and Cultural Centre, Port Vila, Kenneth Roga, Western Province Cultural Centre, Gizo, Victor Totu, Gaudalcanal Cultural Centre, Honiara, Mali Voi, UNESCO Office for the Pacific States, Apia (and for his comments on my draft), and Sidney Moko Mead, Victoria University, Wellington.

For Chapter 4: Pat Cooke, Curator of the Pearse Museum and Kilmainham Gaol, Dublin (and for his comments on my draft), Micheal de Mòrdha, Manager, The

Blasket Centre, Dún Chaoin, Kieran O'Connor, Architects' Department and Jim Blye, Information Office, both at the Office of Public Works, Dublin, Peter Walker, Manager, The Big Pit, Bleanafon (and for his comments on my draft).

For Chapter 5: Bill Cranmer, Chairman, The U'mista Cultural Centre, Alert Bay, British Columbia, Doug Cranmer, Alert Bay, BC, Gloria Cranmer Webster, former curator of The U'msta Cultural Centre, Alert Bay, BC (and for her comments on my draft), Peter Macnair, Keeper of Ethnography, Royal British Columbia Museum, Victoria, BC, Joy Hendry, Oxford Brookes University, Oxford (and for her comments on my draft), and Stephen D. Smith of Beth Shalom Holocaust Memorial Centre, Newark.

I apologise to those whom I may have inadvertently forgotten.

Earlier versions of material in these chapters have appeared in the following forms:

'Old collections and new connections: innovations in the South Pacific' in K. Schofield (ed.) *Connections and Collections: Museums, Galleries and Education, London*, London University, Institute of Education, 1997.

'The new indigènes: Culture, Politics and Representation', *Journal of Art & Design Education*, 1997, 16:3.

(with Siu, King Chung) 'ZaiXian ZhongGuoWenHua: Shenzhen Zhong-GuoMinsuWenHuaCun ShuPing ['(Re)presenting Chinese culture: a discourse on the Shenzhen Chinese Folk Culture Villages'] in Stephen C K Chan *ShenFenRenTong Yu GongGongKongJian: WenHuaYanJin LunWenJi [Identity and Public Culture: Critical Essays in Cultural Studies]*, Hong Kong, Oxford University Press (China) Ltd,1997.

(with M Hitchcock and Siu, King Chung) 'On the South-East Asian "Living Museum" and its Antecedents' in Simone Abram, Jacqueline Waldren and Donald Macleod *Tourists and Tourism: Identifying with People and Places*, Oxford, Berg Publications, 1997.

'Chinese theme parks and national identity' in R. Riley and T. Young (eds.) *The Landscapes of Theme Parks: Antecedents and Variations*, Studies in Landscape Architecture, Cambridge, Harvard University Press, 1998.

# Dedication

for Karl, Jane, King and Sarat

# Preface

Museum, Chicago

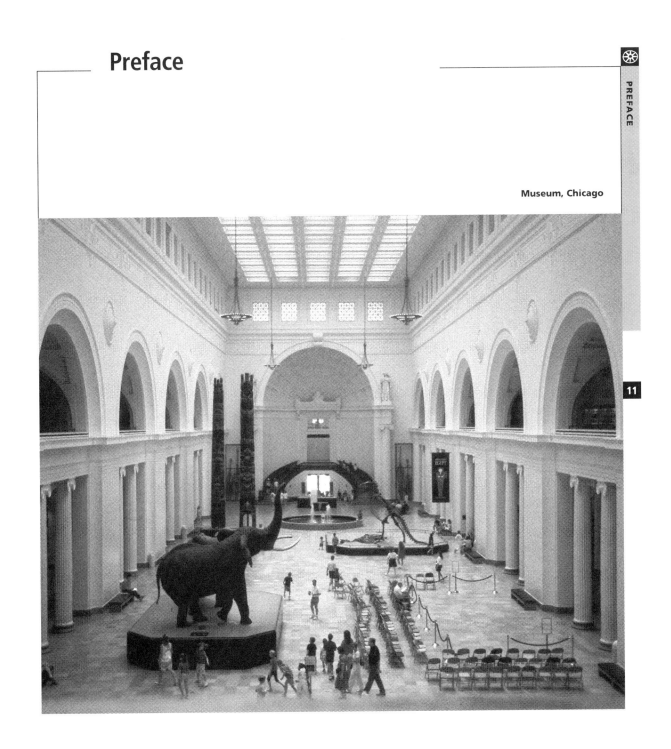

## Cultural performance and the spectacularisation of culture

Most studies of tourism deal with the tourist's experience.[1] This study concentrates on the other part of the equation – the providers of the experience, and in particular it considers the strategies that performers adopt to make themselves the content of tourist experience. This study seeks to create a general typology of performance related to anthropological and ethnographic approaches employed self-consciously in all cases. This is very much a study of 'anthropology in action'. All of the settings and arrangements analysed here are of ethnographic spectacles staffed by volunteers; that is to say that the people offering themselves for cultural inspection do willingly and usually with some pride. Yet these spectacles are not necessarily easy to typify, account for or evaluate. The first example that I encountered before contemplating this work has left questions unresolved in my mind. These are questions that I have taken into the study proper. Although I now know a considerable amount more contextual detail, the event I first witnessed still perplexes me in terms of how I read and respond to it.

In July 1991 whilst visiting the Field Museum in Chicago to see the newly opened and mildly controversial Regenstein Halls of the Pacific.[2] I was surprised to hear a series of loud sounds coming from the large central hall. I went quickly to the nearest balcony and from there had an excellent view of a performance by a group of lightly clothed performers adorned with beads, shells and feathers and carrying rattles and spears. They were performing a series of dances and songs before a leaf house which served as proscenium, stage set and changing room for each new performance. My interest and puzzlement was such that I became engrossed in the spectacle. I was totally unprepared when, momentarily turning to see who was looking over my shoulder, I discovered that my neighbour in the balcony, similarly intent on the performance, was a member of the troupe, dressed identically to those below. This unexpected conjuncture led me to ask myself what he and I were engaged in and how we came to be in such a singular situation.

The answer was superficially easy to answer. I had, through pure serendipity, stumbled upon the last week's programme of a four week tour by a group of Asmat and Dani performers in major US museums as part of the 1990–91 Festival of Indonesia.[3] The leaflet handed out to visitors explained it all succinctly: 'thirty-five tribespeople from Irian Jaya, Indonesia, the western half of the island of New Guinea will visit Field Museum as part of a cultural friendship tour of the United States to celebrate the 1990–91 Festival of Indonesia'.[4]

[1] The most notable examples I have in mind are, within sociological theory the works of John Urry, in tourism research that of Eric Cohen, and in visual studies the photography of Martin Parr.

[2] see the catalogue by Ron Dorfman (ed.) *Pacific: A Companion to the Regenstein Halls of the Pacific*, Chicago, Field Museum of Natural History, 1991 for an example of a novel approach to displaying culture. This is also developed more extensively in *Field Museum of Natural History Bulletin*, November 1989. For an impressive critique see Roger G. Rose 'Exhibiting the Pacific in American Museums: Review of 'Pacific Spirits: Life, Death and the Supernatural' Field Museum' *Pacific Arts*, 4, 1991, 1–7.

But, how did these thirty-five tribespeople (and how were they so designated?) from two different regions (the Asmat from the Southwest coast, the Dani from Baliem Valley in the Jayawijaya Mountains) become involved in a 'cultural friendship tour' together? The answer evidently involved the Festival of Indonesia, yet why amongst the one hundred million population of Indonesia were these two representative groups accorded such a prominent place in cementing US–Indonesian friendship? The answer may be partly to do with visual representation, and partly the residue of academic research.

Irian Jaya represents as a province, a cultural and geographic entity largely unincorporated in the Indonesian self-image (as I will go on to detail in Chapter 2). The contrast between Melanesian culture and the domestic life of the majority of the population of Indonesia living in the western provinces is sufficiently acute to create in this majority a fascination.[5] This is the fascination that is exploited in the Festival of Indonesia. The Asmat and the Dani occupy significant places in the Indonesian imagination. The Dani are regularly depicted as highland warriors wearing penis sheaths and feather head-dresses. The Asmat have become identified as virtuoso carvers of ceremonial shields and decorated ancestor poles. But who so identified them?

A few Dutch ethnographers and curators were struck by the decorative and sculptural achievements of the Asmat as early as 1830. During the first half of this century a considerable body of literature and visual reference was built up, devoted to Asmat carving.[6] This created an international recognition for Asmat craftsmanship which was employed by both missionaries and the Indonesian government when it acquired Irian Jaya in 1962[7] to promulgate an Asmat Art Project in 1968 in association with the United Nations Development Programme.[8] By 1985 the Asmat Art Project developed into an Indonesian government-sponsored Asmat Progress and Development Foundation with the President of Indonesia's wife, Ibu Tien, as patron.

The Asmat Foundation established a cultural centre and handicraft shop in Agats in Irian Jaya in 1986 and in the same year supplied the exhibits for a new Asmat Museum in a cultural park in Jakarta[10] (discussed in detail in Chapter 2) both established by Ibu Tien. The cultural centre museum at Agats now holds annual carving contest and the winning pieces are sold at auction to dealers from throughout Indonesia.[11] The Foundation also promotes 'travelling exhibits, performances, demonstrations and lectures' such as the one I attended in Chicago.

[3] The four museums were The National Museum of Natural History, The Smithsonian Institution, Washington DC; The American Museum of Natural History, New York; New Orleans Museum of Art; the Field Museum. A small catalogue accompanied the tour written by Tobias Schneebaum entitled The Asmat: *Dynamics of Irian*. Another lavish exhibition was also touring North America at the same time which dealt briefly with a northern Irian Jaya. See Paul M. Taylor and Lorraine V. Aragon *Beyond the Java Sea: Art of Indonesia's Other Islands*, National Museum of Natural History, Smithsonian Institution in association with Harry N. Abrams, New York 1991.

[4] 'Asmat: Dynamics of Irian Jaya at Field Museum. Traditional Dancers and Artisans of Irian Jaya, Indonesia. July 25–August 4, 1991 (leaflet).

The terminology employed to characterise 'otherness' is itself worthy of note. 'Aboriginal', 'fist nation', and 'indigenous' have been used as self-conscious alternatives to the earlier terms 'primitive' and 'savage'. To mark the artifice involved in such appelations I use the term 'indigène' throughout. 'Indigène' leans in two directions – on the one hand, it refers to self-description on behalf of the group under discussion – on the other, it suggests the frame created by the viewer.

[5] Mike Hitchcock provides an interesting case study of Indonesian images of Irian Jaya in his 'Images of an ethnic minority in Indonesia' *Anthropology Today*, 1, 1, 1985, 1–4.

[6] see Dirk A. M. Smidt (ed.) *Asmat Art: Woodcarvings of Southwest New Guinea*, New York, Braziller in association with the Rijksmuseum voor Volkenkunde, Leiden, 1993.

[7] the date of accession is given as 1962 by the Indonesian government, and 1969 by the departing Dutch.

[8] Ignatius Suharno and Bernard Mitaart *Ukiran-Ukiran Kayn, Irian Jaya/The Art of Woodcarving in Irian Jaya*, Jayapura, Regional Government of Irian Jaya, 1977 n.p.

[9] Asmat Progress and Development Foundation Asmat, Jakarta, n.d. (1990?), 33.

[10] Tobias Schneebaum 'Touring Asmat' *Pacific Arts*, 7, 1993, 54.

[11] James Clifford *Routes: Travel and Translation in the Late Twentieth Century*, 165.

The Asmat and Dani may be described as 'stone age people' in domestic Indonesian literature but they have a symbolic importance in Indonesia's claim to cultural pluralism across the whole extent of national territory. The inhabitants of Irian Jaya provide a visual reference which emphasises not so much an illustration of cultural theories of evolution but more a topographic, cultural and ecological challenge to the taken-for-granted certainties of a modern Asian nation. The Asmat and the Dani are not readily assimilable into the self-image of Indonesia. They provide in their very presence, a challenge to all who come to see them on tour.

The final irony of my unexpected meeting was that it should be in, of all places, Chicago, the site of the great Colombian Exposition of 1893, and at the Field Museum, the repository of the fair's anthropological exhibitions. But perhaps there is no real irony involved. The shows put on by the Asmat and Dani in 1991 might not have looked out of place in 1893 in Chicago, Washington or New York. What is different is the political and geographic context within which the show now takes place; what remains stable is the visual image. It is the relationship between the two that remains problematic. It was, perhaps, this recognition that provided food for thought as I glanced at my Asmat neighbour in the Regenstein Hall.

My account of the Asmat and Dani performance up to this point makes a tacit assumption, that they are strangers in Chicago. They are, at best, exotic visitors whose presence is the result of the largesse of some benefactor. Such an assumption is odd in at least two ways. Firstly, one only has to consider the geographic origins of the population in this midwestern capital to recognise that many people from the Pacific already live there. Secondly, Melanesians live with contemporary expectations of the modern world in Irian Jaya as much as anywhere else. In becoming world renowned, group members come to expect to visit the places where their accomplishments are recorded in collections. This represents a form of cultural reciprocity. In Papua New Guinea, on the other side of the political divide of the island of New Guinea, the 141st parallel, the Wahgi people entertained the ethnographer and curator, Michael O'Hanlon during his two year's field work (1979–81) and whilst he was collecting for an exhibition in London held in 1993 (discussed in Chapter 2) they clearly saw themselves as involved in an international relationship. As one commentator has remarked, 'The Wahgi, for example, saw themselves as already in relations with London, albeit indirectly, through the prior visit there of their neighbours, the Mount Hagen dancers. They expected O'Hanlon to organise their own trip'. Similarly, the Asmat Progress and Development Foundation, however circumscribed by political and religious agendas, provides for the Asmat and Dani, on the very basis of the performances, occasions to develop complex relationships with peoples outside Irian Jaya, and beyond Indonesia. To perceive them as passive pawns in nationalist representation is to ignore the dynamic of social transactions involved in setting up such events.

The remaining questions relate to my presence at the spectacle. Why was I there and why was I surprised? My reason for visiting Chicago was to examine how artefacts from the Pacific past were employed in an exhibition of present day Oceania. To meet a group very evidently both contemporary and yet performing in a way redolent of the past (the lack of interpretation or explanation of the performance linked it to prior versions in the same venue a century earlier) risked, I felt, implicating the members of the audience in a range of prior assumptions. Why should people, I wondered, perform in such a manner today? The source of my discomfort was difficult to pin down accurately. At best I could remind myself that cross-cultural comparisons are tricky at the best of times, and required further study both in depth and in detail. The Asmat performance was, in effect, the unanticipated opportunity to provoke a rethink about the whole nature of cultural representation, and especially self-representation.

Recent trends in anthropology have led to a re-examination of much of the epistemological basis for the discipline itself. In particular, with the work of Geertz, attention has been paid to the problematic nature of making cross-culturally valid judgements.[12] Such judgements have been rendered even more insecure by those who remind their peers that their accounts are, at best, literary constructions and follow the rules of literary form more closely than they might care to admit.[13] In an analogous movement, partly influenced by this anthropological critique, a new sensitivity has arisen within museology and especially in the display of culture.[14] And yet neither of these parallel developments has had much impact on the general population in the developed world where, although interest in anthropology has remained continuously high over the past century, this curiosity continues to be satisfied by a range of often decidedly non-academic means. The most popular of these have been anthropological displays in a variety of commercial venues. However, none of these shows has been innocent of anthropological methods nor unsupported by members of the profession. Anthropology has been and continues to be used as a kind of nostrum to give a veneer of respectability to these forms of

[12] in particular I refer to his article 'Being there: whose life is it anyway?' in his *Works and Lives: the Anthropologist as Author*, Oxford, Polity Press, 1988, pp 129–49.

[13] The work of George Marcus is highly significant here. James Clifford and George Marcus *Writing Culture: The Poetics and Politics of Ethnography*, University of California Press, Berkeley, 1986; George E. Marcus and Michael M. J. Fischer *Anthropology as Cultural Critique: An Experimental Moment in the Human Sciences*, University of Chicago Press, 1986.

[14] Among the exponents of this approach Ivan Karp is most noteworthy. See Ivan Karp and Steven D Lavine (eds.) *Exhibiting Cultures: The Poetics and Politics of Museum Display*, Smithsonian Institution Press, Washington DC, 1991. But journals like *The Journal of Museum Ethnography* (UK) and *Museum Anthropology* (US) signify this change.

popular representation but it has also made those attending these exhibitions 'anthropologically knowing'. These spectacles are the subject of this study.

I have employed the title 'Being Ourselves For You' to encapsulate the features that these phenomena share. Firstly, the phrase suggests a self-conscious-ness on the part of performers who by their actions, appearance and description are defined as memorably different from their audience. The most obvious example is to be found in the imperial and colonial expositions from the end of the nineteenth century until 1939. Here colonial subjects would entertain a paying audience in a metropolitan country by simply enacting domestic home life in a 'village'. The ensemble of such villages provided the audience with an image of the heterogeneity of peoples united under imperial rule. These expositions are discussed in Chapter 1 as a major source from which popular representations of culture and otherness were drawn. The title also implies that the actors are engaged in some sort of enter-tainment and seek to appeal to the tastes of the audience. Finally, the title suggests a high degree of truth or realism. The audience is promised 'the genuine article'. This is regularly stressed in a variety of ways. For example, performers' costume provides an example native and pre-industrial manufacture. This reminds the audience that other aspects of appearance and behaviour contribute to the display. Authenticity is not only to be found in the performers but also in their environs. The construction of dwellings on the sites of these Expositions, and at the arguably more commercial World's Fairs, made further claims for the veracity of the spectacle to an original, often in some other part of the globe.

But the phenomena discussed in this work are significantly different from the imperial 'villages' that were constantly reassembled as the exposition moved from one venue to the next like a circus. These are permanent exhibitions. In this respect they are akin to the tradition of Skansen, the first open-air museum of regional architecture in Sweden devoted to preserving the past in physical form. From Skansen derives an interest in cultural preservation in the face of industriali-sation, urbanisation and the development of a modernist culture. This approach James Clifford has described as 'salvage ethnography'[15] in which cultures, prac-tices, and even people are rescued 'before they disappear'. A number of the displays that I will discuss share this justification for their existence.

It might be thought that such phenomena would have disappeared with the demise of imperial rule. In a strict sense they have. There are, of course, no more universal imperial and colonial expositions and World's Fairs have been suitably

[15] in his 'On ethnographic allegory' in Clifford and Marcus *Writing Culture*, p 113.

reformed to extirpate such crude examples of vulgar evolutionism. But this certainly does not mean that the spectacularisation of culture has faded away.[16] What has happened is that it has found some surprising new forms. Some of the ideologies underlying these new displays have been superceded, but the displays have also retained a residue of these earlier forms.

Is the spectacularisation of culture, particularly in some of the more garishly commercial displays, more than a footnote to the history of popular entertainment? The argument of this book is emphatically that it is. It is on the basis and the persistence of such forms that significant new kinds of cultural construction are taking place in many parts of the world. I claim that, if the major contemporary sites of 'Being Ourselves For You' are to be found associated with religious or, more commonly, political and nationalist ideas, there nevertheless remains a set of problems for those who would wish to spectacularise culture for other ends. I offer in Chapter 3 the example of 'Kastom' and its growth in the Pacific to outline this case. Where there are few economically sustainable alternatives to tourism, forms of spectacular cultural display take on a singular importance at the same time as they raise new and daunting problems.

In case it appears that this work is only devoted to tracing such performances 'home' as it were from the imperial show to the ex-colonial venue, two further themes are developed. The first, in Chapter 4, I have entitled 'Beyond the Modern Paradigm'. I argue that some current exhibitions in Western Europe raise the same range of issues about authenticity and the display of culture as considered earlier in the work. The second reason, discussed in Chapter 5, that I suggest the phenomenon described as 'Being Ourselves For You' is worth consideration is that it literally cannot be avoided. Thanks largely to the imagineers of Disney, certain forms of spectacularisation, and particularly those with an anthropological slant, have led to a widespread tendency to approach the world as spectacle. This has a profound implication for views of history and how it is to be conceived as well as, of course, how we look at each other. As a final admonition I offer a couple of architectural examples of where the movement can take any who wish to consider seriously the postmodern potential not yet realised within anthropology proper: the ability to don a culture as readily as clothes.[17]

I should also remind the reader that the topic throughout the work is and remains the very process of spectacularization of culture. As I hope will become apparent, there are some common issues that the various attempts to do this have

[16] Catherine A. Lutz and Jane L. Collins argue that major magazines like National Geographic have an important role in establishing fashions of representing the other. See their *Reading National Geographic*, University of Chicago Press 1993.

[17] Though Erving Goffman's work with its insistence on the significance of performance and the theatrical treatment of culture already offers some interesting challenges as is recognised by such authors as Dean MacCannell. However, there is a further thread to trace back from dramaturgic analysis to politeness theory in the concluding chapter.

had to face as well as a surprisingly similar set of solutions adopted despite some quite different circumstances and settings. This does not, of course, mean that the representations can be treated as pieces of standard anthropological field work (whatever that might be). Those looking for characterisations that they may recognise from their experience in a society represented in any of these parks will be doomed to disappointment, unless, that is, that their experience encompasses spectacular performances. I think that it is partly this desire for strict congruence with personal memory that keeps many anthropologists from visiting and nearly all from crediting what is on offer in ethnographic theme parks. But what such intellectual integrity fails to remark is the anthropological interest that resides in attempts to visualise culture. This work provides no comment on the particular anthropology of the societies discussed nor does it claim specialist knowledge in so many different cultures. I hope, however, that it lays out some of the issues that confront any who wish to go about providing such visual displays of culture and the way that these representations may contribute to the vision that members of a society form of themselves.

# 1

# Why should we look at each other?

## The subjects of ethnography

In his pilgrimage to American theme park entertainment Umberto Eco describes the experience as a journey into hyper-reality. This form of reality is based on a notion of culture familiar to students of the Frankfurt School, a false consciousness, but one which is willingly embraced. What so fascinates Eco is the new form of mixed genre: 'the American imagination demands the real thing and, to attain it, must fabricate the absolute fake; where the boundaries between game and illusion are blurred, the art museum is contaminated by the freak show, and falsehood is enjoyed in a situation of "fullness," of *horror vacui*.'[1] He illustrates the confusion between dissimulation and reality with an example from a popular 'Western' park, Knotts Berry Farm in Buena Vista, California: 'The village school, reconstructed with hyper-realistic detail, has behind the desk a schoolmarm wearing a bonnet and an ample checked skirt, but the children on the benches are little passing visitors, and I heard one tourist asking his wife if the children were real or "fake"'.[2] This picture can be repeated in many other historical reconstructions around the world. The Board School at Beamish Museum in County Durham even offers 'strict discipline and learning by rote',[3] thereby transporting today's children in educational time travel.

Eco's thesis is that it is no longer possible in a postmodern world to be an innocent spectator of entertainment that draws us into enjoyment itself and where the content is no longer important. What Eco and other commentators are proclaiming is the end of history, the fracture of the narrative and the denial of privilege to any single account. What is important in this view of postmodernity is the reference to the world of Disney that either subliminally or explicitly underlies the proposition, which has developed a vocabulary to underline the theatricality of its exhibitions. These are 'illusioneered' by 'imagineers' who indulge in 'whimsification',[4] transforming the landscape into a recognisable version of the cartoons and films. What will become evident in this chapter and throughout the work is the impossibility of excluding 'Disney theory' from any discussion of human display but equally, the partiality and limitation of this approach, however widespread its manifestations are throughout the world. To contradict Eco, there are many significant alternative visions to Disney which do not rely on the knowing playfulness of hyper-reality. Whilst it would be foolish to claim that such examples are 'uncontaminated' by any reference to the world of the 'imagineers', this study explores their vitality, their variability and their implicit rejection of postmodernity in favour of a vision based on the traditions and the methods of classical anthropology.

[1] Umberto Eco *Travels in Hyper-reality* Picador, London 1987, 8.

[2] Eco *Travels in Hyper-reality*, 42

[3] Peter Lewis *Welcome to Beamish* The North of England Open Air Museum, Beamish, County Durham, 1995, n.p.

[4] Alexander Wilson 'Technological Utopias' *South Atlantic Quarterly*, 1993, 93:1 pp 157, 164.

In this study I look at a series of attempts by a variety of people, mainly in South East Asia and the Pacific, to create a visual anthropology which explains to the domestic population, and sometimes to foreign tourists, how the society is constituted and what it looks like.[5] From Indonesia, from China and Taiwan, from Hawai'i and elsewhere in Western and Central Polynesia, from Solomon Islands, Vanuatu and Kanaky (New Caledonia) in Melanesia, and from the North East Pacific (the Kwakiutl people), representations of their inhabitants are currently offered as ethnographic subjects for a variety of reasons, some political, others economic or religious. Among the earlier examples, such as Taman Mini Indonesia in Jakarta, a strong sense of post-colonial nationalism is present. The examples in China also show a more modern and complex ethnic nationalism. These are discussed in the next chapter. The earliest of all these ethnographic parks, the Polynesian Cultural Center, anticipates some of the more self-conscious attempts made in Melanesia in the last decade to question seriously the basis upon which post-colonial societies are constituted.

All of these case studies share some common defining features. Beside a commitment to an anthropological vision, they argue that their representations are based upon indigenous field work. This claim is double-edged. On the one hand it implies that there is a deeper reality that previous anthropology from the colonial era missed, largely because the gap between informant and ethnographer was so deep. But indigenous field work is also proposed as a way of resolving current problems confronting ex-colonial societies. Looking back 'behind' colonialism offers a bridge to reunite and restore the damage done subsequent to the advent of colonialism. But all of these cases also subvert the anthropological project in the rejection of the traditional notion of 'the other'. Augé states the normal proposition clearly: 'the question of the other is not just a theme that anthropology encounters from time to time; it is its sole intellectual object, the basis on which different fields of investigation may be defined.'[6] Modern tourism has, some commentators maintain, only reinforced the intellectual divorce between the anthropologist and his (an explicitly gendered pronoun much explored in contemporary methodological texts in anthropology) object. Anthropologists like tourists, from this perspective, 'objectify those they observe, regarding the other as available for their acquisition and use. In this process, the other, stripped of power and volition, becomes defined to meet Western standards of conceptual unity.'[7]

[5] I follow Marcus Banks and Howard Morphy's usage: 'visual anthropology as we define it becomes the anthropology of visual systems or, more broadly, visible and cultural forms' *Rethinking Visual Anthropology*, 5.

[6] Marc Augé *Non-Places: Introduction to an Anthropology of Supermodernity*, Verso, London, 1995, 18.

[7] Frederick Errington and Deborah Gewertz 'Tourism and anthropology in a postmodern world', *Oceania*, 60, 1989, 38.

Bolton argues that becoming the subject as well as the object of ethnography provides some indigenous people in the South Pacific with a transformed potential.[8] It could be argued that this freedom may extend not only to re-portraying themselves but even, when circumstances are right, to offering a revisionist picture of visitors and former colonial officials.[9] This potentially exciting and risky business represents the ultimate subversion which hides behind smiles in most performances of 'being ourselves for you.'

## Historical precedents for ethnographic representation

It is perhaps somewhat surprising that there has been a renaissance in ethnographic representation in the last two decades, particularly since there persists such a prominent tradition from the period of high imperialism so hostile to the intentions of the regenerators of the project. Paradoxically, precisely the same motivations were responsible for the original versions of ethnographic spectacle as those that drive the new generation. Political, economic and religious rationales were regularly employed in the late nineteenth and early twentieth centuries to justify spectacles that unashamedly sought to entertain whilst purporting to educate. The problem for contemporary exponents of this form of visual anthropology is that the traditions associated with earlier manifestations refuse often to fade away in the light of contemporary cultural pluralism. Indeed, nestling in some apparently uncontroversial displays are to be found some very old-fashioned values. One of the most interesting of features that this study seeks to explore is the cognitive dissonance built into the very notion of display. Put at its most simple, despite the attention that the authors of these latter-day spectacles pay to contemporary approaches to anthropological or cultural theory, viewers may stubbornly refuse to follow such thinking and stick, instead, stubbornly to a preconceived set of visual stereotypes. These stereotypes do not even have to be consistent with each other, but can be reached for by their employers as 'appropriate' to each occasion. It is, therefore, important for the new exponents to consider briefly the source of many of these visual stereotypes, particularly as they may themselves be using them unwittingly, unaware of the hidden charge that they contain.

One of the original sources of ethnographic display was the international exhibition which from the last quarter of the nineteenth century until the First World War became not only a vehicle for merchandising but an occasion for the

[8] Lissant Bolton 'Dancing in Mats: Extending *Kastom* to women in Vanuatu' PhD Thesis, University of Manchester 1993. This point is extended in the discussion in Chapter 3.

[9] 'Native people relatively rarely represent themselves, at least not in the major mass media, but are frequently represented by others. They even more rarely, if at all, represent others, that is, members of the majority population or foreigners, at least as long as they are a relatively underdeveloped, marginal minority.' Eric Cohen 'The study of touristic images of native people: mitigating the stereotype of a stereotype.' in Douglas G. Pearce and Richard W. Butler *Tourism Research: Critiques and Challenges* Routledge, London 1993, 40.

celebration of imperial majesty and rule. Benedict locates the origin of this development in the arrival of 'human showcases' at the Paris Exposition of 1889.[10] Here 'people from all over the world were brought to sites in order to be seen by others for their gratification and education.' Gratification rather than education was the main theme for a number of reasons. Firstly, there occurred over the period of the universal exhibitions the filling out of the trope of otherness. Secondly, a form of realism associated with the display of 'authentic sites' helped emphasise the distinction between those who were displayed and those who viewed. Finally, the displays being living, became actors and performed 'appropriate' daily tasks thus reinforcing the distinction already made.

Otherness became inextricably entwined with issues of progress and specifically with a crude form of evolutionism. At the St Louis Exposition of 1904 villages were displayed in evolutionary fashion:

> A department of anthropology aimed to display 'representatives of all the world's races, ranging from the smallest pygmies to the most gigantic peoples, from the darkest blacks to the dominant whites and from the lowest known culture (the dawn of the stone age) to its highest culmination in that Age of Metal which, as this Exposition shows, is now maturing in the Age of Power.'[11]

Beside the showmanship of the traditional fairground manifest by reference to taxonomies of body size and degrees of civilisation this quotation emphasises the significance of anthropology in sustaining this evolutionary tableau. Professor W. J. McGee, President of the American Anthropological Association was in charge of the anthropology department at the St Louis Exposition. Under his tutelage the 'more advanced tribes' were near the centre of display and the pygmies and the Igorots from the Philippines were consigned to the extremity.[12] The Igorots came in for much attention from commentators on the exhibition, mainly on account of their near-nakedness. But anthropologists were significant not only in the construction of the ethnographic displays, they became authoritative interpreters. Sometimes they organised extramural and summer courses at the exhibitions,[13] but they, like the Orientalists described by Mitchell,[14] might also employ native actors as illustrations in the presentation of academic papers. In 1900 W. H. Rivers suggested to the Anthropological Institute in London that anthropologists should 'seek special permission from the exhibition proprietors in order to 'inspect' these

[10] Paul Greenhalgh *Ephemeral Vistas: The Expositions Universelles, Great Exhibitions and World's Fairs, 1851–1939*, Manchester University Press, Manchester, 1988, 82.

[11] J. W. Buel *Louisiana and the Fair*, vol. 5, iii cited by Burton Benedict *The Anthropology of World's Fairs: San Francisco's Panama Pacific International Exposition of 1915*, Lowie Museum of Anthropology, Berkeley, 1983, 34.

[12] Benedict, 266. Perhaps characteristically the Igorots continue to suffer their fate as exotic exhibits. Marcus and Fischer's *Anthropology as Cultural Critique*, University of Chicago Press 1986, sports a photograph on the front cover of an Igorot man from the Fair though he is not discussed in the text.

[13] Robert W. Rydell 'The culture of imperial abundance: World's Fairs in the making of American culture' in Simon J. Bronner *Consuming Visions: Accumulation and display of Goods in America 1880–1920*, W. W. Norton, New York, 1989, 197, 194.

[14] Timothy Mitchell 'The world as exhibition' *Comparative Studies of Society and History* 1989 3:2, 218.

people prior to the exhibit's opening to the general public'.[15] This juxtaposition of ethnography and academic disciplines became routinised by World's Fairs. As Ley and Olds record, 'by 1915, over 900 congresses convened at the San Francisco Fair, representing medicine, science, religion, social policy and the arts'.[16] However scrupulous the anthropologists might have been in distancing themselves from the spirit of Barnum and Bailey's Great Show, the effects of this form of display had serious deleterious consequences on the visitors. Rydel provides the most trenchant criticism: 'whether one refers to the Seattle fair where schoolchildren poked Igorot women with straw or the Omaha, Buffalo, and St Louis fairs where Geronimo sold his autograph for ten cents, the expositions, and especially the midways, gave millions of Americans firsthand experience with treating non-white from around the world as commodities'.[17]

Anthropologists and ethnologists were responsible for the mental image of otherness which they helped elaborate through their involvement in the creation of dioramas and wax models in exhibitions in museums and elsewhere.[18] As late as 1931 in the Paris Exposition Coloniale, Balinese dancers were employed to provide in their performances visual emblems of the exotic[19]. 'La Femme Hotentotte' at the entrance of the Musée de l'Homme in Paris, still to be seen in the 1960s, served as a shorthand for everything African and strange, involving issues of gender and, above all, body shape. But these dioramas and models in turn were based upon anthropological photographs taken either by academics as part of field work documentation or by administrators, members of the military or by missionaries,[20] Anthropologists proved little more resistant to the temptation to take a 'telling pictures' than non-specialists and frequently had more opportunity to publish them. And telling pictures could buttress extant stereotypes. For example, the dinner invitation printed to welcome Professor Haddon back from Australia in 1890 has a list of diners on the front cover and one of Haddon's photographs entitled 'Group of Cannibals' on the back cover[21] Humourous images can hide deep disquiet. Cannibalism remains one of the hidden topics regularly dismissed but discussed in secret in many areas of the world.

Photographic imagery provided a link between popularly circulated visions of incivility and the recreations of colonial living in the tableaux at the expositions and fairs. The tableaux could be justified by their faithfulness to photographs of indigenous topography and subjects. Thus visual tropes could be constantly recycled from the framing of the photographer to the setting of the exhibition.

[15] Annie E. Coombes *Reinventing Africa: Museums, Material Culture and Popular Imagination*, Yale University Press, New Haven, 1994, 88.

[16] D. Ley and K. Olds 'Landscape as spectacle: world's fairs and the culture of heroic consumption', *Environment and Planning D: Space and Society*, 1988, 6, 191–212.

[17] Rydel 'The culture of imperial abundance', 197–8.

[18] Roslyn Poignant records that tableaux of ethnic models were exhibited at Colonial and International exhibitions and that the destruction of such models in the Crystal Palace fire of 1866 was considered in the anthropological press as a considerable loss. R. Poignant 'Photography and anthropology' in *Observers of Man*, Royal Anthropological Institute, London, 1980, 5.

[19] M. Hitchcock and L. Norris *Bali: The Imaginary Museum*, 29 and 68.

[20]  see Roslyn Poignant 'Surveying the field of view: the making of the RAI photographic collection' in Elizabeth Edwards (ed.) *Anthropology and Photography 1860–1920*, Yale University Press, New Haven, 1992, 42–73. The articles by Terence Wright and Christopher Pinney in the same volume extend the discussion of the relationship between anthropology, anthropologists and photography. I deal with missionary images and photography in 'Melanesian artifacts as cultural markers' in Stephen H. Riggins (ed.) *The Socialness of Things: Essays on the Socio-Semiotics of Objects*, Mouton De Gruyter, Berlin, 1994. 186–90.

[21]  illustrated in *The Impossible Science of Being: Dialogues between Anthropology and Photography*, The Photographers' Gallery London, 1995, 9.

[22]  see Ismael bin Abdullah 'Documentary photography: a study of nineteenth century photography with special reference to West Malaysian historical photographs 1874–1910' University of London, Goldsmiths College PhD thesis 1995.

[23]  Mitchell 'The world as exhibition', 229.

[24]  Mitchell *Colonising Egypt*, Cambridge University Press, Cambridge, 1988, 60.

[25]  Benedict, 58.

[26]  Coombes *Reinventing Africa*, 88.

Photographs taken by members of colonial populations were to remain largely hidden and ignored until after the colonial era.[22] For photographers and for the architects of the anthropological exhibits alike a problem about the nature of representation occurred. As Mitchell has noted in his study of representations of Egypt in Imperial exhibitions, 'one can copy or represent only what appears already to exist representationally – as a picture. The problem, in other words, was to create a distance between oneself and the world, and thus to constitute it as something picture-like – as an object on exhibit. This required what was now called a "point of view": a position set apart and outside.'[23]

For visitors to the ethnographic displays physical distance and metaphoric as well as literal superiority were provided by two techniques found in photographic practice, framing and positioning of the observing subject; 'the world is set up before an observing subject as though it were the picture of something'.[24] The frame was provided by the design of the sector, with villages providing the containing concept. All of the inhabitants 'dwelt' in their realistic representations of huts, shelters or bazaars, and there they stayed to be viewed by the visitor who could wander round the village peering into every nook and cranny, in a way not dissimilar from the ethnographer in the 'real world'. Nevertheless, the visitor was never confused by the spectacle because, and this point of Mitchell's is crucial, the village like the rest of the anthropological world was presented as an exhibit. Although in theatrical terms the village and its inhabitants might correspond mimetically with a village in Egypt, or as in Chicago in 1893, 'a Bedouin camp, a Winnebago Indian village, a Lapland village, a Persian palace, a Chinese market, an Algerian–Tunisian village, a Japanese bazaar, an Austrian village and villages from Samoa, Germany, Ireland, Java, Dahomy and Turkey',[25] yet their propinquity to their village neighbours in the exposition reminded the visitor of the artificiality of the representation they were examining.

There were nevertheless, two other forces that sought to distract the visitor from perceiving the artifice of the occasion, architectural detailing and performance by the village inhabitants. Programmes of the exhibitions emphasised the authenticity of the display. Coombes notes that in exhibition programmes, 'a frequent feature of this discourse is the claim that the verisimilitude of the scene is so complete that the occupants themselves fail to recognise that they are living in a simulated environment'.[26] If the architectural features were sufficiently accurate then the inhabitants would be likely to 'feel at home'. This is a proposition not unlike ones still offered for the ecological virtues of zoos and wildlife parks today.

In order to ensure veracity villagers were frequently employed in the construction of their own dwellings. The construction of the Paris Exhibition of 1900 demonstrates the complexity of the undertaking and some unexpected consequences. Colonial workers were imported to labour under the direction of French architects but to supply themselves the final detailing of the buildings. These workers then lived in the constructions they had made for the duration the exhibition. In the case of the Dahomey pavilion they then dismantled it so that it could be shipped home and used as a Post Office.[27] Others had a longer though less glorious life. For example, the Somali village that had appeared at the Bradford exhibition of 1904 and Dublin in 1907 was destined to end its days at Douglas in the Isle of Man in 1912 as part of a holiday attraction.[28] The recycling of exhibits became a regular feature in the routine of local, national and imperial exhibitions.

It was the activity of these inhabitants that brought these tableaux from the realm of the natural history museum to the entertainment of the show ground and gave them text. At the Chicago Colombian Exposition of 1893 the formula was created that all subsequent exhibitions followed fairly faithfully. Each day there was a parade of the village inhabitants on the Midway Plaisance. This was a performance area distinct from the 'ethnic villages', and more clearly associated with fairground activities. On the Midway professional showmen from forty nations lived with their families and 'goats, donkeys, camels, dogs and birds'[29] much as though in a circus, but on display rather than behind the scenes, and so demonstrating the 'back stage' of ethnic display. It was here that rides and other performances for the visitors were arranged, many of them indistinguishable from attractions at ordinary show grounds.

At the end of the ethnic parade the performers would return to their villages to start public living. This was the point at which ethnography was to take over. Aspects of social and religious beliefs were demonstrated by performances of ritual events. At the St Louis World Fair the Philippines were made the central attraction. Over one million dollars were spent in bringing 7,500 exhibits and attendants to people six villages in an area of 47 acres. It was here that the Igorot were the stars of the show. In the Negrito village the daily performance included 'the celebration of marriages, celebrations of annual memorials for deceased relatives, general dances in which all sing, shooting with arrows, making fire and hunting with wild dogs'.[30]

[27] Benedict p 49.

[28] Greenhalgh p 93.

[29] Steve NELSON 'Walt Disney's EPCOT and the World's Fair Performance tradition' *Drama Review* 1986 Winter, 112.

[30] Bureau of Insular Affairs, War Department, Washington DC Philippine Exposition Building for the Louisiana Purchase Exposition, 1905, cited by Benedict Burton, 50.

This range of performance followed rather loosely the interests of professional anthropology. But there were more exciting events to witness, including for the Egyptians, Nubians and Sudanese 'fights, weddings, sword and candle dances'[31] regularly performed since the Chicago show of 1893.

In the villages there were also photograph stalls which offered opportunities for visitors to purchase copies of postcards either of the villagers' portraits or of them engaged in photographically engaging cultural activities. Another feature of these photographic sessions was the frisson of excitement for visitors to be gained by having their picture taken with the villagers, thus exemplifying for posterity their temerity in crossing the barrier between exhibit and viewer. Such photographs represent a commonplace in colonial representation,[32] but here the visitor could travel symbolically to the furthest reaches of the world whilst enjoying the authority of the viewer over the spectacle. It was the ease of this appropriation of power by any fairground visitor that raised disquiet in some commentators. For them the theatricality of the show implicated all involved. As Greenhalgh reflects somewhat poignantly

> One can only speculate on what the Senegalese man thought, as he looked back at the gaping expressions of the Parisian crowd, a pale and unhealthy looking mob shrouded in gaudy dresses and frock-coats, laughing and sneering at what they demonstrably considered the just spoils of war. Perhaps the culture gap was too wide for him to ponder upon anything more than the eccentricity of the garb, the dullness of the climate and the predictability of the crowd's response to him.[33]

Of course, what this picture hints at obliquely is the dimension of power, a feature of central significance in the discussion of anthropological display of any kind. The Senegalese view can only be one of pathos, for those to whom he returns the gaze are not themselves self-reflectively ethnic. Only he remains this which makes the notion of a subverted ethnography of display such a problematic possibility.

The range of cultures displayed in these expositions is cause for similar reflection. Some examples fit easily into the 'imperial portfolio' of the nations sponsoring them. So Dahomey and Senegal were obvious candidates for inclusion in the French expositions, but the Scottish and Irish villages and the Kalmuck camp (of 'nomadic Tartars' exhibited by the Russian Empire) shown at the 1909 Imperial International Exhibition at White City, London, require more thought. A basic

[31] Nelson 'Walt Disney's EPCOT', 116–17.

[32] Nicholas Thomas provides one of the clearest of such examples on the front cover of his *Colonialism's Culture* with a Methodist Missionary postcard entitled 'A Study in Black and White' of a small white child in full white dress and hat holding hands with two Melanesian children.

[33] Greenhalgh, 84.

distinction nevertheless obtains between the industrial imperial civilisation sponsoring the exhibition and the non-industrial whether nomadic or agrarian being displayed. Such a distinction raises afresh the central issue of ethnicity and power. MacCannell strikes to the heart of the issue when he asks, 'in their interaction with others, how can groups in power manage to convey the impression that they are less ethnic than those over whom they exercise their power; in other words how can they foster the impression that their own traits and qualities are merely correct, while the corresponding qualities of others are "ethnic"?'.[34] The test of this proposition is whether the expectation of viewer and performer can be upset. I have only found one very late example of such a reversal, at the 1939 New York World's Fair. Here, the Small American Homes exhibit consisted of two fully equipped and furnished houses that were inhabited by two families (parents and two children) chosen from newspaper competition to live on the fairground for a week at a time. At the end of the season the 'most typical American family' was to be selected, though the publicity material failed to specify how this was to be done.[35] This form of 'reverse ethnography' did, however, have exponents in Britain and North America in the late thirties, of which Mass-Observation is probably the most successful example.[36] It was to be this challenge that much post-colonial ethnographic display was to turn.

## The alternative tradition: Skansen

The creators of the new ethnographic spectacle have not been forced to rely upon the political and economic imperatives to be seen in the universal expositions and World's Fairs. There is another tradition which seeks to provide a more realistic version of domestic ethnography, that of the folk museum. Artur Hazelius is credited with creating the form which combines the transferring to a single open-air site of a range of culturally and architecturally interesting buildings from a wide range of geographic sources. These buildings are then filled with relevant items of material culture, and, of particular interest here, are shown as inhabited. Hazelius was involved in putting on a display of items from his collection at the Nordic Museum in Stockholm in a diorama at the Paris International Exhibition of 1878. Two types of dioramas were shown. The first showed Lapps working in a display entitled 'The Autumn Move in Lule Lappmark' but others were interiors: 'one famous example is a scene from a cottage in Halland:

[34] Dean MacCannell, *Empty Meeting Grounds: The Tourist Papers*, Routledge, London 1992, 121–2.

[35] NELSON 'Walt Disney's EPCOT', 124–5.

here the people are eternally prepared for a feast in a setting that never becomes smoky, drafty, foul-smelling or dirty'.[36]

Hazelius went on to found in 1891 an open-air museum named Skansen in central Stockholm where such tableaux became permanent. Dolls were placed in regional garb in the buildings that had been moved from rural provincial sites to Skansen. In 1926 the dolls were replaced by living examples of regional folk resident in Stockholm. At this time there was a large influx of rural migrants to the capital.[38] The intention behind Skansen was the salvage not only of rapidly disappearing regional architectural forms but the cultures associated with them. Hazelius was passionately interested in the rural dialects of Sweden and their relationship to Norse. It was from this rural base that Hazelius and Skansen sought the material for the construction of Swedish identity. Over time this notion of nationality has been broken down even further into regional identity. So for example, in the province of Östergötland, Old Linköping Open Air Museum proudly announces 'a special feature of Old Linköping is that over fifty people actually live here: so life is in full swing. There are lights in the windows in the evenings and in the summer-time the breeze blows the curtains through open windows. There are also craftsmen living here with workshops selling things – a reminder of the old town craftsmen, and that the majority of buildings here were actually put up by craftsmen and lived in by craftsmen'.[39]

The purpose of peopling of Old Linköping is to reminds one of the relationship between inhabitants and their environment – these are not merely actors, but individuals who live and work in the museum. They are the rationale for the label 'living museum'. Both they and the activities at Skansen serve to underlie the importance of performance to enliven the settings. At Skansen the Missionhuset (meetinghouse) holds services on Sunday, as does the Seglora Church which also provides the setting for weddings.[40] The establishment of an open-air theatre in 1911, choral singing on six evenings and dances held three times a week in the 1930s further cemented the museum into the structure of public entertainment in the capital.[41] All of these activities served to provide a more popular ambience than the maypole dance and the summer festival had traditionally enjoyed.

The significance of the Swedish ventures lies particularly in their weave of architectural and artifact salvage with a similar salvage ethnography. These when united with an emphasis on folklore provide material for a new kind of ethnography which is in turn a potent source for developing ethnic nationalism.

[36] see particularly *First Year's Work* by Mass-Observation edited by Charles Madge and Tom Harrisson, Lindsay Drummond, London, 1938, *Britain* by Mass-Observation, Penguin, Harmondsworth, 1939, and Tom Harrisson *Britain Revisited*, Victor Gollancz, London, 1961. This approach was, however, self-consciously conceived as a continuation of 'real anthropology' undertaken in the South Pacific. See Tom Harrisson *Savage Civilisation*, Victor Gollancz, 1937.

[37] Barbro Klein and Mats Widbom (eds.) *Swedish Folk Art: All Tradition is Change*, Harry N. Abrams in association with Kulturhuset, Stockholm, 1994, 25.

[38] Michel Conan, personal communication, 1996.

[39] Gunnar Elfström *Old Linköping*, Gamla Linköping, Linköping, n.d. p 2.

[40] Ralph Edenheim, Lars-Erik Larsson and Christina Westberg *Skansen*, Stockholm, 1991, 21, 27.

[41] Michel Conan 'The fiddler's indecorous nostalgia' paper delivered at Dumbarton Oaks Studies in Landscape Architecture 1996 Symposium.

The permanence of the site and the close attention paid to historic design features at Skansen offers a marked contrast to the almost medieval forms of caravan that characterises even the most contemporary World Fair, ever recombining popular features of previous shows in more extravagant pageants. Skansen and its successors like Arnhem (1911) and Bucharest (1936) establish a model for post-war successors to emulate, and then to outgrow.

The formula consists of a physical representation of the variety of structures to be found in the country (Skansen) or region (Linköping), including dwellings, farms, workshops, villages and urban districts. Topography is suggested by their siting. So, for example, the Skansen catalogue states

> Skansen is intended to be Sweden in miniature and tries to demonstrate this in both the built-up and the natural landscape. And so the Skåne farm from the southernmost Swedish province is also at Skansen sited as far south as possible, surrounded by willows and beeches, while the Delsbo farm from the northern province of Hälsingland, lies to the north of the Skansen site, with its birches and pines.'[42]

Both Skansen and Linköping reinforce this metonymy: the original buildings from a previous age, whether peasant or industrial, all concentrated on the one spot, provide visual evidence of truth and honesty. Visitors are offered proof through visible remains of how people have lived in the past as well as what remain today. This provides a privileged entry and a means of both understanding the culture and a of recapturing the essence of that life. Skansen is also keen to exhibit the linguistic and cultural minorities in Sweden. There is therefore a Finn settlement and a Lapp camp, though the reader of the brochure is reminded that Lapp seasonal life has changed greatly with the advent of new forms of all-weather transport. Lapps, this commentary suggests, are subject to modern developments like modern travelling slaughter-houses for their reindeer and they use snow scooters.

Skansen insists that sites and buildings filled with historic and contemporary artefacts provide a real panorama of Swedish life. The Zoo at Skansen offers simultaneously an ethnographic contradiction and simile: 'practically every day another animal species becomes endangered, threatened by confrontation with the most successful of all animals – man'[43] What distinguishes Skansen's view from that of the evolutionist universal expositions is that humans are adaptable to circumstance but dependent upon tradition which, if lost, diminishes cultural wealth.

[42] Edenheim et al *Skansen*, 6.

[43] Edenheim et al *Skansen*, 54.

## The unavoidable alternative: Disney ethnography

At the beginning of the Chapter, I characterised the world of Disney as the very antithesis of ethnographic realism. There is no anthropology in the world of pleasure and innocence. The Magic Kingdom at Disney World has been likened to 'a movie that can be walked into'.[44] The Magic Kingdom offers a synecdoche of Disney utopianism. Here images are recycled and precipitated afresh into new displays. The current tales of parents suing the Disney Corporation for 'loss of innocence' because children were scandalised when a 'Mouse' took of his headgear in full view of visitors, nicely epitomises the unreality cherished at Disney.[45]

Yet Disney has its academic pretensions and its own version of ethnography. At Disney World the EPCOT (Experimental Prototype Community of Tomorrow) Center opened in 1982. There are two displays, Future World – 'real futures brought to you by real corporations'[46] and World Showcase which offers a new form of Midway Plaisance with pavilions for eleven nations. The layout of the Showcase is instructive as is the selection of nationalities strung around the central lake. The topography of these relates more closely to the history of representation in World's Fairs and the realities of US trade rather than to any other consideration. The United States dominates the show with 'The American Adventure'. It is flanked by Italy and Japan. Italy is followed by Germany, China, Norway and Mexico, whilst on the other shore Japan is succeeded by Morocco, France, an International Gateway, The United Kingdom and Canada. The clichéd architecture provides 'an Eiffel Tower here, a Chateau Frontenac or Japanese garden there.'[47] The official guide warns visitors that they will not find 'real' countries at the EPCOT Center, but only their 'essence, much as a traveller returning from a visit might remember what he or she saw'.[48] The performers, teenagers from the various countries represented,[49] arranged for each country 'are mostly glorified costume parades intended more as lures for the food and souvenirs than as self-sufficient entertainment. Costumed "strolling players" appear throughout World Showcase to perform comic interludes in the style of each nation.'[50]

The EPCOT displays are not, however, symmetrical in their content. The industrialised countries, Germany, Italy, France, Britain and Canada have restaurants and shops (Canada and France also have film shows). Britain is represented by a pub 'with authentically surly bar staff'.[51] As Kratz and Karp document in their study of EPCOT, it is those countries that seem most exotic and foreign that have museums attached; China, Japan, Mexico, Morocco and, by some particular ironic

[44] Thomas Hine cited by Scott Bukatman 'There's always tomorrowland: Disney and the hypercinemiatic experience' *October*, 57, 1991, 61.

[45] Jane Kuenz 'Working at the Rat', and Susan Willis 'Public Use/Private State' in Project on Disney *Inside the Mouse*, 136–7; 196.

[46] Butakman 'There's always tomorrowland', 56.

[47] Alexander Wilson *The Culture of Nature: North American Landscape from Disney to the Exxon Valdez*, Cambridge MA, 1992, 179.

[48] Stephen Birnbaum *Walt Disney World: The Official Guide New York 1990* cited in J. Kuentz 'It's a Small World After All: Disney and the pleasures of identification' *South Atlantic Quarterly*, 92:1, 1993, 86.

[49] Butakman 'There's always tomorowland, 66.

[50] Nelson 'Walt Disney's EPCOT', 139.

[51] Simon Hoggart 'Man or mouse on Space Mountain' *The Guardian*, London, 14 June 1995.

revenge on Skansen, Norway where the museum is housed in a replica of a stavekirke beside a version of Akershus Castle. The Norwegian museum in its display 'relied heavily on dioramas; a near life-size one of explorer Roald Amundsen with a packed dog sled, and miniature models of a boat designed to sail to the North Pole. Another case showed objects, with skis, paddles and heavy clothing used in early Norwegian polar exploration.'[52] Perhaps to be expected, in the light of World's Fair traditions, the most exotic and therefore the one treated most strictly in ethnographic terms is the Moroccan. Kratz and Karp describe their experience of it thus: 'the centerpiece was a diorama of a Fassi wedding with the bride, her dowry, and a long label on Moroccan wedding customs. Two small rooms displayed metal work, jewelry, and musical instruments. Vitrine displays highlighted craftsmanship and artistry, but labels also told us about types of music and the ethnic groups of Morocco.'[53] In further homage to the World's Fair tradition there are apparently plans for a twelfth exhibit, Equatorial Africa, to replace a totem pole 'surrounded by the music of drums'[54] that currently provides the icon for sub-Saharan Africa.

The significance of EPCOT is not so much that it offers 'authentic ethnography' (a term discussed in more detail in Chapter 5). Indeed, it has been argued the World Showcase has transmuted ethnography into the normal theme park experience. Bukatman argues that 'the World Showcase represents a peculiar implosion of American tourism: foreign lands are further reduced and domesticated, rendered safe whilst remaining absurdly picturesque (*with actual natives*).'[55] Shelton Waldrep has also argued that at EPCOT 'the aura of a country, place, or time – or at least a fictionalised mystique of the same – is tapped into most successfully by theming that doesn't remind you of something that actually exists, something you may have seen in the original'.[56] What perhaps is new and audacious is the subversion of the authority of the conventional museum that these exhibits offer. The national tableaux and pageants at Disney World attempt to cross the traditions of World's Fairs with those of Skansen. As Kratz and Karp document, the museum displays at World Showcase include objects on loan from the Smithsonian Museum of Natural History, the Fowler Museum at UCLA, Denver Art Museum, the Southwest Museum, and further afield, the Palace Museum, Beijing. Such items, and particularly their labels, provide a spurious authority to the displays. This in turn makes the hyper-reality of Disney the more extreme.

What EPCOT has achieved is the demonstration that the contents of ethnographic display can be subsumed into illusioneered fantasy and pleasure. This is not

[52] Corinne A. Kratz and Ivan Karp 'Wonder and worth: Disney museums in World Showcase' *Museum Anthropology*, 17:3, 1993, 37.

[53] Kratz and Karp 'Wonder and worth', 38.

[54] J. Kuentz 'It's a small world after all', 81.

[55] Bukatman 'There's always tomorrowland', 66 (emphasis as in the original).

[56] Shelton Waldrep 'Monuments to Walt in *Inside the Mouse*, 205.

greeted with great pleasure by those who had thought that the tradition of the universal expositions and the World's Fairs had been finally extinguished. Nor does it auger well for those who are committed to developing exhibitions that seek to educate and transform stereotypes into topics of reflective inquiry. But once out of the bottle, the genie cannot be put back in. The tradition of Disney continues that of the World Fair, perhaps with gentler and more ironic stereotypes, but nevertheless it is not only available, but it is the largest and arguably the most pervasive vision enjoyed by more people in the various versions of Disney than has ever been possible before in world history.

# Ethnographic theme parks:
## the emergence of a global paradigm

## The advent of theme parks

The Second World War spelt the death of Imperial Display. The Festival of Britain of 1951 harked back to the first of all such displays, the Great Exhibition in Hyde Park a century earlier, and contained a small Centenary Pavilion in the shape of the Crystal Palace.[1] But already the traditional relations between imperial power and colonial possessions had been sundered during the nineteen forties. The Commonwealth, for example, was in The Lion and the Unicorn pavilion devoted to British political might, reduced to the abstraction of a 'tall mast of polished hardwood and brass, bearing a trophy of flags.'[2]

An exception to this general development was the United States, and it was here that the tradition of ethnographic display survived, albeit with significant changes. Disneyland, established in 1955, continued the tradition of the Midway Plaisance in all its bewildering variety, but employed new technology. The most spectacular example of this recreation was in a much visited and commented-on ride entitled It's A Small World. One guidebook summarises the show thus:

> The ride itself is a leisurely cruise in sherbet-coloured boats that take you through glittery scenes of hundreds of Audio-Animatronic singing-and-dancing dolls, all attired in their national costumes. There are Canadian Mounties, hip-swaying hula girls, leprechauns, kings and queens, snake charmers, flying carpets, pyramids, sphinxes, giraffes and hippos, volcanoes, sombreros and even an 'underwater' scene representing Hawai'i. The theme of world unity shines through in the detailed costumes and settings from countries around the globe.[3]

And, to prefigure the later ethnographic extension at Disney World, there is an evocation of exotic sites. Eco notes how these exude authenticity (as stridently as at any World's Fair), and offers as an illustration the Polynesian restaurant which 'will have, in addition to a fairly authentic menu, Tahitian waitresses in costume, appropriate vegetation, rock walls with little cascades, and once you are inside nothing must lead you to suspect that outside there is anything but Polynesia.'[4]

This evocation of Polynesia was, of course, itself part of a long tradition. Samoans had their own village at the World's Columbia Exposition in 1893,[5] The Hawai'ians, ever popular, struck one particular visitor to the Panama Pacific International Exposition of 1915 particularly:

[1] South Bank Exhibition Plan, Festival of Britain, H.M. Stationery Office, London, 1951.

[2] Mary Banham and Bevis Hillier *A Tonic to the Nation: The Festival of Britain 1951*, 1976.

[3] Judy Wade et al *Disneyland and Beyond: the Ultimate Family Guidebook*, 50.

[4] Eco *Travels in Hyper-reality*, 44.

[5] Nelson 'Walt Disney's EPCOT' provides an illustration of Samoan actors posing for a photograph, 108.

They had Hawai'ian music, a Hawai'ian band playing ukeleles and girls singing. The Dole pineapple people gave you a free drink of Pineapple juice which I had never had before and you would sit there for free, and you would listen to the music . . . The first live music I remember enjoying so much was this daily concert they had. Oh, that Hawai'ian girl, can you imagine, a beautiful young girl doing the hula and singing. What it meant for a hick from the country, drinking pineapple juice to the tune of Hawai'ian music.[6]

But if people could travel to California to experience Hawai'i and other islands of the Pacific why not venture further? The Disney response was to purchase a large chunk of Florida to give more of the same, in greater detail and therefore more semblance of the Pacific and other places. The popularity of mass jet travel which had begun the 1960s helped Disney's plans to draw the world to Florida but it also meant that the tourist world might itself extend beyond the continental United States. Vacationers could now experience Hawai'i for themselves. Once Hawai'i had become a routine destiny for North Americans (and Florida had replaced Spain for British holiday makers!) similar destinies in the Pacific were to beckon the Meganesians, Fiji for Australians, and somewhat later, the Cook Islands for New Zealanders.

In these new destinations all of the normal trappings of tourism were reproduced – beaches cleaned every day, golf courses, shopping malls, evening entertainment and sites of local interest. But, to remind the visitors that they had made a special journey to somewhere exotic the sites and entertainment were to have a special inflection. Fiji has two rival attractions which offer a snapshot of Fijian life. The first of these, Orchid Island, has 'a typical Fijian village where people live and work. A life so deeply bedded in tradition, a heathen temple, a Chief's house exactly as it existed in the last century, traditional Fijian handicraft demonstrations, a mini Museum revealing a vivid history of Fiji and, to top it all, a Fijian Spectacular you'll never forget'[7] Orchid Island provides most of the paraphernalia associated with World's Fair displays[8] but with one additional attraction, the locality. Here people are to be seen, in their native habitat, one which, in true show ground tradition, the brochure slyly insinuates, has a 'cannibalistic connection'. To reinforce the topicality of the setting, collections of local flora and fauna are displayed in an agricultural section and mini Zoo.

[6] quoted by Benedict, x.

[7] Orchid Island Fijian Cultural Centre brochure, Suva, n.d. (1995).

[8] Fiji was also the subject of imperial and colonial displays. See N. Thomas Entangled Objects, 175–7.

Pacific Harbour Cultural Centre and Marketplace goes one better. Tourists are seated in canoes and then transported on water around a set of displays. The brochure promises:

> Step into a twin-hulled canoe poled by warriors for your island tour.
> It is your time-machine, taking you back 3,000 years to observe culture which came from the sea, blended with the beauty and grandeur of these islands, where people learned to live with richness and dignity.
> A Fijian warrior in traditional dress will go with you on your voyage into the past. He will tell of his people's voyages and legends. You will see men creating fire, building an outrigger canoe with stone axes, women making pottery without a wheel, beating masi, weaving sennet. Look at a Fijian kitchen, the war fence protecting the chief's house, medicinal herbs growing, Fijians with war clubs and long spears, on guard.'[9]

The exoticism of the culture is demonstrated by a performance of firewalking, which brings the excitement of circus performance with the authority of tradition.

Both Pacific Harbour and Orchid Island package in a half day's visit the local culture, costume, architecture, history, zoology and artefact manufacture that tourists might expect at the Australian Museum or the Smithsonian. But they also suggest that the locality provides for additional authenticity. Orchid Island even invokes the sanction of the Fiji Museum in its reconstruction of a chief's Bure. The evening show at Pacific Harbour is performed by the Dance Theatre of Fiji which seeks to create *mekes* (performances) based on academically researched song and dance routines.

For both venues historical reconstruction of architectural features is brought into the present by the performance of indigènes. What is self-consciously absent from these reconstructions is reference to contemporary reality in Fiji and the history of the island since 1879 when indentured labourers were first introduced from India to work the sugar plantations. Today the Indian population is larger that that of Fijian ancestry and this demographic transformation has been the source of much tension. Fiji has also been watched with great interest by other states in the South Pacific, notably Tonga where the sale of passports to non-Tongans raises the spectre of 'another Fiji' with its constitutional coup of 1987.[10] Representations of 'historic Fiji' have a political edge or purpose that may be imperceptible to tourist spectators, but which has a vivid contemporary significance to

[9] Welcome to Another World: A Fascinating Look at Fiji's Past and Present', brochure, Pacific Harbour, n.d. (1995).

[10] Paul Theroux's bad-tempered travel book on the South Pacific *The Happy Isles of Oceania*, Penguin, 1992 makes for very uncomfortable reading in its unflattering depiction of many island states; however, it is indispensable for its detail of contemporary life, and provides some unsurpassable insights. For Tongan passports, see p 360.

the performers, as well as to the Indians who work backstage in the tourist industry. As Fiji lies at the intersection of Melanesia and Polynesia its cultural policy and its politics are of heightened interest to the whole of the Pacific, particularly the issue of indigenousness. Questions of 'indigenous performance' and who has such rights will be the subject of Chapter 3.

## A religious experience?: the Polynesian Cultural Center

The Fijian cultural centres, and the others like them that have sprung up across the Pacific, in Rarotonga, Noumea, Apia, or Honiara have not appeared from out of thin air. For those who know of it, the Polynesian Cultural Center at Lai'e on Oahu on the other side of the island from Honolulu and Waikiki is the obvious original from which they all draw, a visible and powerful template. As tourism in the Pacific effectively began in Hawai'i and remains both pre-eminent and pivotal it is not surprising that ethnographic tourism has its roots here. What is perhaps most remarkable is the impact elsewhere of the PCC, given its very singular historic origins and purpose.

Ross starts his definitive and intellectually provocative study of the Polynesian Cultural Center (hereafter PCC) with a rationale for such a study. He says;

> Nowhere, one would think, are the contradictions shared by both the anthropologist and the tourist more visible than in the 'cultural parks' of ethnographic tourism, that sector of the industry which brings the tourist into contact with performances of traditional cultures . . . Cultural theme parks or centers – 'living museums' of traditional culture without any actual resident inhabitants – are the primary spectacle of ethnographic tourism.[11]

This definition of ethnographic tourism is extremely helpful. Ross distinguishes it from other sorts which abut onto it like cultural tourism which is based on landscape, archaeological tourism, religious tourism or pilgrimages, recreational and even sex tourism. Needless to say, such a distinction also provides a checklist of other possible directions that ethnographic tourism might be diverted into.

Ross's definition highlights the two major elements that are everywhere combined in such parks, namely performance and architecture. What he also suggests is that such parks are the principal arena of contestation between anthropology and tourism with its associated specialisms of leisure development and

[11]  Andrew Ross *The Chicago Gangster Theory of Life*, 43. Though, as Geoff White notes, in the case of the PCC, the students live next door at Brigham Young University (personal communication September 1997).

39

management. As tourism is now the largest global industry (including warfare) such a contest is likely to be gladiatorial and bloody. The stakes become inestimably higher on both sides when the *causus belli* is the very rationale of the industry, its ethical, economic, cultural and political agendas. Anthropologists risk, in the very assault, being forced back onto a conservative agenda in which every change is a change for the worse. Both parties polarise and simplify a discussion over what are complex issues. These are also issues that are of the utmost significance to those performers who provide the human material on which the whole edifice of ethnographic tourism is itself constructed.

The Polynesian Cultural Center provides an excellent terrain to inspect the debate and the mutual disdain generated in such a struggle. Two particular reasons can also be given for selecting this case. Firstly, the PCC is the most successful such park in the world with nearly one million visitors per year. It is the longest established and firmly integrated as the second largest attraction in Hawai'i (surpassed only by the U.S.S. *Arizona* Memorial at Pearl Harbor),[12] and Hawai'i is the leader of world tourism. Secondly, the PCC is no ordinary theme park; it has academic pretensions both in terms of cultural theory and presentation as well as, for good measure, providing a critique of its anthropological critics as well as of other forms of religion in the Pacific region. Being attached to a campus of Brigham Young University and committed to the principles of Mormonism has created for the PCC a final gulf between it and its detractors.

The Mormons established the Church College of Hawai'i at Lai'e in 1955 to educate students from the Pacific region. In its early days students supplemented their income by working in the pineapple fields which was not only arduous labour, beginning at three o'clock in the morning, but expensive of study time.[13] A more intermittent source of funds came from a monthly fishing day at the coast where the catch was served at a communal meal, for all who chose to come, on the beach accompanied by songs from the Pacific island students. Another more secure means of earnings may well have grown out of the beach show, a Polynesian dance troupe which started in 1959 travelling twice a week to Honolulu to perform.[14] Although, as Stanton states, this was a highly successful and popular venture it was also a logistical ordeal to transport a large troupe, the support staff and all the staging and equipment to the other coast. A decision was taken to bring tourists to Lai'e. Whilst this was an apparently risky strategy, locating the site as far away from Waikiki as possible, it was to prove an excellent logistical decision. The PCC provided

[12] M. Stanton *The PCC* 193.

[13] M. Stanton personal interview 20 April 1995.

[14] M. Stanton *The PCC*, 195.

**PCC performance at Royal Hawai'ian Shopping Center, Waikiki**

a destination for organised tours and car hire out of Honolulu and a full day's excursion. Today the PCC has a ticketing office at the Royal Hawai'ian Shopping Centre in Waikiki beside which a taster show of Polynesian dances is regularly performed.[15]

The PCC opened in 1963. Its threefold mission was to 'preserve and portray the cultures, arts and crafts of Polynesia, contribute to the educational development and growth of all people who attend Brigham Young University-Hawai'i and the Polynesian Cultural Center, and to demonstrate and radiate the spirit of love and service which will contribute to the betterment, uplifting and blessing of all who visit this special place.'[16] The religious intention made explicit in the third statement provides one of the performance indicators of all performers and guides as PCC. Although discreet, there are opportunities to see the Mormon Temple and its visitor centre to watch a film and 'to learn more about the Church of Jesus Christ of Latter-day Saints.'[17] But for many tourists there will be little if anything that explicitly reminds them that they are in a venue with a religious affiliation.

Nevertheless, the PCC's religious and cultural agenda is on view in the Center. At the heart of the park is a display entitled '1850s Mission Complex'. Surprisingly, this is not an account of Mormon evangelisation of the Pacific but of

[15] opened in 1981, PCC *The Villager* (employee newsletter) June 1981.

[16] PCC Mission Statement, 1955.

[17] R. Ariyoshi PCC: *All the Spirit of the Islands*, 48.

Evangelical Missions. A mission house is shown with a European-style interior which has a 1950s period feel. The text on the panel outside is instructive:

> This is an example of an Evangelical Missionary home found throughout Polynesia in the middle of the late 1800s. Evangelical missionaries usually came as couples and strived to establish homes similar to those they left behind. As Polynesia became more cosmopolitan, Christian churches soon looked like copies of their New England counterparts.
>
> Missionaries of the Church of Jesus Christ of Latter-day Saints (Mormons) were usually single young men who lived with the people, adopting their life-styles and their languages.

This is no minor piece of religious point-scoring but a declaration of cultural policy and relates to the first mission statement. The PCC is a visual manifestation of the church's concern with cultural preservation. Earlier brochures for the PCC were explicit in declaring this: 'These men and women, in our time, have done something about it. they've helped to preserve – for all the world – these dying island cultures as precious fragments of a heroic and all-but-gone-forever past.'[18] The current emphasis is less melodramatic but in the same spirit. 'In many areas of the Pacific, the Polynesian way of life has changed dramatically. Not only do the Polynesians often find themselves on the outskirts of the economic mainstream in their own homelands but their ancient culture is in danger of being entirely eclipsed by modern society. These changes have come within living memory of the older generations.'[19]

Culture is to be preserved in two distinctive ways at the PCC. As the above quotations suggest, it is in symbolic and mental culture that people's memories and traditions are maintained and preserved, but for this to be possible material culture is crucial. The PCC addresses both aspects of culture by visual and aural means. These can be considered in terms of construction and performance. The construction of the Center epitomises the intentions of its planners. On the 42 acre plot a lake was constructed the whole length of the site and around it are strung a series of seven villages representing the main Polynesian cultures. On the northern shore are representations of The islands of Samoa (glossing the political and increasingly significant economic distinction between Western Samoa and American Samoa), Islands of New Zealand (sub-titled Aotearoa-New Zealand to reinforce its Polynesian pedigree), on an island of its own joined to the shore by bridges are the Islands of Fiji

[18] R. O'Brien *Hands Across the Water: The Story of The Polynesian Cultural Center*, 3. Noel McGrevy's earlier 'The PCC: a model for cultural consensus,' also discusses cultural preservation extensively.

[19] R. Ariyoshi PCC: *All the Spirit of the Islands*, 5.

and, and next door, again stressing its Polynesian credentials, the Islands of Old Hawai'i. On the southern shore are the Islands of Tonga, Islands of Tahiti and Islands of the Marquesas. Supporting this cluster of villages are a range of snack bars, restaurants, shops, an IMAX cinema and a large outdoor covered theatre.

Much is made of the authenticity of the construction of the villages. The Fale Fakatui in the Tongan village 'is an exact replica of the late Queen Salote's summer house,' but at a quarter scale. The material for the reed walls was imported and used by Tongan constructors.[20] Similarly the Fijian Chief's house and meeting house were built by 'a non-Mormon specialist in Fijian culture', whilst the Maori carvings were painstakingly made in New Zealand and then transported onto site.[21] The Samoan house is built with sennet rope lashing the poles together. Some changes are admitted. For example, US building codes and fire regulations have meant that sugar cane has been substituted for leaf.[22] The current guide concedes that the Marquesan compound is made of coral rather than basalt on the rather ingenious reasoning that 'the decision to use coral is one the practical Polynesians would have made, for they were adept at using locally available material.'[23]

Critics of the Center question the authenticity of the display. Some concentrate on the materials used for construction. One member of the Samoan village is credited with two reproaches; the inauthentic use of plywood in the walls and the height of the Chief's house from the ground. 'The foundations are very high in Samoa. Chiefs always like to be higher than anybody else.'[24] Other critics concentrate on the landscaping. One of the great surprises when visiting the PCC for the first time after experiencing other ethnographic parks is its smallness. Most parks are 70 acres or more; Taman Mini Indonesia is 425 acres. This means that the villages in the PCC are not so much on a sea as round a pond. This has serious repercussions for any understanding of one of the chief features of the Pacific states, their distance from each other on the largest of the world's oceans. As Webb remarks, 'the lagoon contributes to the impression conveyed throughout the center that the Polynesian cultures represented by the villages are very similar and very close.'[25]

The PCC administration is aware of the problems that any visual representation contains. The question of time period in the display is the most significant. The general solution adopted is to construct the buildings according to archaeological and anthropological records of precontact life.[26] This, of course, risks further questions about the appropriateness of this solution for any understanding of the contemporary Pacific where with rapid centralisation and urbanisation the

[20] A-M. Robinson 'The PCC: a Study in Authenticity', 33.

[21] R. O'Brien Hands Across the Water, 79.

[22] Dale Robertson, personal interview 20 April 1995.

[23] R. Ariyoshi PCC: All the Spirit of the Islands, 29.

[24] T. D. Webb 'Highly structured tourist art', 66.

[25] T. D. Webb 'Highly structured tourist art', 65.

[26] A. Ross The Chicago Gangster Theory, 45, 'A great deal of scholarly attention has been devoted to ensuring the detailed architectural, ecological, and artifactual authenticity in the villages. This task is overseen by an environmental historian from Easter Island, Sergio Rapu, the Director of the Institute of Polynesian Studies at BYU and Director of Cultural Development at the PCC'.

greatest proportion of populations often live under galvanised roofs with cement walls, as visitors to either of the Fijian cultural centres can hardly have failed to notice on their way from their hotel. The same, of course is true for visitors to the PCC, as Stanton observes. In this context it has been wise of the designers to describe the Hawai'ian encampment as 'Old Hawai'i'. To circumvent this problem tour guides at the PCC remind visitors of this visual discrepancy but note that it is impossible to represent change in time in such a small venue.[27]

So the problems of Skansen stalk its successors. The difference however between Skansen and the PCC is not so much that the methodology is different. Both are, after all, committed to a salvage architecture and ethnography. The difference lies essentially in who is represented. In Skansen the answer is the Swedes. This fact is emphasised by the changes that had to be made at Skansen post 1905 when Norway ceded from Sweden. The PCC, however is not providing an ethnographic and architectural mirror only to Hawai'i but employing building materials, artefacts and people from other Pacific states. Nevertheless, this is a selection. As Jonassen, a political scientist at Brigham Young University-Hawai'i and a citizen of the Cook Islands notes bitterly, there is no village for Cook Islanders,[28] nor for that matter, he could have added, are there for Niue, or Rapa Nui (Easter Island). But the PCC defends its representation of the past in terms of its commitment to preservation. Preservation and conservation may also be brought together. The architecture and design details throughout the Center are one of the foremost ways that both visitors and 'villagers' are reminded of the legacy which all the literature stresses, risks being lost but which is recoverable.

Of course, few critics of the PCC are Pacific archaeologists or architectural historians. This form of criticism is only part of a larger complaint over authenticity and ethics. What is perhaps surprising in this context is how few academic critics venture into the field of their criticism to confirm their censures. This is particularly true of anthropologists who are conspicuous by their absence from this area of contemporary cultural criticism, one in which they have specialist knowledge. However, there are some strong views held about the propriety of what goes on at the PCC. Identical criticisms surface in all the cultural theme parks discussed in this study. They relate to the notions of culture that such institutions promote and how they do it. Put simply the complaint might be expressed thus: 'You manipulate your performers to create a travesty of the society that they traduce in stereotyped impersonations'. Few express this view as bluntly but most would subscribe to it.

[27] M. Stanton *The PCC*, 199.

[28] Jon Jonassen 'Politics and culture in the Pacific Islands', 5.

What troubles the critics about these parks, and this is as true of the PCC as in Indonesia or China, is the theatricality of the presentation and the implications that this has for the authentic treatment of cultures, as well as the spontaneity and freedom of the performers. In many minds there is a lurking suspicion that the performers are in some way captive, perhaps in a way analogous to the actors of Imperial expositions. Furthermore, the performances themselves are geared to tourist expectations. These are the central issues and they raise questions particularly about the status of culture, the nature of the performance, the role of the student actors, and the expectations of visitors.

There are varying degrees of assertiveness expressed by PCC personnel on the question of cultural authenticity. At its most triumphalist is the reported slogan of a Fijian villager, 'if you want to see Fiji, go the PCC',[29] a sentiment that will be echoed in other parks. Wineara, the current Director of Polynesians Studies at the university and long associated with the PCC, has described the PCC as providing an opportunity for Pacific Islanders to tell their own story. 'The imposition of one culture upon another is, in many ways, a burden which is only fully revealed as those imposed upon tell their own story. There are few places in the world which allow minority peoples this opportunity. The PCC is one of them.'[30] This claim is based on the relationships established in the villages. Each village is headed by a chief (often one of chiefly status at home) who is responsible for the students and ex-students who perform there. The PCC makes much of these relationships. The brochure announces 'The Polynesian Cultural Center emphasises close relationships between older, respected Polynesian leaders and young students as a way of preserving Polynesian heritage.'[31] It is through this contact and learning that cultural continuity is maintained. As McGrevy has stated, 'conservation can vitalize past objects by reviving the skills that produced them and then, by incorporating these skills into present practice, thus deepen and enlarge upon our cultural perceptions and thereby our awareness of our identity.'[32] It is with some pride that the PCC records that a BYU-PCC employee was chosen to head Tonga's National Culture Centre.[33]

Preservation and continuity of culture at the PCC are contrasted with the rapidly-changing world of the Pacific Islands. Fijian students, for example, learn rope making in the PCC with traditional materials rather than with the prevalent synthetic fibres. These same students themselves become 'cultural repositories'.[34] 'Though outnumbered in their homeland, Fijians with the encouragement of their

[29] Jessie Maiwiriwiri cited in A-M. Robinson 'The PCC; A study in authenticity', 53.

[30] V. Pere (now Wineara) 'The Villager' 20 March 1981, 3.

[31] R. Ariyoshi The PCC (1987 edition), 12.

[32] N. McGrevy The PCC, 18.

[33] A-M. Robinson 'The PCC: a study in authenticity', 52.

[34] M. Stanton The PCC, 201.

elders, and through the young people educated at the Polynesian Cultural Center, are saving their arts and beautiful meke (song-dances) for posterity.'[35] But the religious framework of Lai'e makes it possible for nationals not of Polynesian origin to study the Polynesian tradition of their home island group. 'East Indians from Fiji, Filipinos from Hawai'i, and Chinese from French Polynesia have an opportunity, often for the first time in their lives, to cross the cultural line and gain insight and even participate in the dominant culture', in a way that would often be impossible at home.'[36] But this learning is also put to use in the PCC. For example, Hawai'ian students of Japanese extraction conduct hula dancing classes for Japanese tourists. This is the cause of some disquiet and leads to Hawai'ian performers distinguishing between a haole (white) hula and a real one.[37]

A further multicultural virtue claimed for the PCC is that people from different island groups live and work together. This familiarity is further reinforced by

**Fijian (left) and Samoan performers at Samoan village**

[35] R. Ariyoshi *The PCC*, 20.

[36] M. Stanton *The PCC*, 204.

[37] T. D. Webb 'Highly structured tourist art', 67.

traditions of being missionaries on each other's islands. So, a Fijian when asked why he was spending his time in the Samoan village replied that he liked Samoan life having spent two years there as part of his missionary work.

Island culture is further recognised by the holding of national days (Kamehama Day for Hawai'i, Waitangi Day for New Zealand, Fijian Independence Day etc.) which are celebrated by the staff of the PCC. Equally importantly, cultural approval from the rulers of the Pacific States is actively sought at PCC. As Hawai'i is the principal hub of cross-Pacific air traffic, dignitaries from all the island states of necessity visit Oahu on their travels. So King Tuafa'ahau Tupou IV visited the Tongan village in 1976; the New Zealand Maori Queen Dame Te Atairangikaahu visited the PCC in 1979 accompanied by the Minister of Maori Affairs; and Malietoa Tanumafili II of Samoa in 1981.[38] These and other island dignitaries attend cultural performances put on in their honour. Whether they actively comment on what they see or refrain out of politeness is an interesting question. It is likely that etiquette prevents much critical comment particularly as in states such as Samoa and Tonga Mormons hold significant public offices.

This, in turn, raises issues about whose image the culture is to be preserved in. There have already been skirmishes between Mormons and their critics about authentic dress. The full body cover required of actors (particularly females) in all villages is in marked contrast with other tourist shows elsewhere in Hawai'i. It certainly is at odds with most records of precontact dress but is nevertheless truly representative of most current island life, particularly in urban areas. What makes the debate further complicated is that the PCC operates different time references in architecture and costume, the first precontact, the second contemporary. This conflation makes it difficult to establish a basis on which to discuss authenticity. Webb cites one villager's views on this point: 'Culturally the costumes that we wear are close. Sometimes it's not as close as it should be because of the restrictions that the church has on it. And at that point the culture kind of takes a back seat to the way of the church.'[39]

To some extent the issues of culture and cultural preservation, although important in themselves and certainly significant in the PCC's orientation, are secondary to the style of presentation made to the audience. It matters little whether performers are well versed in their own culture if what they do does not reflect this cultural competence. The PCC acknowledges this. Stanton speaks of the culture on show at the PCC as a 'model culture and not the reality, the process of

[38] A-M. Robinson 'The PCC: a study in authenticity' p 33, *The Villager* September 1979, and August 1981.

[39] T. D. Webb 'Highly structured tourist art', 68.

selecting the cultural elements to be shown admittedly creates a "fake culture", one which would not be found today anywhere in the various Polynesian Islands.'[40] He, nevertheless, defends this form of presentation as providing a synthetic experience for visitors bringing together a panorama of historical forms which have been preserved to the present.

What is certainly true is that the catalogue which the visitor is provided with is a remarkably academic piece of popular ethnography far removed from any normal tourist brochure. This in itself, however, creates a problem. The sectioning of the catalogue, mirroring the geography of the villages, reinforces what Ross calls 'the Western paradigm of ethnicity.'[41] The interconnectedness of linguistic, kinship and economic networks across the Polynesian islands becomes erased in favour of culturally specific practices, architecture and dress. Such distinctions are precisely what the post-colonial elites of these Pacific states stress in their attempts to create a new sense of nationalism. This will be considered further in the next chapter, particularly with reference to the development of culture and kastom in Vanuatu. What might be significant here is that, in their attempt to epitomise particular cultures, the village displays resort to a form of cultural shorthand notation which risks collapse into stereotype. Stanton explains the mechanism:

> As a cultural model or 'living museum', the Center uses a thematic
> approach which concentrates on certain dynamic and tangible aspects
> of culture. In an effort to make the visit more meaningful, each
> of the 'villages' has developed some specific activity such as husking a
> coconut, learning to use a certain percussion instrument, involvement
> in a game of skill, or performing a dance that encourages tourist
> participation.[42]

The examples that Stanton offers are significant. The husking a coconut provides a good opportunity to inspect what issues may arise in performance at the PCC.

The first village that tourists are likely to encounter as they enter the PCC is the Samoan. Here they inevitably join the crowd to see what is going on. What they will find is a Samoan man in the middle of the site, often flanked by a Japanese interpreter, performing a comic routine demonstrating how to husk a coconut. Ross provides an example of a script.[43] This is a dangerous act, not in the physical activity which is admittedly skilfully executed as becomes evident as soon as a victim from the audience makes a pitifully bungled attempt to open the coconut, but in the liber-

[40] M. Stanton *The PCC*, 197.

[41] A. Ross *The Chicago Gangster Theory*, 50.

[42] M. Stanton *The PCC*, 199–200.

[43] A. Ross *The Chicago Gangster Theory* pp 47–8; also in a briefer version in O'Brien,15.

**Samoan husking coconuts**

ties that the Samoan takes with his audience. He selects a stooge, often Japanese, usually female, and asks her about where she lives, what she does and about her holiday in Hawai'i. This is a sophisticated piece of reverse ethnography in which the stooge confirms a series of negative stereotypes about her culture and herself, as well as her incompetence to perform physical tasks requiring strength and dexterity. The script is highly charged with reference to skin colour. The Samoan's punch line on cleaving a coconut and offering it to members of the audience is 'Drink this and you'll become brown like me'. Many of the asides that the performer addresses to his stooge are couched in terms of ethnic stereotypes, some highly unflattering, particularly those directed at the Chinese and Japanese members of the audience. By liberally spreading his insults across the audience the Samoan husker draws squeals of embarrassment from every one. This is an act which is regularly policed and sometimes censored (especially for jokes against gays and Japanese).[44] The question that arises is why the PCC should give such prominence to an act like this. For answer one has to surmise that it represents a response to the kind of evening entertainment that tourists have come to expect of the floor show, but it is certainly

[44]  V. Wineara, personal communication.

a perplexing spectacle in the context of the PCC which contains nothing else even remotely similar.

If the visitors' timing has been right the first experience at the PCC could be quite different. The afternoon starts with a performance called 'The Pageant of the Long Canoes'. This form of presentation was conceived at the PCC and has been copied and adapted widely in other cultural theme parks. Pacific Harbour in Fiji, already described, provides one of the later adaptations of this themed entertainment. 'The Pageant of the Long Canoes' offers tourists who are stationed along the lake shore a moving spectacle of village performances. O'Brien gives a good account of the first canoe to emerge:

> On the platform, still and statuesque, are five figures: a *kahuna* holding aloft a royal *kahili*, or standard, of red and yellow feathers; behind him a tall, athletic *ali'i*, or high chief, wearing a golden *malo* and regal helmet and a cloak of golden feathers; the chief's dark-haired consort, crowned with a *lei* of golden feathers, a necklace of whale-tooth ivory at her throat; and behind them, two ladies-in-waiting in long golden gowns.[45]

This is the prelude to a performance of the Hawai'ian myth 'The Goddess of the Feathery Rain'. This short vignette sets the scene for five similar floating tableaux staffed by clean-limbed and athletic performers. The Fijian float is devoted to the story of the origins of firewalking, the Samoan shows a myth of an eel god and his love for a mortal, the Maori float has a similar theme whilst the Tongan dwells on the divine origins of its kingship. Tahiti is represented by the enactment of the story of the freeing by a chief of his parents from a giant bird. There are not enough Marquesans resident at PCC to mount their own float. Other Marquesan performances rely upon 'borrowing' actors from other villages.

'The Pageant of the Long Canoes' acts as a prelude to the much longer, fully orchestrated evening show. But some of the same considerations apply to both. The style of performance is similar, with a rapid set of dance routines all crisply executed by young actors with much energy and skill. A narrow range of theatrically engaging presentations reminds the audience who is performing at any one time. So in the evening show Sielu Avea from Samoa, 1993–94 world fire-knife champion (featured on the cover of the PPC publicity leaflet, 'What to See and Do in Polynesia') and the coconut husking performer already discussed, steals the show with his lighted torch performances, repeating the firewalking reference from the

[45] O'Brien *Hands Across the Water*, 7.

afternoon pageant. The choreography for both shows is credited to the instructors from each culture, all resident elders at the PCC, the most recent having joined in 1971. Authenticity in performance is stressed in the evening show guide, 'Instructor Josefatu Tulele from Gau, Lomaviti, Fiji, joined the PCC staff in 1975. "Joe" says he tries to go back to Fiji every year "to keep our dances current and authentic. Visitors from Fiji who see the show are always amazed at how well our young Polynesian Cultural Center dancers are able to perform." '[46]

Whilst the songs and dances range from the avowedly traditional to 'high energy group dance' it is difficult for an audience to see them as the catalogue suggests, giving 'lessons in love, duty, faith and honor . . . easily absorbed and embraced.'[47] The problems for the audience are too complex. Firstly, the different sections, although clearly marked by an announcer, follow each other so fast and concentratedly that there is insufficient time to assimilate. The evening show allocates between six and twelve different routines to each of the six island groups represented in a programme little more than 90 minutes in total duration. But there are other reasons that an unsophisticated audience might experience difficulty in absorbing the various mythological or ethnographic references, and these are related to the limited demands made upon viewers.

Two considerations are important when reviewing the impact of the performances. Firstly, these shows do not look markedly different from any others that the audience might have seen, with one exception, the inflection of exotic cultural references. There are however, good reasons for the audience to ignore such references: they are subservient to the ethos of the show, which is contained within a familiar format, with pre-recorded music, sentimental ballads, show turns like firedances, simulated volcanic eruptions, and a curtain of water raised and lowered between acts.[48]

If the music is all produced in the same format, the appearance of the performers is oddly familiar too. This is because the costumes although varied according to national style, resemble each other in their manufacture. Although research goes into the history of each culture, the costumes are made from new fabrics and contemporary dyes. The latter, in particular, provide a tonal similarity to the ensemble. The underlying problem in offering daily performances throughout the year is that traditional materials will not stand up to the stress. A solution adopted at the PCC is to make a costume using near traditional materials for special occasions and another of man-made fibre for regular performances.[49]

[46]  PCC *Mana: The Spirit of Our People* n.p.

[47]  R. Ariyoshi *PCC: All the Spirits and the Islands*, 41.

[48]  This renovates a World's Fair innovation, the Acquacade at the 1939 New York Fair which had curtains of water 200 hundred feet wide. Nelson 'Walt Disney's EPCOT', 123.

[49]  R. Epping, personal communication.

To the more culturally literate other incongruities stand out. Although the performers are required by the manager to study Anthropology 101 as part of their degree and they undertake a ninety day probation, this does not prevent substitution and borrowing in the show.[50] Substitution is sometimes obvious even to the foreigner to the Pacific, particularly when pale skinned actors appear first as Maori then as Tahiti which can result in quite different standards of performance in a single troupe. But the practice is widespread and only of deep concern to those who insist on cultural copyright. But borrowing songs, dance movements, drum rhythms do raise concern among critics and some performers. As will be discussed in the next chapter cultural copyright and royalty payment for performance has always been practised in many parts of the Pacific and there are those now who ask why lucrative tourist performances should be exempt from such agreements. Cultural copyright is becoming as much an issue in the Pacific as in the litigious world of Disney.

Some of the borrowings at PCC shows are slight, even unintentional. Tongan male dancers when performing a Samoan dance will tend to use Tongan head movements.[51] Others are more significant and involve misattribution even if from ignorance. Jonassen, a Cook Islands drummer as well as a member of faculty of BYU, was employed as a student at the PCC. He records his surprise and disquiet at hearing Cook Island drumming and songs described and performed as Tahitian.[52] There is, of course, nothing new about cultural borrowings. It happens all the time in Pacific cultures. The distinction, however, is that the borrower is usually aware that an item has been borrowed and from whom. So, normally, is the audience. Such confidence cannot be assured in the commercial world of the PCC with its near one million visitors.

Does all this matter? It could be argued that the criticisms raised so far are rather purist. Critics either pretend that one can offer a more complex view of cultural entertainment than is in fact possible, or they grumpily turn their back on the enterprise and deem the whole thing unethical and unworthy. These criticisms, it might be suggested ignore both the nature of tourism as well as most of the realities of Pacific life, particularly that experienced by the student performers.

There is, the apologists for ethnographic tourism would maintain, something naïve about turning one's back on the phenomenon as though by doing so, it will disappear. Furthermore, so the defence might continue, there is at the back of much criticism a kind of romanticism which creates a manichaean vision of

[50] L. Apolo, personal communication.

[51] J. Jonassen, personal interview, 20 April 1995.

[52] J. Jonassen *Cook Island Drums*, Ministry of Cultural Development, Rarotonga, 1991, 12.

authenticity which is opposed to the modern world. There is also an implication that such performances only provide a parody which demeans those that act in it. Therein lie the real reasons for such disquiet at students at the PCC performing for paying visitors. There is something akin to indenture or peonage in the minds of the critics when they conjure up a vision of performance at the PCC. To counter these views the critics are invited to consider the reality of life at the PCC and how it relates to its sister institution Brigham Young University-Hawai'i (BYU-H) next door. 2,000 students are enrolled at BYU-H. Some 800 come from the Hawai'ian islands, 600 from elsewhere in the Pacific such as Samoa, Tonga, Fiji, New Zealand, Tahiti, the Cook Islands and some islanders from the Pacific diaspora, principally Los Angeles. There are also Japanese from Los Angeles and Samoans and Filipinos from Hawai'i. The rest of the students come from the continental United States as well as from Asia.[53] Students come to BYU-H as one of the few providers of a tertiary education in the Pacific. Apart from New Zealand and Hawai'i there is only one other university teaching in the English language, the University of the South Pacific with its main campus in Suva, Fiji. A higher education is as prized in the island states as elsewhere and much more difficult to acquire than in many places because of the small populations, weak economies and great distances between places.

Students are interviewed by university personnel at home at their church according to academic criteria. In the early 1980s a shortage of performers from Tahiti and Fiji led those interviewing to seek students with a good grasp of song, dances and drumming to bring to Lai'e. But the policy was abandoned in 1985 when it was decided that it was far easier to train academically gifted students necessary cultural skills rather than the other way round.

Of the 2,000 some 700 students elect to work at the PCC for up to twenty hours per week. Of these 150 are performers in the villages and the evening show, the rest work backstage in support roles. The PCC provides scholarships for a third of the students of $3800 per annum for four years. Why do students elect to work in the PCC? Beside the desire for education, the principal reason must be financial, either to support themselves or to help out at home. Stanton records that all full-time adult workers from the Tongan village remit home $100 per month. This helps either their family or their own bank account, and hence the country's balance of trade.[54] Another powerful attraction is vocational training. Performers may well plan to enter tourist entertainment back home either in a similar role or as managers. Craftworkers may look for openings in workshops. Similarly those who

[53] J. Muaina, personal communication.

[54] M. Stanton *The PCC*, 200.

53

have worked in ticketing, financial control, catering or transport will have expertise that is transferable. Economic justifications are not hard to make when island per capita income is extremely low. The fact that only as little as 20 per cent of students do return home serves as a reminder that they have indeed become career oriented.[55] It further suggests that they become active agents on their own account.

Students at the PCC are also sophisticated adults who have often been involved in tourism before attending university. Stanton gives an example of the irony to be perceived in tourist-performer encounters. 'On numerous occasions, visitors have exhibited loud outbursts of exuberance because they have seen "real natives at work in their own grass huts." Most workers at the Center are accustomed to such rather naïve behavior and recognize that this type of reaction is intended to be complimentary.'[56] Not all their responses are as mute. Ross offers an example of a PCC joke that situates the tourist in a rather less flattering light:

> A 1993 April Fool's issue of the BYU campus newspaper *Ke Alaka'i* – dated April 1, 2013 – ran a feature on the addition to the PCC of Haole Suburbs as another model village, featuring identical tract houses. Performances included 'walking like a haole', 'using a remote control', and 'dancing out of rhythm', while the food offerings included macaroni and cheese, and peanut and jelly sandwiches.[57]

Is the work undertaken by the students demeaning and undignified? How free are they? The answer depends upon the position of the questioner. From the perspective of the student working through college it is essentially work, work like any other, less dirty and tiring than some and less well paid than much other. It is also undertaken from within the ambit of the church and with a very strong emphasis upon the value of culture *per se*. Thus the chiefs and elders in the villages share culture with students and as the brochure announces, 'the Polynesian villages at the Center are not only museums, they are living, vital links to home. They are crucibles of culture.'[58]

What lies behind some of the criticism about the authenticity in architecture, performance, and cultural policy at the PCC is a dislike of the Mormon Church itself and its activities throughout the Pacific. Some critics are firmly of the opinion that the church has been instrumental in destroying much traditional life throughout Polynesia. It comes as an ironic perversity, such critics would maintain, for the church now to be proclaiming itself the saviour of traditional life. Once this view is

[55] A. Ross *The Chicago Gangster Theory*, 44.

[56] M. Stanton *The PCC*, 194.

[57] A. Ross *The Chicago Gangster Theory*, 46.

[58] R. Ariyoshi *PCC: All the Spirit of the Islands*, 5.

[59] A typical example looks like this: 'The Mongolian President will attend a luncheon hosted by the Indonesian Chamber of Commerce at the Hilton Hotel before the entourage visits Taman Mini Indonesia Indah. Last night the state guests attended a function which Vice President Try Sutrisno and other high-ranking Indonesian officials attended. The function started with an exchange of souvenirs and ended with a cultural show'. *The Jakarta Post*, 4 March 1997.

put on the table it becomes possible to see the full degree of distrust and distaste that is felt. What the criticism does suggest is that the Mormon church is somehow not part of Pacific life. However since 1850 it has had a major presence in the region and is lived by a significant population. No doubt, within the church there are differences and disputes between adherents from different island states, but the church has made a point of emphasising what unites Polynesians. This is attractive to Polynesians within the church but also without.

The ethnographic spectacle at the PCC at Lai'e provides material for debate, disagreement and struggle. What it at stake is a tussle between parties with different interests. The very success of the venture has sharpened the criticism. Poorly attended and run-down shows do not attract the same notice, nor the degree of censure. But a major tourist attraction run as an educational charity by a missionary church with indigenous actors from across the Pacific stacks up the list of issues for dispute in a singular manner. What is surprising is how, despite this range of contentious elements, the PCC has become the model emulated by other cultural theme parks throughout the world. Neither ideology, nor religious affiliation, have made the PCC less attractive to such an unlikely follower as the Chinese government, as will be detailed later in this chapter.

### Bhineka tunggal ika (although different we are united)

Taman Mini Indonesia Indah (Beautiful Indonesia in Miniature Park), always referred to in its abbreviated form as Taman Mini, looks as unlike the Polynesian Cultural Center as is conceivable. Its sheer size, 425 acres, dwarfs the PCC. It is an official government sponsored institution and has great symbolic, cultural and even political significance. Like the PCC it offers a range of ethnographic representations around a lake and it has a religious message. But it is an institution created to exemplify to Indonesians and the world at large the simultaneous diversity and unity in material form. Taman Mini is the official repository for culture, and foreign dignitaries are regularly taken to visit as part of their official programme.[59] They may be somewhat bewildered by what they see. Not only will they be exposed to a range of ethnographic displays and enactments from all over Indonesia but they will also see soldiers 'being ourselves for you' at the Military Museum and a series of huge monuments to episodes during the war of independence as well as statuary commemorating Buddhist and Hindu cosmology.

**Military Museum, Taman Mini**

A monument to the Non-aligned Nations further emphasises the political context within which culture is displayed.

On entering to the park the official visitor or the ordinary tourist will encounter Pancasila, the state-promoted doctrine which combines the five major religions of Indonesia under an umbrella synthesis.[60] There is a large statue entitled 'Monument of the Flame of Pancasila' providing Pancasila with the imagery commonly associated with war memorials.[61] To reinforce the military symbolism there are two large murals flanking this entrance entitled 'Relief of the Indonesian Struggle' underscoring the nationalist anticolonial message. Beyond the statue, in the park the visitor will see represented Protestantism, and Catholicism with their churches, Islam with Pangeran Diponegoro mosque, a Hindu Dharma temple as well as a Buddhist Wihara. The Protestant church can be booked for weddings on Saturdays. This group of religious buildings acts as a visual reminder to the visitor of the official state doctrine of Pancasila which recognises and syncretises all of these faiths under the slogan 'Unity in Diversity'. This is the central and ubiquitous theme underlying the design of Taman Mini. Religious endorsement is particularly important. So a plaque commemorating the planting of a tree by Pope John Paul II

[60] The five tenets of Pancasila are, belief in one God, a just and civilized humanity, the unity of Indonesia, democracy guided by the wisdom of measures taken by deliberation/representation, social justice for all Indonesian people (translation: Acciaiola).

[61] J. Pemberton in his 'Recollections from "Beautiful Indonesia",' 246, discusses the symbolic significance of the dimensions of the statue as being both a reference to the date of the declaration of independence as well as a conjunction of sacred numbers.

on his visit in October 1989 also doubles up as not only as approval of the Catholic church at Taman Mini but it also signifies approval of its setting within Pancasila.

Cultural importance is provided for the park through the Indonesian Museum which is situated just inside the entrance. There are another ten specialist museums within the grounds of Taman Mini, each offering a different gloss on the official agenda of nationalism. Some are obvious; a forbidding low, large square crenellated pentagon-shaped fortress is naturally a museum of the armed forces; a building with tanks and external scaffolding and pipework serves as a museum for oil and gas. A sport museum and a stamp museum offer other metaphors for nationality. The simile is pushed further. A Fauna museum is constructed in the shape of a giant lizard or Komodo Giant, a reptile specific to central Indonesia. The Asmat museum seems out of register but, as will become apparent, is very much part of the visualisation of Indonesian identity.

But these contemporary emblems of nationalism are not immediately visible to visitors. Beyond the Indonesian Museum and the Pancasila religious buildings the site opens up to offer a twenty acre lake with the Indonesian archipelago superimposed on it to a scale to fit within the lake surface. Along the shores of the lake are situated 27 Rumah Adat (Customary Houses or pavilions). Tucked into the far corner is a late addition, Timor Timur (East Timor). At the far end of the lake is a large monument and garden dedicated to the non-aligned movement. There is already firmly built into the layout of Taman Mini an historically specific as well as a political rhetoric. All of this is far too large for the viewer to take in at one glance. To get an overall view visitors are advised to take a cable car which will take them across the lake and thus traverse the geography of the country in one sweep taking in the variety of its inhabitants through the architecture of the regional pavilions on the way. For a closer look, but with a speed sufficient to reinforce the unity of the experience, there is also a monorail circling the lake. These are important devices because the normal method of transport, taxi or shuttle bus, takes too long to retain any semblance of the map. What visitors receive from their aerial perspective is what Hubinger calls a 'literally tangible Indonesian reality'.[62]

The regional pavilions are the central focus of Taman Mini. The official leaflet (brochures are impossible to obtain) reinforces this point:

> The cultural heritage of Indonesia is an invaluable wealth and pride. The legacy which consists of diverse customs spreads extensively throughout

[62] V. Hubinger 'The creation of Indonesian national identity' Prague Occasional Papers in Ethnology, 1 1992, 2.

the Indonesian archipelago. However, due to the wide spreading and various customs, only a few people have the opportunity to witness the appearance and existence of the overall cultural heritage. 'Mini Indonesia' endeavors to bring closer and unite this diverse cultural heritage in one place, with which increasingly, people of Indonesia may become closely acquainted.[63]

This declaration suggests the purpose of the park, to create a visual and conceptual unity from an extraordinary diversity. Hubinger neatly sums up the problem confronting Indonesian nationalism and thus Pancasila. He notes that Indonesia was arguably unique in Southeast Asia in having no dominant ethnically definable group or culture, using a language not a mother tongue of any of its members, and without any political identity before European conquest.[64] It is hardly surprising that Taman Mini should exemplify the various steps to unify such a diversity of people in one of the most physically attenuated geographies in the world with one the largest populations. Six million Indonesians visit Taman Mini every year to celebrate 'unity in diversity', all through the lens of anthropology. Here they are entertained by the range of what Hubinger calls 'hitherto living traditions' in a form redolent of the imperial convention which celebrates 'the brilliant present as well as admirable past of a nation'.[65]

Taman Mini does not come without historical pedigree. The most evident is Disneyland. The Children's Palace comes from Ludwig of Bavaria's fairy palace at Neuschwanstein via Disneyworld. It reminds the visitor where the idea originated. Mrs Soeharto was moved by her visit to Disneyland to declare in 1971 'I was inspired to build a project of that sort in Indonesia, only *more* complete and *more* perfect, adapted to fit the situation and developments in Indonesia, both materially and spiritually'.[66] This was not a project to be trifled with. Inhabitants of the area were evicted, student protests were put down by soldiers in Jakarta, and the opposition in the press to what was seen as a massive waste of money was rejected not only by Mrs Soeharto but firmly by the President himself who warned those opposing the plan, 'Quite frankly, I'll deal with them! No matter who they are! Anyone who refuses to understand this warning, frankly, I'll deal with them'.[67] From this point on the construction became a matter of national prestige. To underline its symbolic importance Taman Mini was inscribed in the rhetoric of political theatre. Provincial governors were summoned to ceremonially hand over their 'provinces' at Taman

[63] Taman Mini 'Indonesia Indah' leaflet, n.d. (1992?).

[64] V. Hubinger 'The creation', 4.

[65] V. Hubinger 'The creation', 7.

[66] cited by J. Pemberton 'Recollections', 241. There is some uncertainty about the pedigree of the idea. Benedict Anderson speculates that she may have got the idea from a visit to Timland, a similar development in Bangkok in March 1970. see his 'Notes on contemporary Indonesian political communication' *Indonesia* 16, 1973, 64.

[67] B. Anderson 'Notes', 65.

Mini to Mrs Soeharto before the grand opening in 1975. For this they were required to don 'their' provincial costume for the event, despite the fact that they were mostly Javanese generals.[68] It comes as little surprise that learn that Taman Mini was chosen in 1983 as the venue for the wedding of the Soeharto's daughter, Siti Hediati. This was to be, of course, a traditional wedding following Javanese custom, attended by members of the government, traditional rulers and the diplomatic corps. What is perhaps somewhat unexpected is that the ceremony should be planned with military precision following a specially commissioned manual complete with sketches of manoeuvres planned at various stages of the ceremony.[69]

Performances of this kind provide a poor substitute for the normal expectation of a cultural park. There are, admittedly, regular musical and other forms of performance at Taman Mini. But there are few residents in any pavilions. Each province hosts in its pavilion an annual 'full scale special program when artists, musicians and dancers are brought in to re-create an authentic regional culture experience'.[70] The description is significant. People are imported for the occasion, one described as a 'regional culture experience'. Each of the terms singly and the phrase as a whole bears inspection.

There is at the heart of Taman Mini a glaring anthropological contradiction.[71] There is no such thing as regional culture. Some Indonesian cultures, or languages, like Javanese cover more than one province; the larger islands have three provinces. But, more importantly, others like Irian Jaya, contain a large number of quite distinct and unrelated peoples. Decisions have to be made at Taman Mini, in a way reminiscent of those at the Polynesian Cultural Center, as to which cultures to privilege and which to ignore. The major way that this has been done is through architecture. It is the most designed and eye-catching of architectural examples that find a place in Taman Mini. This in turn has some interesting repercussions. Anderson maintains that the constructions at Taman Mini form the template on which regional architecture itself becomes based. He states 'in Jakarta, Surabaya, Medan and Makasar, new urban dwellings are being built which provide a clear stylistic link between the rumah adat and Mini's "rumah adat".[72] It is as if Swedish regional architects copied from Skansen but with one significant difference – the Skansen examples are genuine buildings resited. The regional pavilions at Taman Mini, as the promotional literature admits, 'duplicate traditional houses constructed from authentic materials' and to emphasise and augment this authenticity, they contain 'handicraft displays, traditional costumes and other artifacts

[68] J. Pemberton 'Recollections', 247.

[69] J. Pemberton On the subject of 'Java'' Cornell University Press, 1994, 178–9; 'Recollections', 254–5.

[70] 'Taman Mini Parks is Indonesia's centre of "Unity in Diversity"', Exciting Jakarta, Jakarta City Government Tourist Office, 1992, 16.

[71] Hitchcock expresses the political issues involved succinctly: 'In order to achieve the regime's objectives, a "batik curtain" was lowered to obscure the anthropolgical similarities of the nation's diverse ethnic groups' M J Hitchcock 'The Indonesian cultural village museum and its forebears' 23.

[72] 'Notes', 70.

particular to that province'.[73] Anderson is scathing about this form of display: 'warehouses of regional artifacts, they will in effect be icons of ethnicity.'[74]

Visitors are not left to look on baffled at these largely empty cultural warehouses, they are instructed. This is a literary as well as visual education. Panels of text adorn the walls, labels are attached to artefacts, mannequins populate the building clad in ethnic garb which is often described in detail. A label in the North Sumatra pavilion informs the visitor, 'the people are hospitable and warm. Arts and cultures make this region a paradise for social scientists'. Sometimes there are surprises: the South Sumatra pavilion, for example, contains a set of cases with miniature dioramas of vignettes depicting the war of independence. Everything is there to instruct, indeed, unalloyed entertainment is notable by its near invisibility at Taman Mini.

Miniaturisation has a particular educational purpose as Pemberton demonstrates with reference to a Ministry of Education and Culture text book. In this introduction to Indonesian culture students are taken to Taman Mini where they inspect the miniature version of Borobudur, the famous Buddhist construction in Central Java. They express delight at the replica, as they have only seen a photograph of it before. It is also better than the real thing because, since it is reduced in scale they can see it all at once.[75] Taman Mini features more generally in educating young children in recognising ethnic identity. One commentator gives a graphic illustration:

> The government's concern with promoting (and controlling) ethnic diversity is reflected in schoolbooks which teach 'moral education'. The first lesson schoolchildren learn is that Indonesia is "different but also one" (berbeda beda tapi satu juga). Their first classroom assignment is to cut out pictures of houses, dances costumes of Minangkabau, Toraja, Balinese, and other officially designated 'ethnic groups.' The list coincides with the groups represented at Taman Mini.[76]

Such is the power of Taman Mini's authority that individuals from a region will look to the park to provide an authentic version of ethnography.[77] It has become a signal of the coming into acceptance of a culture for it to receive this kind of official recognition. So, for example, as part of its bid for official recognition, Sulawesi has instituted plans for a 'South Sulawesi in miniature'.[78] This is, however, to follow an already well-established tradition. 'Balinisation' in the early nineteen thirties was

[73] 'Taman Mini Parks', 16.

[74] 'Notes', 70.

[75] 'Recollections', 157; 'On the Subject', 157.

[76] T. A. Volkman 'Vision and revisions: Toraja culture and the tourist gaze', 108.

[77] J. Pemberton 'Reflections', 248–9.

[78] T. A. Volkman 'Visions and revisions' p 109. Though she thoughtfully adds 'Each of the province's "four major ethnic groups" is to be represented by its distinctive house: Toraja, Makassar, Bugis, and Mandar. Debates about the project reveal the particular politics of representation. How, for example, can one explain the absence of a Toraja planner to represent the region's major tourist attraction and its most famous house? How can one justify evicting seventy Makassarese families from their land and lived-in houses to build four model houses on the proposed park site? How can one persuade a Bugis noble to sell his own ancestral (lived-in) house so that it may become the exemplary (empty) Bugis house for tourists? And in Mandar, an area where neither politicians, tourists, nor anthropologists have yet defined "the Mandar house," how can one discover one?'.

promoted by the Dutch to instil an appropriate image of the island for tourists. As Hitchcock remarks, 'the Balinese were to be taught by their new masters how to become more authentically Balinese'.[79] The movement of adat from being the description of cultural practice or 'the natural way to act' to the point where 'culture has become art, ritual become theatre, and practice has become performance'[80] has become widespread in the Indonesian reformulation of culture. This suits spectacles like Taman Mini very well, but it can also be considered, as Acciaioli suggests, as a form of symbolic violence created by the co-option and redescription of elements of daily life by official cultural experts. But the importance for the populace of this transformation cannot be overlooked.

What Taman Mini creates is an anthropological cast to everyday thinking. It also makes Indonesians ethnographic virtuosos and even travellers. Diversity, particularly when well marked, recognisable, distinctive in visual terms, but controllable, becomes an object of fascination. All of the immigrants to the huge megalopolis of Jakarta can go to Taman Mini if they are homesick, and, of course, if their home culture is itself represented. But some may like the representations of themselves more than others. There is, despite and perhaps because of the visual rhetoric of Taman Mini more than a hint of the imperial expositions and pre-Second World War in the park. Pemberton notes the uncanny resemblance between the architecture of the Indonesia Museum and the Nederlandsche Paviljoen at the 1931 International Colonial Exhibition in Paris. But there is a more tangible link to be found and it is located in the special treatment that one province receives at Taman Mini. The province is Irian Jaya and it is accorded far more than its fair share of space and consideration than any other.

One reason for such particular attention might be its honoured place in Indonesian history. As Anderson has noted, West Irian (as it was known in colonial days) was where nationalists were incarcerated by the Dutch and they frequently died there.[81] The colonial authority of the Dutch was restored in West Irian when Indonesia seized its independence in 1945, and Dutch rule continued (in name at least) in the vast jungles and mountains of Western Papua until 1963. For these reasons West Irian symbolised the final step in the consummation of Indonesian nationhood. The imposing Irian Barat monument in Jakarta is an echo of what Anderson calls a monumentalist 'speech'.[82] Whilst all of this may well be true, it diverts attention from what is really going on at Taman Mini.

[79] M. J. Hitchcock and L. Norris *Bali: The Imaginary Museum*, 24.

[80] G. Acciaioli 'Culture as art: from practice to spectacle in Indonesia' 153.

[81] B. Anderson *Imagined Communities: Reflections on the Origin and Spread of Nationalism*, 176.

[82] B. Anderson 'Notes', 61.

**'Melanesians' at Irian Jaya pavilion, Taman Mini**

At first sight it might strike one merely as a curiosity that postcard stands in Jakarta, Bali and even Lombok should sport so many cards depicting the Dani from Irian Jaya.[83] But publicity for Taman Mini promising 'the primitive arts of Irian Jaya'[84] suggests an all-too familiar set of references, as noted earlier. But this image was built into the official structuring of Taman Mini. The Irian Jaya Provincial Governor, General Sutran, was decked out at the solemn inauguration of Taman Mini, 'with a fur crown and a large ornamental nose bone',[85] a particularly piquant performance for a Javanese man.

Irian Jaya (literally 'glorious Irian) represents the ultimate challenge of Indonesian inclusive nationalism as the inhabitants indigenous to this place were not Malay but Melanesian. So striking is this fact that the display, forlorn though it is, at the Irian Jaya pavilion includes a canoe on a lake containing a group of Melanesians holding spears. This group has been cast in concrete from what appears to be a photographic original but they have been supplied with cotton shorts. Associated with these people are the 'primitive arts' for sale in a kiosk and an Asmat carver in full head dress often to be seen whittling away new wooden artefacts in the compound.

[83] I have in mind particularly the Impact Postcard series featuring the photography of Karl Muller, but other publishers like SVR produce identical products. see also E Edwards 'Postcards: greetings from another world' *Journal of Museum Ethnography* 1993.

[84] 'Taman Mini parks', 16.

[85] J. Pemberton 'Recollections', 247.

A question remains as to whether the visitors to Taman Mini can incorporate the image of Irian Jaya within the framework of Indonesian nationality whatever the official rhetoric. It seems likely that this might be a case of what I have described earlier as the stubborn resistance of an audience to revise its stereotype. To that extent the issue of difference provides a perplexing issue for Indonesians wishing to demonstrate that they are united in nationality. Irian Jayanese continuing irredentism in the face of population transfer into the province and the constant warfare with multinational mining companies makes the issue the more delicate and perplexing. One of the possibly unconsidered consequences of anthropological heightened awareness is that it may make the cultural distinctions a source of disquiet and disdain rather than wonder.

**Asmat carver at Irian Jaya pavilion, Taman Mini**

**Chinese style
tourism**

During the past decade China has followed Indonesia's example in offering visitors a range of visual presentations of its theories and policies on ethnic issues. The fifty four minority nationalities have produced 'not only hard currency but also important symbolic capital'.[86] It is the proud boast of the Communist Party of China that from the founding of the People's Republic the equal status and autonomous rights of all were recognised. These rights were enshrined in the 1949 constitution when minority nationalities were specifically mentioned.[87] A department of state, the State Nationalities Affairs Commission, promotes the autonomy of minority nationalities and their equal rights.[88] Throughout the past fifty years ethnicity has, despite the oppressive anti-minority period of the Cultural Revolution, remained a self-proclaimed feature of Chinese official life. The fact that these 54 recognised nationalities, comprising 6 per cent of the population, inhabit some of China's most sensitive frontier regions and many continue to prove restive (Xinjiang and Tibet are the most prominent but by no means only examples) makes the equivalent of 'unity in diversity' a vital strategic policy in China.

In its determined strides towards modernisation China has also developed tourism. In this movement China has had to decide, at an official level, like Indonesia, whether to consign the minority nationalities to history or to encompass them in new plans. It is something of a surprise to discover that China has chosen to spearhead its drive for modernity with its minorities. Chinese tourism is synonymous with the visual display of ethnography. Some areas have been dedicated as special regions for tourism, particularly Hainan Island off the South East shore which is the site of mass tourism construction and Yunnan in the Southwest because of its cultural diversity and beautiful mountainous scenery in the cockpit between Vietnam, Laos, Myanmar and Tibet.[89] But Yunnan's rugged geography makes tourist travel difficult and time-consuming. So in the regional capital, Kunming, a sample of minority peoples have been brought together in a 'village'. The description has a familiar ring:

> Covering an area of 2.7 hectares the village has, in addition to the White Pagoda, five residential houses, two Dai-style buildings and other constructions including a Burmese-style temple and a so-called Wind and Rain Bridge. The first residents were fifty Dai people. Next to the Dai village a 6.7 hectare Bai village has begun to take shape . . . Local officials say that Yunnan province has 26 ethnic groups and each has its

[86] D. Gladney 'Representing nationality in China', 95.

[87] *People's Republic of China Year Book*, 1990, 91.

[88] *Directory of Chinese Government Organs*, 1989/90, 44.

[89] M. B. Swain 'Commoditizing ethnicity in Southwest China', 26.

own colourful customs and practices. Thus 26 different ethnic villages will be built beside Lake Dianchi to form a unique cultural scenic group.[90]

Similarly, in the neighbouring province of Guizhou, a village, Xijiang, chosen as 'a natural museum of traditional Miao lifestyle' has been electrified and had tourist facilities attached.[91]

But the logic of such ethnically-inflected tourism is ever more centripetal: why not bring together the ethnic population of China in one place? This is exactly what has been done at Shenzhen, the fastest growing and most advanced city in Guangdong Province, South East China, right next to Hong Kong. Here the China Travel Company, registered in Hong Kong has been involved in the construction of not one but three parks, Splendid China (1989), China Folk Culture Villages (1991) and Window of the World (1995). These have been built with Hong Kong capital. This does not mean, however, that they necessarily have to follow the example of Disney. There remains in each of the parks a strong sense of Chinese identity. As the architect of the Shenzhen complex remarked 'every element in the display should consistently exclude foreign and non-folk tendencies; no foreign handicrafts, no Macdonald's hamburgers.'[92]

There is considerable tension between the educational, cultural and even political purposes that these phenomena serve and the popular entertainment offered to attract a mass audience. Each park offers a distinctive mix of landscape, architecture and performance. It is the weave of these three features that provides the specificity of what I term 'Chinese Style Tourism'. All attempt a form of ethnographic realism; the visitor is invited not only to inspect but to enter the theatrical sense of the occasion. This theatricality is made possible through three-dimensional sets

It can be argued that Splendid China offers the clearest case of Chinese style tourism philosophy in action. It is also, in many ways, the most traditional and yet the nearest to the European original from which it derives. Like Mrs Soeharto, Mr Ma, the architect of the Splendid China project had a dream,

> During my trip to Europe in 1985, I visited the famous Madurodam 'Lilliputian Land' in Holland when an idea came to me and I was thinking how great it would be if we could build a miniature scenic spot

90  Kou Zhengling 'Kunming Builds Ethnic Culture Tourist Zone', 29.

91  T. S. Oakes 'The cultural space of modernity: ethnic tourism and place identity in China', 6.

92  Ma Chi Man cited in N. Stanley and Siu, King Chung 'Representing the Past as the Future: The Shenzhen Chinese Folk Culture Villages and the Marketing of Chinese Identity', 38.

in which China's renowned scenic attractions and historical sites could be concentratedly displayed so that people could admire and know more about China's beautiful wonders, splendid history and culture as well as various national customs and habits in shorter time.[93]

Miniaturisation, as at Taman Mini, permitted Ma to offer within the space of 75 acres fifteen major landscape features including mountain ranges and passes, the famous stone forest at Lunan, Yunnan, the Yangste gorges and a working copy of the Huangguoshu Falls, Guizhou. On this landscape are placed 48 major historic Chinese constructions with the Great Wall encompassing a quarter of the site. Many of these are religious structures (temples, mosques, pagodas, stupas), other are imperial (The Imperial Palace and the Temple of Heaven). Because the site is smaller than Taman Mini visitors in Splendid China do not need an aerial perspective to encompass the whole. Chinese topography and architecture are literally at the visitors' feet. To reinforce the sense of Chinese-ness another feature of Madurodam is introduced – the figurine. '65,000 life-like pottery figurines spreading over in groups in front of the magnificent ancient buildings, in the picturesque natural spots and dwelling houses with unique local characteristics . . . (They) are harmoniously and skilfully integrated with the scenic attractions to form a pleasing whole, expressing the cream of glorious culture and the long history of the Chinese nation.'[94] These figurines are also used to populate the minority regions. The peoples of the Southwest are represented by costumed miniatures of Bai and Dai people whilst Mongolians are shown at a fair on the Mongolian grassland (entitled 'Joyful Nadamu Fair'). Visitors are reminded in this most oxymoronic of parks that they are in the presence of authority – 'The World's Largest Miniature Spot.'[95]

Splendid China nevertheless remains a highly didactic experience for the visitor. The marketing plan behind the tourist attraction was 'to give more people of the world better understanding of China, and thus promote the friendly contacts between the peoples of China and other countries and give great impetus to the development of China's tourism.'[96] However, the lessons to be learned at Splendid China are not obvious to the stranger. Why certain topographical features and architecture were selected is nowhere explained, nor the purpose of the display of minority peoples. In order to understand these features the viewer has to become acquainted with both details of Chinese territorial claims (hence the significance of the Potala Palace) and contemporary readings of Chinese history (the figurines in

[93] Ma Chi Man 'Let the World Know More About China' in *Splendid China: Miniature Scenic Spot Grand Opening Souvenir*, 5.

[94] 'Lilliputian Pottery Figurines' in *Splendid China*, 37.

[95] *The World's Largest Miniature Scenic Spot – Splendid China Catalogue* 1990.

[96] *World's Largest Miniature Scenic Spot*, p 6.

**Waterfall on Ciuhu lake, China Folk Culture Villages**

historic dress 'holding a memorial ceremony for Confucius'). Chinese style tourism appears to work best for those who know their Chinese history. This problem is one that it shares with Taman Mini: the key to interpretation is elusive. This may explain some of the difficulty of transporting and translating Splendid China to Orlando in 1992.

When it came to providing the 'real ethnographic experience' the architects looked abroad for ideas and 'a great amount of first-hand valuable information was gathered about the local ethnic cultural tourist attractions.'[97] Foremost among those consulted was the Polynesian Cultural Center, especially for ideas about training, personnel policy and tourism management.[98] China Folk Culture Villages (henceforth FCV) set about providing a fuller sense of visitor engagement when it opened in 1991. Although only half the size of Splendid China (45 acres) it nevertheless sought to create a 'beautiful landscape'. 'The landscape of the villages, which is the product of the clever use of the natural environment and architectural

[97] Shen Ping and Chueng Yuet Sim (eds.) *China Folk Culture Villages*, 4.

[98] I. Rene Yang, personal communication. This was to lead to a formal training programme in hospitality for FCV employees at Brigham Young University-Hawai'i which is still in force.

features of various villages, reproduces in a creative way the natural wonders of mountains and rivers, thus heightening the expressive effect of the customs and conditions of different nationalities'.[99] Although no attempt is made to suggest geographical accuracy, a lake of one and a half miles length provides a central focus. Around Ciuhu lake are strung the natural and human constructions. At the northern end is a large waterfall which is set against a model of Yunnan's Stone Forest. The strategy is the opposite of that at Splendid China. Although miniaturised, the physical features remain at large enough a scale to engulf visitors. The real Stone Forest is a spot much visited by Chinese and international tourists and subject to major development.[100] Near this model stone forest the Yi, the inhabitants of the Stone Forest district, have their village. Ciuhu lake not only provides a landscape backdrop but also supports architecture and people. Twelve different bridges are strung over it in varying regional and historic styles and both performers (e.g. Cormorant fishers) and visitors navigate its surface. The lake also sports the most Chinese of aesthetic developments – the Folk Laser Music Fountain. This paradoxically-named entertainment consists of a range of computer-controlled

**'Reformed architecture' compound at Zhuang Village**

[99] Shen Ping and Chueng Yuet Sim (eds.) *China Folk Culture Villages*, 19.

[100] M. Swain 'Staging Sites/Sights of Yunnan China's Stone Forest: Whither Post-Modern Authenticity?'.

**Shaman scaling ladder of swords beside the Dong Drum Tower**

water jets which are lit with changing colours. Shape, colour and rhythm can be supplemented by lasers and synchronised with music. Such fountains although technically highly sophisticated are already highly popular in China and offer a safer variant on fireworks displays.

Around the lake there are twenty other well known scenic places from around China and twenty four villages built in the architectural vernacular of twenty-one selected ethnic minority. There is no attempt to simulate antiquity in these buildings. In FCV contemporary ethnic architecture is shown. For example The Zhuang compound follows the principles of 'reformed architecture'. The traditional intermingling of people with animals is replaced with segregated premises with animals beneath and humans on the first floor. Similarly, the Mongolian Yurt sports an air conditioning unit as do reformed architecture yurt settlements in Mongolia. The interiors insist that tradition is consistent with modernisation. Similarly, the structures can be seen as part of a contemporary architectural trend in China, the 'old town' idiom, which is used widely to a provide a conscious copy of antique building in the design of streets and neighbourhoods.[101] Reconstruction, even if it means bulldozing ruins, is seen as part of modernisation. As Oakes has expressed this paradox, 'far from threatening a traditional landscape, modernisation was awaited as the impetus for rebuilding what outsiders expected to be there.'[102] However, reconstructions also come with a political agenda in FCV as in Splendid China. Two of the largest structures, a stone watch tower and a lamasery, come from Tibet. It is in 'Tibet' that official visits by Chinese leaders are often posed, though, perhaps surprisingly, when Deng Xiaoping visited

[101] A. Anagnost 'The Nationscape: Movement in the Field of Vision', 592.

[102] T. Oakes 'Cultural Geography and Chinese Ethnic Tourism', 11.

**Mongolian yurt attendant** (photo Siu, King Chuag)

FCV in January 1992 he was taken to see a shaman performing a traditional scaling of a ladder of swords. Yet there are signs that landscape, architecture and people do not always marry as happily as the creators of the park would wish. Four of the twenty one nationalities represented are Muslim, yet none are so identified. The mosque, finished two years after the rest of the park, only has an exterior. The interior is merely a shop for Uygur products.

Performance in FCV feels more like the PCC than Taman Mini, and it cements the experience in a way impossible in Splendid China. Firstly, all the villages are inhabited by their respective minority people. Most are amazingly welcoming and willing to patiently answer questions about the topography, architecture, crafts and way of life. These attendants provide what the Midway Plaisance and the earlier imperial expositions were never able to do – to let the ethnographic subjects become interpreters rather than objects. The performers engage the tourists not only as site interpreters but also through the regular performances in the village during the day and at the Folk Arts Parade and Performance in the evening at the Central Theatre. The village performances spill out from the village and become musical processions around the lake and take the visitors with them. Performers thus offer a vital mediating role, interpreting their culture, situating it within that of other Chinese people and offering human form to the landscape, architecture and interior design. The overwhelming majority of visitors to FCV are themselves Chinese, mostly from the surrounding provinces in the most developed region of China. What the visitors are acquiring is a mode of tourist experience, itself a form of modernity, where this form of cultural consumption has great novelty for well-paid workers, officials and the military. The representation of the far reaches of China is as much part of contemporary display as the Folk Laser

**Hoarding advertising 'Window of the World' Kowloon, Hong Kong**

Music Fountain. Minority regions are as subject to reform and renewal as the Special Economic Zone in which FCV is situated.

Visitors have an opportunity denied in the PCC or Taman Mini. They can literally disappear from sight. Whilst at the PCC tourists can avail themselves of photo-opportunities and have themselves photographed with 'Polynesian' accoutrements, in FCV they can do far better. They can select from a menu the minority costume that appeals most and hire it for the day. Thus when there are performances at the various villages one needs to look for hairstyles and shoes to detect the inhabitants from the interlopers.

The last of the Shenzhen parks, Window of the World, offers the sharpest of contrasts, yet it completes, albeit in negative form, the picture of Chinese style tourism. This, the largest of the parks in Shenzhen (120 acres), was opened in 1995. The logic of the enterprise is simple. If Splendid China provides a trip round

**I M Pei pyramid at entrance to 'Window of the World'**

**View from the 'Eiffel Tower', 'Window of the World'**

China's topography and culture, and the Folk Culture Villages extend the notion of Chinese-ness to the non-Han citizens living mostly in the farthest reaches of China's authority as well as providing an opportunity for the visitor to interact and learn from the minority people themselves, then Window of the World brings the rest of the world to China, but, it should be stressed, strictly on Chinese terms. It is in Window of the World that the full picture of Chinese style tourism becomes evident. The promotional poster for the park reminds the viewer that the rest of the world is seen in relation to China. The entrance reinforces the point. One emerges from the subway into I. M. Pei's pyramid at the Louvre. This is work of a US citizen of Chinese parentage and the architect of the Bank of China's building in Hong Kong. To underscore the point, the title of the park in Chinese characters is in the hand of the President of China, Jiang Zemin, composed on the occasion of his visit.

The park is likely to bewilder the unprepared visitor. Although twice the size of Splendid China it appears cramped and the logic of display is hard to grasp. The only way to get any sense of the topography is from the top of the Eiffel Tower which, like its original, as Barthes suggests, enables the viewer to distinguish and link the features beneath 'an object virtually *prepared*, exposed to the intelligence, but which he must himself construct by a final activity of the mind'.[103] There is a rather vague geographic sense to the ensemble. The Americas are to the West of Africa and Europe. The South Pacific is likewise banished to the South East though Europe extends to meet it. Miniaturisation is employed to pack in as much material as possible. The immensity of the Africa Safari Park, Kenya is suggested by huge herds of miniature wildlife. Scale changes make for some surprises. The juxtaposition of Stonehenge (1:2) and Buckingham Palace (1:15) and in the Americas of Manhattan (1:100), the Capitol (1:15), Mount Rushmore and the Grand Canyon require the viewer to refocus constantly. Some of the effects are, however, theatrically exciting, especially the waterfall representing Niagara Falls. It could be argued that this confusion of scale is only troublesome for those who know the originals. The landscape at Window of the World is not designed to produce verisimilitude but to provide a photographically recognisable set of structures. Scale is of no significance. Items can be cropped, enlarged, reduced and collaged at will by the photographer. Windows of the World offers a feast of photo opportunities.

The same may be said of performance. Chinese female performers as equestrian horseguards or sentries at the Arc de Triomphe provide entertainment but hardly suggest serious imitation. However, there is an interesting lack of congruence between the attention paid to a continent or country and the peopling of it. Europe has thirty six structures and two performances (stiff, military and formal). Asia has thirty five buildings. Only the Japanese complex is staffed, mostly by Chinese minority young women and men. North America, with twenty two buildings is represented by its ethnic minority, 'North American Indians', not specified but undoubtedly from the Pacific North West. These performers are, again, Chinese minority people. The Maori performance before the Marae – one of only five Oceanic structures, is staffed by dancers from Yunnan. Their performance, bewildering though it is in its choreographic references, reminds the knowing viewer again of the Polynesian Cultural Center. Africa has only eight structures but again it is the site of a major series of performances, by members of the Wa people, chosen, no doubt for the hue of their skin. The evening show owes a lot to the Polynesian Cultural Center in its choreography and costume. But again ethnicity is highly stresses.[104]

There are two contradictory ways of reading Window of the World. On the one hand, it can be seen as a deliciously ironic parody and riposte to the World's Fairs tradition. There is evidence to substantiate such a view. It is consistent with

103 R. Barthes 'The Eiffel Tower', 243.

104 'Talented singers and dancers of different colours of skin perform wonderful programs on the grand stage of the World Square.' Ma Chin Man *Window of the World* (special presentation edition with English text), Shenzhen, 1995, p 53.

**'Maori stick dance' at Area of the Pacific**

the treatment in Splendid China and the Folk Culture Villages to pay special attention to minority cultures. The 'Maoris' and the 'American Indians' remind the viewer of continuities in the world as well as the physical differences. However, the treatment of Africans reminds us that the residue of imperial tradition with its evolutionary schema finds a home in China. As the catalogue states:

> Living in such a severe environment as black Africa, its people, however, store infinite vitalities. On festival nights, they always make bonfires beside their camps, singing and dancing, in a speed and rhythm simple but wild, which reflect the primitive impulse and talent from the bottom of life.[105]

Evidently, this Chinese interest in minority peoples in Western societies is no defence against a very old fashioned view of Africa. The African performances are among the most popular and most discussed by visitors at Windows of the World. Here there is no invitation to be a Maori nor an African. They serve as a reminder that the traditions of World's Fairs have by no means disappeared, nor have traditional responses to Black people in China.[106]

[105] Ma Chi Man *Window of the World*, p 35.

[106] Black slaves appeared in China at the end of the Tang Dynasty. Portuguese in Macao brought slaves after 1555. As Dikötter notes, 'these African slaves sometimes ran away into China, and eventually constituted a community of their own in a district of Canton' *The Discourse of Race in Modern China*, 17.

**A Chinese variant: Taiwan**

One of the most significant cultural differences that has occurred over the past half century as Taiwan has developed so differently from mainland China can be seen in its ethnographic theme parks. These have taken as their subject the indigenous populations of Austronesians who arrived in Taiwan from the South before the Han crossed the straits to dominate the island. The culture parks in Taiwan lack the exuberance and the showiness of FCV because, despite their attention to issues of nationalism, their agenda has been formulated differently. Firstly, there is a political and cultural question right at the heart of Taiwanese identity which has become more significant over time. The basic question is 'who are the Taiwanese and how do they relate to China?' In different ways each of the Taiwanese parks attempts an answer largely through landscape and architecture supplemented judiciously by forms of human interpretation.

The earliest of the Taiwanese parks has sought a purist approach. The theme park itself is situated in a regional park within the territory of one of the ten non-Chinese peoples collectively known as aboriginals. Taiwan Aboriginal Culture Park (TACP) at Ping Tung was opened in 1987. The park is built into a steep hillside at the edge of a large river valley and is in three parts. At the entrance to the park is a small museum with a traditional exhibition of ethnic minority life and costume (a Yami diorama). Beside the exhibition centre are a range of villages, all reconstructed from the records of Japanese ethnographers earlier in the century. Half a mile away there is a dance performance area with a shop and restaurant. Here members of the local Paiwan people put on performances of their own and other minorities' songs and dances. Another half mile up the trail the remainder of the nine minority mountain tribes are represented by small villages. There are some sixty buildings in all. Each is carefully signed with description of the original's design and purpose. The overall impression of Taiwan Aboriginal Cultural Park is of a thoughtfully landscaped outdoor museum. The buildings are dwarfed by their setting and the remoteness of the park discourages many visitors. The academicism in display makes few concessions to light amusement and in fact underlines the distinction between the aboriginal peoples and other Taiwanese. The faithfulness of the reconstruction of the buildings of the early twentieth century further reinforces this sense of remoteness. It is difficult to agree that the park achieves its declared intention, the familiarisation of the visitor with aboriginal life.[107]

The second park in Taiwan, the Formosan Aboriginal Culture Village (FACV) in Nantou County was completed at roughly the same time as Ping Tung. It

107 'We hope that we can make the characteristics of aboriginal artefacts more understood and appreciated through this park, and accomplish the aims of the culture preservation, the inheritance of culture and the culture education' *Taiwan Aboriginal Cultural Park*, (leaflet) n.p., n.d.

161

**Map of Formosan Aboriginal Culture Village**

is situated close to one of Taiwan's main tourist attractions, the Sun Moon lake, a paradigm of Chinese picturesque, a setting of mountain and water. The overall size of this park is twice that of Splendid China (150 acres). Like Ping Tung, FACV is dedicated to portraying the nine aboriginal peoples of Taiwan in a series of villages down the hill. Academic authority is invoked throughout the hillside display. As the guide notes, 'all aspects of the layout and architecture of the houses have been completed under the guidance of learned experts, so as to convey a genuine idea of traditional aboriginal culture'.[108] The same Japanese ethnographer Chijiiwa Suketaro whose fieldwork and detailed plans of aboriginal villages (1938–43) were employed at TACP are likewise used as a basis for construction here at FACV. Dr Suketaro also acted as a consultant in the design of this park.

The buildings have original and reproduction objects of daily life in them and unlike TACP they are attended by indigenous interpreters. Towards the top of the hill is the Naruwan theatre. 'Here the FACV Youth Troupe, made up of enthusiastic and talented young people from each of the nine Taiwan aboriginal tribes, performs traditional songs and dances for the enjoyment of or guests.'[109] This show

**Skullframe based on original of 1860 studio by D Chiyiwa Sukekaro**

[108] Chang Jung-i 'Preface' in Yao Te-hsiung (ed.) *Formosan Aboriginal Culture Village*, 1.

[109] *Guidebook*, Formosan Aboriginal Culture Village.

employs the format of the Polynesian Cultural Center, combining elements of the Pageant of the Canoes, using a watercourse to bring performers on boats and rafts past the audience in a moving pageant before a stage with its curtain of water jets as at the PCC evening show. Even the costumes look familiar in their bright primary tones. These performers take visitors down to the base of the hill to invite them take part in another performance at the World's Stage. This journey to the foot of the hill serves to link two other elements with the aboriginal culture villages: the Future World and the European Palace Garden. Future World offers rides and other forms of amusement park attractions. It also has a prominent laser fountain. It is the European garden, situated opposite the main entrance to the park, that provides the visual surprise. This fifteen acre site stretched across the valley floor provides an ideal type formal garden. The rationale for the display is itself interesting:

> The area around Sun Moon Lake has long been regarded as one of the finest beauty spots in Taiwan with its attractive combination of mountain and lakeside scenery. However, with overseas tourism on the increase in recent years as local incomes have risen, many Taiwanese have become attracted by historic European culture. Therefore the proprietors have taken advantage of this magnificent setting to create a European-style garden covering six hectares for visitors to enjoy right here at home.'[110]

FACV thus backs a number of options at the same time. Serious purpose and thematic unity are provided by the aboriginal villages, all authentically reproduced. These villages are, however, only one of three elements in the park. On arrival, visitors can choose between the European Palace Garden or the World Plaza. The culture villages lie beyond the World Plaza. It is quite feasible to spend a day at the park enjoying rides and eating in the European Palace without venturing into the villages beyond. To entice visitors to make such an expedition the most immediately recognisable and arguably the most exotic of minorities, the Yami, seafaring fisherman who live on an island off Taiwan's South coast, are placed beside the entrance to the World Plaza. FACV is constantly upgrading the showground so that competition between the various elements of the park become ever more intense. One is tempted to see the aboriginal villages existing because of the other elements but it must be admitted, nevertheless, that aboriginal culture is more visible and accessible here than at Ping Tung.

[110] Yao Te-hsiung, *FACV*, 149.

The third of Taiwan's culture parks takes a different approach. Taiwan Folk Village (TFV) at Changhua opened in 1993. It is roughly the same size as FACV, Nantou County (145 acres). At the top of the park there is the obligatory waterfall and artificial river. Four other small lakes dot the park. At the top of the site there is a section devoted to aboriginal cultures. But the attempt is desultory. The culture at Taiwan Folk Village is Taiwanese Han. The guidebook sets the tone:

> The changes in Taiwanese society have been too drastic. The scenery I knew as a child, bit by bit, has disappeared. Suddenly our lives have become a rift. The establishment of Taiwan Folk Village is to fill the cultural gap in modern Taiwanese life. Here we preserve for you the most complete Taiwan folk culture. Not just buildings or ancient cultural objects for display. More important, we recreate and present for you the true forms of early Taiwan life.'[111]

Taiwanese traditional life is to be found firstly in architecture. The resiting of the two hundred year old Dien Au temple in the park is part of the representation of heritage architecture and is accompanied by examples of 'Old Town' style. Copies of the city's former wall and west gate provide the entrance to the park. Above the gateway copies of Taiwan's most important documents over the past three centuries are displayed in a museum.

Taiwanese culture is represented by individual performances of traditional trades in a village at the foot of the city walls. Here, noodles, wine, camphor and paper are prepared by demonstrators and visitors are invited to try their hand. Cultural performances are offered by troupes such as Cantonese Lion Dancers. Political endorsement is provided by the official portrait of the President of Taiwan visiting the park shortly after its opening. To ensure financial viability the park also houses a fun fair at the top of the hill totally overshadowing the aboriginal village. Unlike its two companions, Taiwan Folk Village constructs the past of Taiwan more in the idiom of mainland China. It is the disappearance of Chinese architecture, way of life and manufacture that provides the logical linkage in the park's presentation. Here, unlike at Ping Tung or Nantou County, performers do not integrate the landscape and architecture. They remain antique relics more akin to those to be found in industrial open air museums in North America or Europe. Nevertheless, the park at Changhua serves to amplify the sense of 'Chinese style tourism'. The treatment of the aboriginal cultures in this park suggests that its authors were less concerned

[111] *Taiwan Folk Village Guide*, 26.

**Cantone lion dance**

[112] This approach reinforces a traditionalist view of Chinese culture 'Hua-hsia' which stresses 'a set of primordial values which is both a source of cultural uniqueness (vis-à-vis other people) as well as a myth of historical origin' A Chun 'The culture industry as national enterprise: the politics of heritage in contemporary Taiwan, 73.

[113] A. and P. Wylson *Theme Parks, Leisure Centres, Zoos and Aquaria*, 24–7 and 34–8.

[114] The catalogue has four sections, reminiscent of Disney promotional literature style: Dream One – Progress and Development; Dream Two – Freedom and Peace; Dream Three – Joy and Happiness; Dream Four – Life and Eternity. Ma Chi Man *Window of the World*.

with the integration of all elements in contemporary Taiwan and more with a traditionalist Chinese view.[112]

What at the end of the day, distinguished Chinese culture parks from others? There is a distinct debt of gratitude to occidental traditions in the design and operation of these parks. Yet, there is also a counter-movement, to use landscape, architecture and performance to generate a specifically Chinese experience. To accomplish this, the architects of these parks have drawn on elements of Chinese formal park and garden planning and combined them with distinct topical reference. This anchoring of landscaping to historic and cultural reference provides the basis for the spelling out of a sense of national identity in Taiwan and China quite as much as in Taman Mini. The European Palace Garden at FACV looks out of place because it jars in its formal abstraction with the sometimes fussy topographic and architectural detail elsewhere in the park and in the others.

It is this visualised sense of nationalism that sets these parks off from other EPCOT style internationalist theme parks like Busch Gardens, or Europa Park, Rust, Germany.[113] Window of the World, turning its back on China, continually emphasises global internationalism, But this universalism is, however, highly abstract[114] in the style of Disney. It is as if the rest of the world can be seen as a series of images which have no anchor in history or geography. This runs directly counter to the topicality of all the other Chinese parks. They have a much less manichaean vision than their occidental counterparts. In the latter the future is juxtaposed in a utopia contrasted with the present. For the Chinese culture parks, the past, the present and the future flow together.

## A worldwide phenomenon

Finally, it could be asked whether these Asian culture parks are anything more than an evolutionary curiosity. Do not the Formosan Aboriginal Culture Village, The Tang Dynasty City, Singapore and The Middle Kingdom at Ocean Park, Hong Kong[115] represent an intermediate form of entertainment on the way to the real utopian and ahistoric world of internationalism and postmodernity? As theme parks mature and become more sophisticated, this argument might run, is the specific local reference likely to evaporate as, say Parc Asterix is doomed to do when confronted with Disney World Paris? Is there an iron law that demands that we progress (or regress) from representation to fantasy? To ask questions in this form may itself betray a parochialism assuming that Disney represents a ubiquitous future. The lesson that these Chinese theme parks offer is that the landscape of modernity may be skilfully married to the politics of enjoyment. Splendid China sets out the alternative agenda clearly, 'to replenish space among scenic spots, "realistic activities" scenes with national flavour also depict vividly the age-old Chinese cultural traditions and local customs. All views are modelled on real objects and based on full and accurate facts. The project thereby is a perfect combination of entertainment and learning, art, knowledge and education'.[116] Whether such a rationale will continue to operate effectively will depend to a large extent on the willingness of citizens in Asian countries to see their world through this particular prism of nationalism. Rather than withering away, such forms of presentation may be strengthened by the skilful admixture of sophisticated funfairs with culturally oriented living dioramas.

The future may not be quite so rosy. There are already some ominous signs. The replica of Splendid China built by Chinese enterprise in Orlando right next to Disney World, has not been a conspicuous success.[117] The didacticism and lack of high technology attractions leaves most visitors bemused and disappointed. Splendid China has not transplanted well to the Disney environment. Attendances

[115] A. and P. Wylson *Theme Parks*, 45–6.

[116] 'The Splendid China Planning' in *Shenzhen Urban Planning and Design: A Compilation for the First Decade Celebration of the Special Economic Zone*, Shenzhen 1990, 98.

[117] A revealing account of the sort of 'hot capital' involved from Beijing is detailed in Harrison Salisbury's *The New Emperors: China in the Era of Mao and Deng*, 424–5.

are also slipping badly at Shenzhen.[118] Partly this decline may reflect the high cost of entrance combined with more choice. From one competitor in 1993, Shenzhen now faces at least twenty others which range from one respectfully devoted to Confucius in Qufu to the excitement of an 'earthquake park' on the site of the major disaster at Tianjin. The desire for entertainment may well be outstripping the appetite for ethnography in the service of nationalism.

Nevertheless, there still seems a keen thirst for ethnographic tourism and display. Two further Asian examples demonstrate the variety of purposes that such developments may serve. The Little World Museum of Man in Central Japan is a large development (over 300 acres) which combines high technology museum displays of such items as evolution, technology, language, social organisation and religion. These natural history displays are introduced by 'young lady companions, "culture mates" wearing ethnic garments'.[119] So ethnic displays come themselves in different modes. But the rest of the park has the expected Skansen-effect of dwellings collected and restored from around the world. The melange recycles many of the spectacles from other parks. A Samoan house is placed next to a Micronesian one under palms by a pool, and a Nyakusa house and woman's house from Tanzania appear to have been transplanted directly from the Tanzanian Village Museum.[120] There appears to be the same scholastic intensity devoted to buildings and explanations at The Little World as at Skansen.

The last example comes from Sarawak and demonstrates quite a different direction for ethnographic interaction. The Sarawak Cultural Village is set next to a beach resort created for Visit Malaysia Year in 1990. This small village has an array of non-Malay ethnic houses, though Malay and Chinese also have their own buildings too.[121] What is distinctive about this development is that the cultural resources of the park are put to a new employment. The Holiday Inn and the Cultural Village take the logic of Taman Mini with that of the Folk Culture Villages and synthesise them in a new attraction for tourists. The personnel from the park provide all the trappings for an exotic tourist wedding. As the brochure announces,

> Together, we offer you a choice of three exotic wedding packages – Malay, Iban (Sea Dayak) and Bidayuh (Land Dayaks) . . . The rituals and customs adopted in each of the three wedding packages are authentic. And the costumes are no less so. And each has its own charm and appeal. All you need do is choose, and leave the rest to us.[122]

[118] Jigang Bao provides the following statistics (given in millions):

Visitors

|  | Overseas | Domestic |
| --- | --- | --- |
| 1990 | 0.65 | 2.67 |
| 1992 | 0.50 | 2.42 |
| 1993 | 0.47 | 2.67 |
| 1994 | 0.41 | 2.34 |
| 1995 | 0.21 | 1.38 |

|  | Window of the World |
| --- | --- |
| June 1995–June 1996 | 5.00 |

[119] The Little World Museum of Man *The First Open-Air Museum of Mankind in the World*, Aichi, n.d. (c1990), 14.

[120] The Little World p 3 map compared with National Museum of Tanzania *Guide to Village Museum*, Dar Es Salaam, p. 15 and map

[121] Kampung Budaya Sarawak: Sarawak Cultural Village *The Living Museum of Sarawak: A Window into Cultural Diversity*, Kuching 1990.

[122] Holiday Inn, Damai Beach *You are invited to a most exotic wedding . . . your own*, Kuching, 1994 n.p.

Thus the thrust of the Midway Plaisance has been at least superficially reversed: European visitors (and they are Europeans in the Holiday Inn literature looking suitably solemn) come to perform their wedding with traditional authority. This does nothing for the inhabitants of Sarawak except provide some passing employment as extras on a theatrical set.[123] This is, of course, the most central of objections to ethnic tourism. By a perverse logic, the more realistic the appearance, the more disquiet is aroused in the mind of anthropologists and ethnographers, if not among the indigenous performers for whom the very question of being themselves becomes a potential sentence imposed by a tourist industry, local or international, bent on using ethnicity as a principal marketing and branding device. A question remains as to whether there are any viable alternatives to this form of imposition created either in the name of nationalism or of tourism proper.

[123] The Sarawak government has instituted an official 'thanksgiving for the harvest' performed by Iban and Dyak, largely for tourists. This, it is reported, does little to dampen the resentment of the Dyak majority for their Malay rulers. I am indebted to Bien Chiang of Academia Sinica, Taipei for this information. But for a discussion of the employment of indigenous minorities within peninsular Malaysia see Wazir Jahan Karim 'Anthropology without tears: how a 'local' sees the 'local' and the global' 'in Henrietta L. Moore *The Future of Anthropological Knowledge* Routledge 1996, 122–3.

# The revolt of the represented:
## the growth of cultural centres in the Pacific

### Situating the problem

[1] see chapter 1 footnote 8.

[2] for a detailed discussion of Pacific islanders' satirised performances of Europeans see Vilsoni Hereniko 'Representations of cultural identities' in K. R. Howe et al *Tides of History: The Pacific Islands in the Twentieth Century*, University of Hawai'i Press, Honolulu 1994, 411.

[3] Caroline Vercoe 'Postcards as signatures of place' *Art Asia Pacific* 3:1 1996, 87.

[4] C. Vercoe 'Postcards' 89. Vercoe also discusses the work of Jim Viviaere who provides a visual critique of Gaugin in his work entitled *6 Tahitians, 2 in Leningrad, 4 in Papeete, 1990*. This image is also discussed by Nicholas Thomas in *Oceanic Art*, Thames and Hudson, 1995, 207.

[5] David Lowenthal *The Past is a Foreign Country*, Cambridge University Press, 1985, 336.

[6] Bernard Smith *European Vision and the South Pacific*, Yale University Press, 1985, 1–7.

[7] But this contention can be modified. 'Local people aren't always *so* interested in their cultural centres that they want to keep them running. In a sense, it is only when it is no longer a matter of everyday lived reality that 'culture' emerges as something that needs 'preserving'. M O'Hanlon, personal communication.

What each of the above ethnographic parks offers in its own idiosyncratic manner, is a constructed programme promoting a version of ethnicity. But in each case its intellectual and theatrical construction is the work of work of professionals. These architects set the terms of what is embraced within the realm of the park. Cohen's contention, that native peoples rarely represent themselves,[1] remains as true today as a century ago. If the performers at the Folk Cultures Villages enthusiastically embrace their roles this is far from universally true. At the Formosan Aboriginal Culture Village the folk demonstrators dissociate themselves from their audience by ignoring them and pretending that they are not there as they chat among themselves whilst they work, or, when visitors become too intrusive, they employ the more radical tactic of turning their chairs and their backs on the audience.

There are other forms of distancing including postmodernist devices satirising the whole business.[2] Vercoe offers an example of performance art entitled 'The Couple in the Cage', in which a couple are exhibited in museums and art galleries as specimens of a mythical Amerindian tribe, the Guatinaui, 'undiscovered by Columbus'.[3] The cage has display boards with detailed false ethnographies of the tribe and the performers' biographies. The actors in turn subject the audience to documentation in 'neo-anthropological fashion'.[4] What this and other artistic forms of critique disclose is the fragility of stereotypes and how they can be subverted. Ethnicity is, in this respect, no different than other supposedly stable cultural and individual identities. But this form of postmodernism is not particularly welcome in areas of the world where issues of identity and cultural ownership remain fraught issues. And these are often places where performance has a vital significance both in re-establishing a sense of continuity with a pre-colonial past as well as refashioning the present.

Lowenthal gets to the heart of the matter when he states that 'those bent on contriving a prideful past may have to mediate between traditionalist and modernist goals. The desire to affirm continuity with a pre-colonial heritage and to 'restore' non-western traditions often conflicts with an equally urgent need to demonstrate that the new country and its people have long been 'modern'.'[5] This chapter details some attempts to rescue the notion of spectacular culture from the grip of theme park entrepreneurs and to restore it to the indigenous population both for its own uses as well as to produce a new form of cultural capital that can be employed in a reformed type of tourist entertainment. Like the Folk Culture Villages personnel, there are others in the western Pacific seeking to embrace tradition in the name of modernity. These are involved in what I term 'indigenous curation'.

There are special reasons why the Pacific should be the site of this development. Firstly, there is the legacy of contact. Smith makes the telling point that the islands of the South Seas are better known than many other parts of the world because they were discovered by westerners late but were subject to intense scrutiny from the combined disciplines of oceanography, botany, zoology and ethnology and depicted faithfully by classically-trained landscape painters.[6] They were also the subject of intensive collecting of any objects which could be used to epitomise the life and culture of the various islands, both by ethnographers and also by those who settled there either to trade, evangelise or impose political regimes. The siphoning off of prize examples of artefactual life meant that the major reference that remains to former pre-European contact life remains through the museums of major imperial powers. For the South Pacific, the creation of Skansen structures is highly problematic because so much has been expropriated but also because climatic conditions in the region, both in terms of catastrophes like cyclones as well as the attrition of humidity and insects, has meant that little that is not made of shell or bone has lasted for much more than thirty years in this environment. As a result there is intense contemporary interest in indigenous physical and mental material and in their interpretation. It can truly be said that museology in the South Pacific is a matter of vital political interest and concern. Interpretation and display are, in their turn, too important to leave only to curators.[7]

## Indigenous curation

In 1983 Sidney Moko Mead wrote an article entitled 'Indigenous models of museums in Oceania'.[8] Here he argued that the Western models of museums were inappropriate to the region because they were designed for an anonymous urban audience by highly trained specialists concerned above all else to conserve the items in their collections. Mead stated, 'If conservation were no longer a prime function of museums, these institutions would be less expensive and look less like a hospital for art objects than they do at present'.[9] A much more useful model was to be found in traditional custom houses that he had studied in Solomon Islands in the 1970s:

[8] Sidney M. Mead 'Indigenous models of museums in Oceania' *Museum* vol. 138, 1983 98–101.

[9] Mead 'Indigenous models' 100.

The two Santa Ana custom houses are structures in which are stored and displayed model canoe ossuaries, skulls in cane containers, decorated bowls, the odd large susugu pudding bowl, a bonito canoe or two and other valued objects. The house posts which supported the roof are often decorated . . . In the context of the village the custom house served a valuable purpose in presenting to the carvers fine examples of the local carving styles. Through the structure the men were able to examine art works done fifty years earlier. The large house posts lasted longer and so provided a greater sense of continuity with the past. There was a wide selection of objects to observe and study.'[10]

The relationship between individuals (in this case men) and objects is structured by principles of tabu or tapu – the objects have a sacred power which derives from their ownership and their employment in particular rituals. Such objects in a traditional setting have no need of cases or security guards. People who do not have the custom right to see them will not enter their presence. What Mead is suggesting has two aspects. On the one hand, traditional structures of pre-contact life persist and offer analogues of Western museums, but without the attendant paraphernalia. At the same time they act as the locus for the reintegration of material objects from the past into contemporary instruction. There have been a number of attempts in widely varying locations in the South Pacific to develop the concept of an indigenous museum. As will become apparent, however, although the examples are truly indigenous, they are never naive. Each has a reference to museological procedures and objectives. What is also interesting in Mead's model is that the term museum itself becomes problematic. Although Mead continues to use the term he suggests that a more democratic approach to the display of culture is more appropriate to the Pacific. It becomes interesting to see the way in which the nomenclature shifts both in time and setting from the early post-colonial national museum to more locally based cultural centres.[11]

Two of the most interesting accounts of 'indigenous museums' come from Papua New Guinea. In his remarkable account of making a collection and then displaying it in Britain, Michael O'Hanlon gives a fascinating account of the Onga Cultural Centre in the New Guinea Highlands. The creator of the centre appears to have been motivated by Mead's intention, as O'Hanlon's account makes clear:

[10] Mead 'Indigenous models' 99, 100; see also S. M. Mead 'Folklore and place names in Santa Ana, Solomon Islands' *Oceania* vol. 43 part 3, 1973, 215–37 for an account of how geography and traditional folklore associated with places are interlinked. Both custom houses were restored through the Australian South Pacific Culture Funds in the late 1980s but they now need rethatching. L Foanaota, personal communication.

[11] I am indebted to Geoff White for this observation.

It was established in the late 1980s by Yap Kupal, a Romonga man of about forty, and comprises a traditional Hagen man's house and a woman's house from the pre-contact period, recreated with what seemed to me exceptional fidelity and stocked with a truly remarkable array of material culture. Yap, who emphasised to me that he was uneducated, said that he wanted to make such a museum after seeing the ones in Port Moresby and elsewhere. His main motive for doing so was precisely so that in future people should know how their forefathers had lived; to get the details right he had gone round interrogating older people.[12]

But Yap Kupal had another reason, to provide a tourist attraction. In this museum cultural performances could be enacted as a tourist spectacle, doubtless employing the materials stored there, whether costume or items used in dances. Thus a second element is added to Mead's model.

A more recent centre has been created in the New Guinea Huon Peninsula where the Nayudos Cultural Centre was completed in 1993. This centre was constructed to foster cultural unity between villages in the vicinity. As a commentator notes:

The compound for the cultural centre was planned to include a house for assemblies of lineage elders as well as youth and women's groups, a workshop and sales outlet for the marketing of traditional items such as bark cloth, stone carvings and string bags, and a small museum.[13]

A guest house with modern facilities was built to accommodate tourists and a dancing area was also added to provide a stage for ceremonial displays. Tied into this complex is a cultural awareness project with special programmes covering oral traditions, genealogies and medicinal plants, thus providing a means of integrating traditions into a contemporary economic and social complex: 'It is a focus of those cultural activities which are encouraged in order to foster integration and consolidation, and because of its combination with a tourist guest house and sales outlet, it is an alternative source of cash income'.[14] Both Nayudos and Onga Cultural Centres provide a new dynamic; the past and tradition are integrated into a forward-looking organisation which accommodates new as well as old.

[12] Michael O'Hanlon *Paradise: Portraying the New Guinea Highlands*, British Museum Press 1993,74.

[13] Christin Kocher Schmid 'Cultural identity as a coping strategy towards modern political structures: the Nayudos case, Papua New Guinea' *Bijdragen Tot de Taal-, Land- en Volkenkunde* vol.149. 4, 1993, 787.

[14] Kocher Schmid 'Cultural identity', 799.

**Vilu War Museum, Guadalcanal**

[15] Catherine Cole and Kenneth Roga 'The relationship between cultural policy and programming in Western Province, Solomon Islands' in L Lindstrom and G. M. White (eds.) *Culture- Kastom-Tradition: Developing Cultural Policy in Melanesia*, Suva, Institute of Pacific Studies, University of the South Pacific, 1994, 10.

[16] 'Fred Kona organized his relatives and neighbors to work at dragging, carrying and trucking an assortment of guns, helmets, mortars, cannon, and crashed planes to a central site – Vilu – where a space was cleared to receive them.' G. M. White 'War remains: the culture of preservation' *Cultural Resource Management* 19, 3, 1996, 53.

The indigenous museum can operate in a converse way. Fred Kona's Vilu War Museum on the plains of Guadalcanal has been assembled to bring together on a custom house site a range of historic objects. At the end of a grassy track in the bush it comes as something of a surprise to be greeted by the relics of some dozen or so US and Japanese fighter planes, large guns and war memorial plaques.[15] The collection was made entirely by the curator without assistance or interference from government. Kona hauled the wrecks from the bush where they had escaped the attentions of scrap dealers in the aftermath of the Second World War, and these objects now integrate world events into a local scenario.[16] To the Western viewer this museum might look like a piece of 'reverse-order salvage ethnography',[17] turning the tables on the normal subjects of ethnography, offering as objects of pathos the military might of Japan and the United States. But this would, I think, be a wrong interpretation. One item holds the key to a new reading, a humble flower urn at the side of a memorial. The urn is, in fact, the case of a spent shell upended and filled with 'artificial flowers' made from tessellated beer cans which provide a most effective syncretic response to the commemoration at a war memorial. The past is very much integrated into the present.[18]

The examples I have offered so far lack official sanction, but similar attempts are made by governments in Melanesia to link back to pre-colonial culture in order to face the future. For both Solomon Islands and Vanuatu cultural centres provide a vital focus in such an enterprise. In Solomon Islands there is an array of cultural centres from the informal and very local such as the Kwaio Cultural Centre on Malaita,[19] and provincial ones in Western Province and Guadalcanal as well as a National Centre attached to the Solomon Islands National Museum.[20] There is a distinct difference in emphasis between provincial centres and the national museum complex which is exacerbated by the prominence of overseas volunteers in the origins and direction of the provincial centres – itself an unintended irony. The programme of the Western Province is fairly typical of the range of activities such centres cover:

The office organizes and delivers an active community education program. Officers tour villages throughout the province encouraging people to learn more about their custom and history, to learn from the

**US memorial Vilu War Museum**

[17] J. Clifford *The Predicament of Culture* Cambridge, Harvard University Press, 1988, 248.

[18] The significance of World War II historic sites as part of the national heritage of Solomon Islands has recently been recognised by the Ministry of Culture, Tourism and Aviation which has set up a committee to identify, develop protect and enhance such sites. Personal communication, Lawrence Foanaota.

[19] D. Akin 'Cultural education at the Kwaio Cultural Centre' in Lindstrom and White *Culture-Kastom-Tradition*, 161–72.

[20] see S. M. Eoe and P Swadling *Museums and Cultural Centres in the Pacific* Port Moresby, Papua New Guinea National Museum, 1991 articles by: L Foanaota 'The Solomon Islands National Museum' (107–12); V. Totu and D. Roe 'The Guadalcanal Cultural Centre, Solomon Islands; R. Keesing 'Custom in the 1980s' (113–31); B. Riley 'Western Province Cultural Affairs Office, Solomon Islands' (152–3).

olos (elders), and to continue to practice customary activities. Annual cultural festivals for secondary school students and registered youth groups, a series of women's custom workshops, annual workshops for volunteers recording oral traditions or assisting in village archaeology surveys, workshops for villagers interested in establishing grassroots museums or cultural centres, and a series of women's custom dance workshops all serve to increase awareness of custom. Officers are regularly asked to judge custom activities, such as crafts or dancing, at community events.'[21]

There is a strongly interventionist ring to this account. It is through education, the recording and publication of events, tales and practices that tradition is captured and made serviceable.

The Guadalcanal Cultural Centre programme wrestles with the same issues though it recognises that there are problems in trying to make tradition 'stand on its own two feet'. As the workers involved comment

It is obviously both naive and unrealistic to expect or suggest a complete re-adoption of traditional culture. However, there does seem to be significant scope for a rejuvenation of those elements of traditional culture which are still of relevance. There is also a need to document those aspects of traditional culture which would otherwise pass inevitably and sadly into oblivion. In other words, those elements of the cultural system which can stand on their own and which remain viable as part of 20th century culture need to be promoted.[22]

Elements of salvage ethnography are enlisted to shore up those aspects of tradition which can be saved. Of course, this raises a very interesting question, one that all active culture preservation programmes face: which elements remain viable, and which cannot be resuscitated?

The Cultural Centre at the National Museum has an agenda that creates tension with provincial ones. Firstly, the Centre acts as a complement to the Museum which since the 1970s has actively collected artefacts from throughout the nation.[23] In this respect it echoes Skansen growing up in parallel with the Nordiska Museet. But in fact the pedigree is more complex. The Cultural Centre is modelled with Pacific Harbour, Fiji, in mind, which in turn is a reflection of the

[21] C. Cole and K. Roga 'The relationship between cultural policy and programming in Western Province, Solomon Islands' in L Lindstrom and G. M. White *Culture-Kastom-Tradition*, 110.

[22] V. Totu and D. Roe 'Guadalcanal Cultural Centre', 115.

[23] Solomon Islands Museum *Handbook for the Preservation of the Solomon Islands Heritage: Smol Fela Buk Hao Fo Kipim Gud Ologeta Impotan Samting Blong Kantri Blong Iumi* Honiara, 1979.

[24] L. Foanaota 'Solomon Islands National Museum and Cultural Centre Policy' Townville, Material Culture Unit, James Cook University, July 1992, 13.

[25] Foanaota loc. cit, 19.

Polynesian Cultural Center. Although there is no lake at Coronation Gardens, Honiara, the same autochthonous architecture is emplaced within the Cultural Village compound, following the by now traditional format of architectural display.

The Cultural Centre is also designed to provide a platform for 'collaboration with indigenous peoples in collecting, exhibiting or publishing their art and cultural work'.[24] The Centre provides in a shop an opportunity for the display of contemporary artefacts 'representing the works of national craftsmen and women'[25] to be seen in eight traditional buildings representing the different provinces within a single space at the back of the museum. Again, the notion of recovery is stressed:

> 'Traditional buildings in Solomon Islands are rich and varied, but because they are usually constructed from natural materials, few examples survive for more than twenty years except in the skills of the people who built them. These skills are gradually disappearing because the knowledgeable old men who have the skills are fast dying out. At

**Typical Makira customhouse and posts**

**Guadalcanal weather coast meeting house**

the same time the idea of houses with permanent modern materials is more prestigious than a thatched building is becoming prominent in the minds of a lot of young people. Since they illustrate something of the society that created them and traditional crafts of building in leaf and timber gathered from the immediate surroundings, they are an important part of the cultural heritage of Solomon Islands'.[26]

The custom house for the province of Makira is based on one from Santa Ana destroyed in the cyclone of 1972, constructed by young men 'trained by village elders in sometimes secret rites of initiation to manhood, and the carved poles supporting the roof represent spirits which were both guides and guards for the young initiates'.[27] The Guadalcanal house was made by a group from Makaruka village, a centre of the Moro movement which in the decade preceding independence offered resistance to the colonial administration.[28] Thus, the choice of architectural example is informed by a lively sense of history.

The structures and their few contents are designed to remind the urban inhabitants that have grown up in the metropolis of their cultural roots. But the

[26] 'Solomon Island Cultural Village' brochure, Honiara, n.d. p 1.

[27] 'Bones on the Roof: Totems in the Garden' *Solomon* No 10 1992, 14.

[28] W. Davenport and G. Çoker 'The Moro movement of Guadalcanal' *Journal of the Polynesian Society*, 76:2, 123–75.

Centre also has another audience: 'since Honiara is the main entry point into Solomon Islands, this cultural centre will be used as an introduction place for the diverse cultures of the people'.[29]

National policy creates conflict with provinces from where the traditions originate. Reproducing material and mental culture in the capital can be seen by provincial centres as a form of neo-colonialism. The publication of the plans for the National Cultural Centre elicited this response from the Guadalcanal Provincial Government:

> 'We view our culture as our whole life, the way we are and who we are, and as an important resource for future development. The 'Cultural Centre' proposed puts the tourist requirements before the concerns of our own people. We are convinced that the commercialisation of our traditions will reduce our heritage to a bastardised form of 'tourist culture'; our custom will be 'on show' like so many animals in a zoo. In short the proposal has no respect for our cultural dignity and exhibits unfortunate elements of a neo-colonial attitude which sees our culture as being an oddity at worst, and quaint at best. Are Solomon Island visitors to Australia and Europe treated to the spectacle of a 'lived-in functional village' where one can observe the 'natives' cooking, washing etc?'[30]

The last comment, of course, provides an ironic and perhaps unintentional reference to the New York's World's Fair of 1939 with its display of the typical American family.

The sharpness of the attack demonstrates that custom and tradition provide the focus for major disagreement. It is probably the shortage of funds available for cultural projects that has so far prevented a more widespread conflict between national and provincial proponents of cultural policy. The involvement of the Tourism Council of the South Pacific in the funding and planning of the National Cultural Centre has done little to reduce provincial anxiety. It would be difficult to agree with the TCSP that festivals for tour ships 'could serve as an opportunity when traditional and modern Solomon Islanders meet their foreign visitors'.[31] Indeed, the commemorations to mark the fiftieth anniversary of the battle of Gaudalcanal in 1992 signalled the displacement of any indigenous agenda in favour of the former combatants. As White remarked of the event: 'combined with

[29] L. Foanaota 'Solomon Islands National Museum and Cultural Centre' in Lindstrom and White, 101.

[30] Guadalcanal Provincial Government Press Release 12/1/10 dated 9/4/90, 3.

[31] F. Schouten 'Solomon Islands Cultural Centre: Management and Operation Plan' Suva, Tourism Council of the South Pacific, July 1992, 11.

the arrival of well over one thousand veterans on tour ships and international flights, the sudden presence of Americans, Australians, and New Zealanders in a town with a population of just over 30,000 constituted a second invasion'.[32] The very question of the relationship between 'traditional' and 'modern' raises as many issues as does the value of the opportunity offered for Solomon Islanders to meet visitors from tour ships.

Vanuatu provides a vivid contrast in the development of indigenous culture and its various manifestations. The Vanuatu Cultural Centre (VCC), until 1995 housed in a rather elderly building containing a museum, the National Library and a craft shop, as Bolton remarks, 'disappoints the tourists who make sorties inside, but it is completely unintimidating to the islanders. Situated next to the taxi rank on the main street of the capital, it draws the most local visitors of any museum I have visited in the Pacific. People wander in and out constantly'.[33] This is an observation that I would endorse. It is to be hoped that this casual but intimate relationship between the collection of items of tradition from many of the islands and their ni-Vanuatu visitors survives the recent move to large new premises out of town near the parliament building and Malvatumauri (Council of Chiefs). There are, however, other reasons that the VCC represents a new direction in the South Pacific.

Kirk Huffman was appointed as curator of the VCC in 1977 and was instrumental in developing an Oral Traditions Project from the Centre. This programme was founded by Peter Crowe and workshops have been continually offered by Darrell Tryon. What was special about this programme was that, although it was national in scope, it was highly localised. Middle-aged rather than young fieldworkers were selected, with advice from the locality, for their involvement and know ledge of traditions or customs. The training was not in Port Vila but in the North of the archipelago and was conducted in Bislama not French or English.[34] Nearly sixty male and ten female fieldworkers from throughout the island chain still meet together annually, usually selecting a particular topic (such as customary rules relating to issues like land tenure or husbandry, pigs and birds, death ceremonies[35]) for discussion. Since 1991 this has been joined by a Women's Culture Project with the triple objective of promotion, documentation and revival of women's cultural knowledge.[36] This project has had as its first task the documentation and revival of women's mat weaving on Ambae, an island in the North of Vanuatu.

Throughout the VCC programme there is a determination to strengthen links back to custom and tradition. This has had effects in Solomon Islands too.

[32] G. White 'Remembering Guadalcanal' *Public Culture*, 7, 1995, 530.

[33] L. Bolton 'The Vanuatu Cultural Centre and its own community' *Journal of Museum Ethnography* No 6. 1994, 75.

[34] L. Bolton 'The Vanuatu Cultural Centre', 71.

[35] M. Jolly 'Custom and the way of the land: past and present in Vanuatu and Fiji' *Oceania* 62, 1992, 343; personal communication Ralph Regenvanu.

[36] L. Bolton 'Bifo Yumi Ting Se Samting Nating: the Women's Culture Project at the Vanuatu Cultural Centre' in Lindstrom and White *Culture-Kastom-Tradition*, 153.

[37] Vanuatu National Cultural Council 'Vanuatu Cultural Research Policy', Port Vila, 1995.

[38] L. Bolton 'Dancing in Mats: Extending Kastom to Women in Vanuatu' PhD thesis, University of Manchester, Department of Social Anthropology, 1993, 66.

Kenneth Roga from Western Province Cultural Affairs Office has attended Huffman's training programme. The Women's history project in Solomon Islands Western Province predates the VCC's by three years. What is evident, however, is that UNESCO's oral traditions training courses from the 1970s have given rise to a very specific form of cultural regeneration in both countries. All of the projects develop a particular concept entitled 'kastom'. The Vanuatu Cultural Research policy document defines the term as 'traditional political, social, religious and economic structures, and their associated practices, systems of knowledge and material items.'[37] Kastom as a concept has a much more than local significance in the Western Pacific. The term itself raises in a very pointed way some specific responses of local peoples to reconnect with aspects of tradition and, as importantly, the elaboration of a demand to broker or decide how their distinctive ways of life are to be interpreted and displayed. Whilst it may be fanciful to expect the South Pacific to answer our concerns about the preservation and reinvigorating of local and regional identity, the strategies employed in the region have more than a casual significance for any who seek to question hegemonic formulations of culture.

### Kastom and the subversion of 'salvage ethnography'

In her discussion of kastom in the context of Vanuatu Bolton distinguishes between two uses of the term, firstly as a noun standing alone, to mean a ceremony as in 'wan smol kastom' (a small ceremony) and secondly, and more usually as an adjective to describe practices before colonisation. She gives examples of the latter: kastom stori (story), kastom singsing (song), kastom lif (medicine), kastom jif (chief), kastom kot (court).[38] Each of these practices is specific to a particular linguist or related group of people. However, Bolton maintains, 'it is not that kastom represents the past. It represents people's notions of what was valuable or important about the past which can be imported, altered or created for use in the present.'[39] This view is a development and reformulation of Keesing's earlier notion of kastom as relatively essentialist and static so that indigenous people externalise their view of their way of life as a 'thing'.[40] What has happened, as Jolly has remarked, is that 'the term has gradually come to take on the anthropological concept of culture or a whole way of life.[41]

This life is contrasted antithetically with modern western. So the Are Are pipers originally from Malaita but resident in Honiara are resplendent in their near-nakedness,[42] but they also feature on the front cover of the current Solomon

[39] L Bolton, personal communication, October 1996.

[40] J. G .Carrier Occidentalism: Images of the West, 6.

[41] M. Jolly 'Custom and the way of the land p 341; R. Keesing 'Creating the past: custom and identity in the contemporary Pacific' The Contemporary Pacific, 1, 1 and 2, 1989, 23–4.

**Are Are pipes**

Telekom phone book alerting us to the ambiguity in the status of kastom. Although kastom is often seen as pagan and opposed to 'skul' (school) or Christianity this has not prevented its being readopted by Christians as Jolly has noted:

> The national revival of kastom in association with Christianity has been paralleled by the revival of kastom in many local Christian communities. Many aspects of such revivals are, within the limits of Christian adherence, optional – revivals of the traditional rites of birth, marriage, funerals, pig-killing, kava-drinking, dancing and singing, and making artifacts.[43]

Kastom is also integrated into politics. It represents the bedrock on which the post-colonial society is constructed and has its own rhetoric. Bolton captures this neatly in a quotation from a rural ni-Vanuatu woman: 'Kastom is the life of the people – as the Government is always saying on the radio.'[44] The Vanuatu constitution builds the preservation of kastom into the offices of government. The Council of Chiefs (Malvatumauri) is responsible for the promotion of all aspects of kastom and

[42] K. Gravelle 'The Pipers of Are Are' *Solomon*, 14, 1994, 9–11.

[43] Jolly 'Custom and the way of the land', 343.

[44] Bolton 'Dancing in Mats', 67.

is entitled to be consulted on all legislation that touches upon customary matters. The Council sits at the top of an elaborate structure of village councils, area councils, island councils and 22 members elected to the Malvatumauri itself.[45] However this institutionalising of traditional agencies in a western constitutional framework is treated as contradictory at best, and farcical at worst by its detractors. Kastom can be employed to stress the specificity of local customs or the unity of each of these in opposition to the western and global. As such it is malleable to suit different circumstance. As Akuila Yabaki ironically has commented, kastom may be used by 'our brown masters' as a cloak of authority to mask the reality of their

**Summoning villagers to a performance, Yakel village, Tanna**

[45] Chief Noel Mariasua, President of the Malvatumauri, personal communication.

**Women setting up craft sale, Yakel Village, Tanna**

elite position.[46] 'Politicians raised in urban settings and educated overseas proclaim the virtues of a kastom they have never known.'[47] This may be an over-cynical view but it attests to the political significance of the concept for any successful politician in Melanesia.

Perhaps more significantly for my purposes here, kastom has another dimension, that of ownership, or as Bolton calls it, the politics of knowledge, 'the right to speak for, to identify with, a continuity with the past'.[48] The example of the Narasirato Are Are Pipers is again instructive in this context. There is some disquiet and disapproval of the troupe performing dances and songs from other people and different provinces in their shows. Despite having their own elders check that their repertoire is genuine and accurate they have not paid for the right to perform, say, the music of Marau Sound.[49] In Melanesia generally the copyright on designs, stories, songs, and dances is well established. To perform or execute anything belonging to another group requires negotiation and the payment of a fee or royalty. As Lindstrom notes, 'Only those people who possess a copyright can talk publicly with legitimacy about the knowledge in question. Copyrights, as property, are inheritable. Rights to produce and talk about genealogy, secret clan names, magical spells and medical therapies, ritual practices and artifacts, canoe

[46] 'Pacific European links for sustainable development and management', paper delivered at the Conference on Environment and Development in the Pacific, School of Oriental and Africa Studies, London, 21 October, 1995.

[47] R. Keesing 'Kastom in Melanesia: an overview' *Mankind* 13. 4 1982, 299.

[48] Bolton 'Dancing in Mats' p 76.

[49] Personal communications from C Teahanu and L Foanaota, Solomon Islands National Museum.

**Dance performance, Yakel Village, Tanna**

manufacture and other technologies pass down within lineages.'[50] Whilst customary land right is a concept readily grasped by the western legal mind, medicinal secrets and potions based on natural plant sources are only now being patented by international drug companies without license from customary owners of this knowledge. The documentation of customary music and performance by the MABO project in conjunction with Solomon Islands National Museum of oral history as well as music by the Vanuatu Cultural Centre helps reassert the performing rights of the customary owners and confirms that kastom lives on as do its owners.

'Living on' can also have graphic exemplification. Tanna, one of the centres of Vanuatu kastom, has a 'kastom village'. Like earlier experiments on Malakula, the inhabitants of Tanna have attempted to isolate themselves from non-kastom by erecting a cultural barrier to ward off outside influences.[51] For visitors there is provided something like a cross between a museum and a cultural centre. Yakel,

[50] L. Lindstrom 'Traditional cultural policy in Melanesia (Kastom polisi long kastom)' in Lindstrom and White *Culture-Kastom-Tradition*, 69.

[51] For a discussion of the Small Nambas cultural quarantine experiment see *Pieces of Paradise* exhibition catalogue, Australian Museum, Sydney, 1988.

near the air strip, offers the visitor 'full kastom' in terms of setting, architecture, artefacts, dress, and, above all, performance. It represents both a form of cultural quarantine – outsiders may peer in but their malign influence is confined and contained by kastom practitioners. Yakel comes without tourist paraphernalia[52] and confronts the visitors with their impertinence in interrupting the lives of the villagers. From the first blow on the gong by the young boy on the approach of the visitor, to the setting up and inspection of the wooden and leaf crafts piled up for sale and the performance of the dances by the villagers in two circles singing and banging the ground rhythmically all the time, visitors are reminded that here are customary people who have made few apparent concessions in living memory.[53] And yet the elder of the adolescent boys giggle and extemporise, distancing themselves from the performance to the annoyance of their elders.

Yakel offers one example of the way that kastom is employed in the contemporary world, offering a museum tourist experience and a source of income for the owners of kastom. This is also the rationale for the Are Are pipers, who are, however, in the vice of unemployment in the metropolis. But kastom can have a more central role in economic development. In both Solomon Islands and Vanuatu logging, principally by Malaysian companies, has already had a devastating effect. One of the principal tasks of all cultural centres in the region is to identify and then preserve archaeological and custom sites. Loggers are not supposed to clear such sites. In an attempt to prevent logging in South West Malakula the Mbatga't have turned to eco-tourism as an antidote. Visitors will be invited to undertake nature walks, stay in replica villages, see and purchase artefacts, and attend customary events.[54] Other villages in Vanuatu are similarly recreating dancing grounds, re-erecting stones and drums.

Eco-tourism can come in different forms. At Port Resolution on the other side of Tanna something has been made of the history of contact between European and indigenous people. As the name implies, Port Resolution was the first landing for Captain Cook's ship HMS Resolution in 1774, a magnificent horseshoe shaped harbour. The geography is made even more splendid by the looming presence of Mount Yasur, a continuously active volcano, as a backdrop. Cook wrote in some detail about his visit to Tanna, and his account reflects some sensitivity to intercultural encounters and the significance of power in such events.[55] The book also provides some of the earliest sketches and drawings of the topography and people of Tanna. Now Port Resolution offers the Napikinamu yacht club with a club house

[52] though it is certainly heavily promoted as a cultural antiquity: 'In Port Vila the last century is only an hour away' Air Vanuatu *Hello Vanuatu: The Essential Visitor Guide 1994*, 74.

[53] Theroux's account of his visit to Yakel is one of profound pessimism dwelling on the effect of the bad weather on the scantily dressed people streaked with mud. *The Happy Isles*, 258.

[54] *Beneficial Environmental Sustainable Tourism Newsletter* Port Vila, April 1995, 1 and 2.

[55] 'It was impossible for them to to know our real design; we enter their ports without their daring to oppose; we endeavour to land in their country as friends, and it is well if this succeeds; we land, nevertheless, and maintain the footing we have got by the superiority of our fire-arms. Under such circumstances, what opinion are they to form of us? Is it not as reasonable for them to think that we come to invade their country, as to pay them a friendly visit? J Cook *A Voyage towards the South Pole*, 66.

**Port Resolution restaurant, Tanna**

exhibiting pendants from yachts that have visited since it opened in 1994, a restaurant and a thatched cabins 'designed by the local village in traditional style'[56] and furniture made of local materials to imitate those to be found at a western resort, including deckchairs. But this is not the standard resort; there is no electricity, though there are, in best eco-tourist fashion, solar showers and solar toilets. Guests are invited to bring their own food as they may not like what they are offered by the villagers.

But geography and the adventure of 'rough tourism' are supplemented by cultural interest because this, one of the largest villages on Tanna with a population of 350, is also a centre for the Jon Frum movement.[57] This is a source of considerable appeal to western visitors as it offers a vivid example of a syncretic religion and political force that turns upside down their own religious landmarks whilst at the same time combining aspects of kastom with modernity. The contrast with the past is made more explicit by a well-tended one hundred year old missionary grave at the centre of the tourist village. Against such religious orthodoxy, the singularity of reinterpretation of the colonial past by the adherents of John Frum is both exciting and disturbing. For them the Garden of Eden was to be found on Tanna from

[56] David Sharland 'Port Resolution Napikinamu Yacht Club and Cabins' leaflet 1995.

[57] Following Lindstrom I use the term 'movement' as a shorthand for a complex set of perspectives on what has been called a cargo cult. Lindstrom offers a convincing set of reasons for being highly suspicious of the label 'cargo'. He shows how a variety of players have used it for their own purposes, from colonial administrators and missionaries to film and television presenters such as David Attenborough. See L. Lindstrom's 'Strange tales from John Frum' in his *Cargo Cult*, 73–145.

**Pentecost land dive on 5,000 Vatu banknote**

58 Joël Bonnemaison *The Tree and the Canoe: History and Ethnogeography of Tanna*, University of Hawai'i Press, 1994, 246.

59 a concept developed by Christina Torin who remarks: 'whenever we assimilate new information we do so in terms of what is already known to us. In respect of cognition, this is perhaps so obvious that it does not require restatement. But its implications tend to get lost when we look at appropriation across cultures. In such cases, the process of appropriation contains a paradoxical reconciliation with a rooted conservatism'. 'Leonardo's " Last Supper" in Fiji' in S Hiller (ed.) *The Myth of Primitivism: Perspectives on Art*, Routledge, 1991, 261.

60 L. Lindstrom 'Cargoism and occidentalism', 55.

61 Lindstrom 'Cargoism and occidentalism', 56.

whence John Frum set forth with his ark to visit the rest of the world. The symbolism of the US flag as a religious rallying point is contrasted with the belief that 'Philip, Duke of Edinburgh, is actually a man from Tanna pretending to be a white man; he is waiting to go back to his island to re-establish his true identity. His real family lives on the slopes of Mt. Tukosmera'.[58] The John Frum movement, not long ago a source of political apprehension to the colonial administration, appears at Port Resolution and elsewhere in Tanna as a fascinating form of appropriation across cultures.[59] Visitors thus get a chance not only to visit an Edenic scenario but an occasion to inspect their own beliefs. Despite its remoteness, this combination of natural splendour and cultural interest drew 200 visitors in its first year of operation in 1994–45.

Lindstrom suggests that cargoism is a category that reveals more about its exponents than the supposed cargoists. 'Whatever else they may tell us, cargoist texts are allegories of desire. Thematically, cultists desire wealth, dignity, freedom, and independence, and the like. Cargo stories present these lists of desired objects or states of being as normal, pan-human focuses of aspiration. But more furtively, Cargoism also essentializes desire itself.'[60] The attraction of John Frum is, from Lindstrom's perspective, that the cult tells us about ourselves. As he puts it: 'We are all cargo cultists in that we wait eternally for an end to desire that will not end. The Melanesian cultist merely reads our lines'.[61]

But kastom in the service of tourism has its attendant problems. The Pentecost land dive (nagol) that Jolly has written about in detail[62] is performed by young Sa speaking adult males in South Pentecost and has become a spectacular tourist attraction. It involves these young men launching themselves from the top of a tower some hundred feet high into a clearing beneath with vine cords attached to the tower and their ankles to prevent them crashing into the ground. Traditionally, however, the dive was only performed during the period of the yam harvest, April, when the lianas are supple. Tourists, however, want to see the spectacle at other times and other places. This has led to considerable conflict between the holders of tradition in South Pentecost and the national tourist authority, Tour Vanuatu, who have sought to extend the season and increase the number of sites, promoting the event as 'an experience of a lifetime; the death-defying Pentecost jump. Not a tourist show but a cultural event. Seeing is believing! Awesome!'[63] The result in 1995 was not only awesome but tragic. Tony Melson was badly injured when the liana broke during a Tour Vanuatu sponsored dive.[64] The elders were quick to place the blame on the demands of the tourist authority who had defied kastom. What is at stake here is the struggle for control between the local and the national interest. As Jolly and Thomas have noted 'diverse local traditions do not easily nestle within the larger traditions appropriate to a nation state or a region'.[65]

Not all the problems with opening custom to tourism are as dramatic, but they can be as serious. There are some structural issues. For example, as Mead has commented recently on his model:

> The one difficulty with the customhouse model was that women were not allowed near it or in it. That is a little problem to be addressed although in some parts of Melanesia it is not an issue. In the Solomons it is definitely an all male institution. So, the problem is how to generalise the model or dress it up in new clothes so as to get around the gender issue. I will leave that matter to you.[66]

This is hardly a small question, but it is one that custom tourism has to confront. In another context Errington and Gewertz state: 'The Chambrai did not understand that if they continued to sell their initiations (and perhaps other ceremonies) as tourist attractions, they would themselves no longer find them convincing and effective.'[67] This, as I have noted, has already started to occur in the dances performed by the Yakel villagers. This ethnographic self-consciousness can extend

[62] M. Jolly 'Kastom as commodity: the land dive as indigenous rite and tourist spectacle in Vanuatu' in Lindstrom and White *Culture-Kastom-Tradition*, 131–44.

[63] Tour Vanuatu, brochure, April 1995.

[64] *Vanuatu Trading Post* 9 April 1995.

[65] M. Jolly and N. Thomas 'The politics of tradition in the Pacific: introduction' *Oceania* 62, 4, 1994, 243.

[66] S. M. Mead personal communication.

[67] F. Errington and D. Gewertz 'Tourism and anthropology in a postmodern world' *Oceania* 60, 1989, 51.

to the manufacture of traditional artefacts as O'Hanlon illustrates for the Wahgi people in Papua New Guinea:

> Demonstrations of how stone axes used to be made, or how highly pearl shells were formerly valued, tended to be carried out with a caricatured seriousness which collapsed into laughter. There was sometimes a sense that people felt they had been absurd to esteem shells in the way they had, to have laboured as long as they did to grind hard stones down to make axes. Now they knew better.[68]

A quite different problem may also arise in precisely the most traditional or customary of locations. As Eber warns in the context of eco-tourism 'demands for reverting to 'tradition' – heard all too often within tourism debates today – might, in effect, contribute to the retention of traditional structures of exploitation and control'.[69] Yet it is undeniable that tourism represents one of the only viable means of sustaining patterns of rural life and generating income in the South Pacific that does not, of necessity, devastate the environment.[70]

### Representing custom and making a living

In her review of the political significance of museums in the Pacific region, Adrienne Kaeppler exemplifies a number of ways in which museums provide a basis for the building of national identity from the complexity of local attachments through visual display.[71] Kaeppler notes how museums in the Pacific have been transformed into cultural centres which have a broader brief, as has been illustrated earlier in this chapter. But Kaeppler goes further and suggests that some quite new features have emerged in such venues: 'Although individual groups of tribes are encouraged to preserve their distinctive cultures as living entities, new institutions have been created that attempt to forge a national identity based on an amalgamation of indigenous concepts.'[72] For example, she cites dance and theatre companies in Papua New Guinea that have created work which 'are not simply composites but are the forging of new artistic forms that are theatrical events representative of the New Guinea nation, understandable to themselves as well as to outsiders.'[73]

The Are Are pipers, the Waghi experience of axe-making, and the Yakel dance performers suggest that this advance may not be easily accomplished. The nagol dispute casts further doubt on Kaeppler's assertion (at least in respect of

[68] O'Hanlon *Paradise*, 74.

[69] S. Eber *Beyond the Green Horizon: Principles for sustainable Tourism* World Wide Fund for Nature, Godalming, 1992, iii.

Vanuatu) that 'cultural traditions are their own and are not promoted for tourist consumption.'[74] What is in question here is the relationship between two different agendas. On the one hand there is the programme of cultural recovery directed to the indigenous population – the prime objective of most Pacific cultural centres[75] – and on the other the employment of cultural performance to generate tourist income.[76] The question is whether the two are simultaneously compatible.

One way of focusing the question is to erect a set of bipolar terms that contrasts emic and etic. If one takes any of the performance examples suggested above the question would be, in each case, the extent to which this cultural performance is directed principally towards one's peers or outwards towards strangers (tourists). Is the performance to be seen from within or from without? Is it an example of a culture in decline and in danger of disappearance or is it a declaration of the life and vitality of the community? Does the performance educate or is it a spectacularized performance? Does the performance take place in a local venue or at a site convenient for outsiders? These are not entirely mutually exclusive categories but posing them in this way raises the issue as to whether, by invoking kastom, cultural regeneration and tourist performance can ever be squared successfully. At its most simple, can a cultural performance ever be of worth to the community and marketable to tourists?[77]

To frame the question in this way relies upon a presumption, one implicitly shared by cultural conservators and tourists alike, that there is something steady, constant, almost tangible, in the traditions of kastom and culture. Linnekin suggests that this is an erroneous assumption to start from. Rather, she suggests, it is more realistic to approach tradition from a cultural constructionist direction. 'Cultural construction implies, instead, that tradition is a selective representation of the past, fashioned in the present, responsive to contemporary priorities and agendas, and politically instrumental'.[78] In this formulation culture is not to be located in a particular set of patterned practices and performances, but is the subject of contestation between those who wish to promote it for their own purposes. Seen this way, the creation of new cultural 'composites' that Kaeppler endorses brings into debate issues of cultural copyright and how they are to be enforced on the one hand, and the elisions, substitutions and changes made to suit tourist taste on the other. As Thomas has pointed out 'Art is increasingly a domain through which people present their culture and heritage; once it is visible, they effectively become actors in the theatre of politics and in the multicultural marketplace'.[79] And, it

[70] Ralph Regenvanu, Director of the VCC commented 'I have discussed cultural tourism with others from the Pacific islands who are much more pessimistic than me – mainly those from Hawai'i who feel that cultural tourism is always a disaster. I am still hopeful and think that in today's reality it is one of the only avenues for income for ni-Vanuatu'. Personal communication.

[71] A. L. Kaeppler 'Paradise regained: the role of Pacific museums in forging national identity' in F. E. S. Kaplan *Museums and the Making of 'Ourselves'* Leicester University Press, 1996, 19–44.

[72] Kaeppler 'Pacific museums', 34.

[73] Kaeppler 'Pacific museums', 35.

[74] Kaeppler 'Pacific museums', 41.

[75] 'The Vanuatu Cultural Centre has resolved . . . to affirm the indigenous ways of living and to work with the community to adapt those traditions to present circumstances as well as recording them for posterity' L. Bolton 'The Vanuatu Cultural Centre', 77

76 'The tourist industry in general, including its entertainment and artefact trades, and the export of dance teams, cultural and artistic specialists, and cultural materials are a real growth industry. It is good business to reward creativity, to pay artists more, and to enhance the quality of their art through training and competition. The artistic industry is becoming a major employer and a generator of income in the smaller island nations – for many of which this is their only unique resource. R Crocombe 'Cultural politics', 32.

77 A similar set of questions concerning authenticity and tourism has regularly been raised in Bali. For a summary of the discussion see M. Hitchcock et al *Tourism in South-East Asia*, 10–11. Waite suggests that occasions like the festival held on Independence Day in Honiara in Solomon Islands may satisfy both. D Waite personal communication. However even such events may lose their attraction. Independence Day celebrations were cancelled in Solomon Islands in 1994.

78 J. Linnekin 'On the theory and politics of cultural construction in the Pacific', 251.

79 N. Thomas *Oceanic Art*, Thames and Hudson, 208.

80 L. Lindstrom 'Traditional cultural policy'. 77.

81 T. Sofield 'The Guadalcanal track ecotourism project in the Solomon Islands' in J. Hay *Ecotourism Business*, 94.

might be added, the same is equally true for performance. The 'multicultural marketplace' is increasingly peopled by more sophisticated operators with backgrounds in kastom and tourist spectacle, competing and collaborating in their marketing of performance. All claim authenticity though the disparity in their claims reminds one that the concept itself is highly contested. But the stakes both political (kastom) and financial (tourism) are so high that neither party is prepared willingly to abandon the marketplace.

The bridge between cultural conservation and tourism is constructed with new synthetic concepts. The neologism 'kastom tourism' is one developed specifically in Melanesia. As Lindstrom notes: 'a strong kastom tourism policy already exists in much of Melanesia that effectively regulates the flow of tourists geographically. Kastom policies also exist to protect sacred places by limiting tourist access to these sites.'[80] This approach is promoted by major players like the Tourism Council of the South Pacific (TCSP) which is in turn sustained by European Union's Pacific Regional Tourism Development Programme. TCSP literature emphasises the importance of indigenous ownership and management.[81] The TCSP also stresses the protection and preservation of traditional cultural patterns, 'in recognition of the importance of traditional cultural heritage and its potential to interface with the growing and ever more prosperous tourist industry in the region.'[82] It is the 'interface' that makes the union between kastom and tourism problematic.

National and regional tourism promoters make much of ecological and human ecological considerations. In most proposals flora, fauna, geography and human conservation are treated in much the same way as a set of natural resources. The ecological lessons are then carried across: kastom folk like the villagers of Tanna, if not preserved will disappear and another 'species' will have been lost. One of the ways of ensuring harmonious development is though consultation. As Eber remarks 'consultation provides local communities with a greater say in the scale, pace and nature of contact with tourists and improves relations between the industry, guests and hosts'.[83] Having a say in development is not, of course, quite the same as controlling it.

There are aspects of tourist development that will be foreign to the owners of kastom. To meet the needs or expectations of tourists may require outside intervention. Just occasionally the TCSP's mask slips and the conflict of interest shows fleetingly as in the exasperated tone of its review of Tanna:

Most famous for its readily accessible active volcano. This is set amidst a moon-like ash plain which also contains a large shallow lake. This area is currently regularly visited by tourists, who frequently complain of the rather exorbitant costs charged by the local custodians. If possible, it would be better for this area to come under Government control by giving it protected area status. Little or none of the money collected from tourists goes into providing facilities for them.[84]

One way of ensuring that visitors will not be disappointed and that their money will be directed to their comfort is through the provision of cultural centres. The TCSP puts its case for such centres in unambiguous terms:

In the time available to them, most visitors will not be willing or able to make several excursions to seek out these aspects (traditional life, music dance and ritual, arts and craft, NS) separately, and they will be unable to make the connections between them for themselves; they will prefer to find them in one location. At the very least they will expect that one location will provide a reasonable understanding of the essence of local culture in its overall sense, especially if that location proclaims itself to be a cultural centre.[85]

To emphasise the point the same report states sternly: 'the commercialization of culture is an inevitable consequence of a failure by official cultural centres to adjust their operations – not their underlying mission in society – to visitors' needs'.[86]

This is a long way from the concept of kastom tourism but the same dynamic is involved, namely the requirement to make displays of indigenous culture comprehensible and accessible to tourists. In order to achieve this two types of experts are employed. From the kastom side are what may be called 'co-opted anthropologists' or development workers who are employed for their ability to participate in the lives of the communities themselves, understand their needs and priorities and then to introduce members of the community into the process of planning and development.[87] As much contemporary anthropology attests, this is a particularly uncomfortable status for the researcher and the community alike. And as Eber warns, 'many conservation schemes, supported by tourism revenue, are directed by expatriate 'experts' who often lack first hand familiarity with local conditions and needs'.[88]

[82] Tourism Council of the South Pacific *Annual Report*, 1993, 14.

[83] S. Eber *Beyond the Green Horizon*, 26.

[84] TCSP 'Guidelines for the integration of tourism development and environmental protection in the South Pacific', Suva, 1990, 101.

[85] V. Middleton *Review of Museums and Cultural Centres in the South Pacific*, TCSP, Suva, 1990, 8.

[86] TCSP Secretariat's preface to Middleton *Review of Museums*, iii.

[87] R. Dodd in RAI/ESRC Workshop *International NGO's and Complex Political Emergencies*, Royal Anthropological Institute, 1995, 4.

[88] S. Eber *Beyond the Green Horizon*, 29.

The second, and arguably the more significant group of experts comes from the field of tourism. The TCSP and the national tourist offices are caught in a bind. Whilst, on the one hand, they need to remain faithful to kastom tourism policies in order to retain political credibility and support at home, they are ultimately judged on fairly crude measures of success, the increased number of tourists attracted and the revenue that they bring. To maximize both of these figures experts are needed with the marketing skills to create a new clientele. These specialists may come from elsewhere in the Pacific, most probably Hawai'i, but as the TCSP is heavily dependant on the European Union it comes as no surprise to find many tourism experts come from the countries that the TCSP wishes to attract. There is, therefore, a cyclical process at work. The Pacific is marketed, understandably, through a European lens. This market is largely composed of nationals who have a colonial memory of the region, France, Germany, Britain and increasingly, their successors, Australia and New Zealand. Eco-tourism projects, in particular, have to appeal to such a fickle and still tiny sector of the market in terms that are recognisable to these tourists. The promotional literature for Port Resolution, Tanna, hints at a recognition of the issue when it states:

> A further suggestion to make your stay a happy one – remember
> you are on Tanna time! In this part of Melanesia we do not have clocks,
> so please expect things to happen, but not necessarily to the minute.
> We shall do our best, but sometimes nature takes a hand and upsets
> our best-laid plans. Don't worry though, we will get you to the plane
> on time.

Although the point is obvious, and one common to many developing tourism zones, it is a highly significant recognition of the collision of different modes of living, with the tourist expectancy ultimately sovereign.

The question remains as to how the demands of tourism are best accommodated. Perhaps the Tonga National Center (funded through a bilateral scheme with Japan), following the example from Sarawak, gets the best of both worlds with its enactment of a 'full-scale traditional Tongan wedding' of a Tongan bride and British groom 'with the strict observation of social decorum and protocol'.[89] But then the Tongan center has workshops led by an expert from the Polynesian Cultural Center. Perhaps this underlines the logical impossibility of providing strict quarantine for 'full kastom', though it might perhaps also alert those who seek salvation in cul-

[89] A. Taumoepeau 'How the Tonga National Center Attempts to do It', in Pacific Museum Directors Workshop, Final Report, UNESCO, Apia 1994, 19.

tural tourism and specifically in developing spectacularized versions of culture that it is useful to look around at others' experience, especially in their encounters with experts.

**Drawing up a balance sheet**

The project suggested by Mead in 1983 has come to fruition in a number of different ways. On the one hand, national museums in the Pacific have acquired more than a trickle of returned items from colonial ethnographic collections. Exhibitions of these collections will reinforce the pressure to repatriate more.[90] These returns have proved significant but not without attendant problems. An example helps show the complexity of issues involved. In the 1991 reprint of Felix Speiser's Ethnology of Vanuatu: an Early Twentieth Century Study, the Vanuatu Minister of Home Affairs provided a preface that sought to distance himself from some of Speiser's terminology in the text,[91] whilst at the same time recognising the contribution that Speiser's work has made to the revival of Kastom: 'the viewing of early cultural photographs, such as those taken by Felix Speiser, has often assisted our people in the revival of certain traditional art forms thought to have been lost forever. For example, using Speiser's sketches of upright hollow drums from the Banks Islands, the Vanuatu Cultural Centre was able to revive the making and use of these 'TIMIAT WOS' on Vanua Lava and Mota Lava in the Banks Group in 1987'.[92]

The problem with Speiser's contribution is its relocation in a setting that is so changed from its original context. The move away from the institutional form of the museum suggested by Mead does not necessarily resolve the issues of 'salvage ethnography', nor easily settle questions of proprietary rights to ownership of objects, knowledge or customary usage. The advent of tourism as a serious aspiration either at the level of national or provincial government may serve to increase dissension over rights. Cultural Centres may risk becoming concentration camps (in the original sense of the term) that condemn indigenous people to residence away from home. The principal difference between the colonial museum and the contemporary cultural centre is that living actors replace historic artefacts. This risks these performers becoming unchangeable artefacts.

Such a gloomy prognosis is rejected by those who claim that they have the vision and power to resist such pressure from the promoters of tourism. There is a strong and well-developed argument that tourism can be put to genuinely

[90] As for example in the major exhibition Arts of Vanuatu See R Regenvanu 'Spirit blong bubu I kam bak' and J Bonnemaison et al Arts of Vanuatu.

[91] For example 'These are completely degenerate and no good works are being produced. Nor is this surprising since, clearly, a healthy art can flourish only on the soil of a healthy culture, and as a culture in the islands is no longer healthy, art must perforce degenerate'. Speiser, Ethnology of Vanuatu, 386

[92] Hon. Iolu Abil preface to Speiser, vii.

productive uses. As one commentator has remarked: 'Tourism projects in Wala [Malakula – NS] and in Tanna have motivated the cultural performance phenomenon, but once created the performances have inspired a genuine revival of interest among the performers, to the extent that the cultural revival and interest has taken on an impetus of its own unrelated to the tourism project, which it still serves'.[93] It is similarly argued that what is of interest to the tourist is of vital importance to the local. So the Vanuatu Protected Area Initiative on Santo seeks to create an environmental education centre to help local people to extend their knowledge and understanding of their environment and to develop solutions to their own environmental challenges.[94]

There are, however, some issues that these proponents of cultural resistance and renaissance might care to consider. Tourism is usually promoted as a means of sustaining both culture and environment through development agencies often under the guise of rural development and generating employment. But eco-tourism is still tourism. Whilst eco-tourists may want to participate in indigenous cultural activities and be enthusiastic in their forgoing of the comforts of developed tourist destinations, their requirements are still those of metropolitan regions. Eco-tourism, paradoxically, with its stress on an inviolate environment may intensify the pressure on indigenous hosts to reach for kastom to provide the visitor with the equivalent of the primeval rain forest and the unpolluted lagoon. Whilst tourists desire to observe and even participate in indigenous life, they do so strictly under their own terms which include clean and plentiful water, pest control, a diet they find palatable, rapid access to medicine and to air transportation. This can be a very high price for nation states characterised by 'ecological fragility, vulnerability, small size, limited resources, geographic dispersion, isolation from markets, disadvantaged economies'.[95] Furthermore, the cultural performances that these tourists expect, serve, as the discussion of kastom in this chapter has highlighted, to encourage either reinforcing the position of the already powerful to the exclusion of others or in the co-option of the local by the nationally powerful. Tourist development aid can further exacerbate this development. This is, of course, no different than elsewhere in the world, but in small states these features become more transparent to the indigenous people. 'Being ourselves' ceases, under these circumstances, to be a unified experience, despite the appearance in performance.

An ironic coda can be added to this picture. A comment on tourism in Java offered by Hughes–Freeland applies equally well throughout the Pacific. She states:

[93] R. Regenvanu, personal communication, December 1996.

[94] *VPAI* 'The First of Its Kind' leaflet, 1996.

[95] M. Fagence 'Ecotourism and Pacific Island Nations', 5

'It is perhaps fair to say that tourism provides the state with an invaluable function: it can be blamed for unanticipated consequences or failure of domestic policy. As well as being able to refract fantasies for the future, tourism can take the blame for problems in the present'.[96] And, we might add, for our image and use of the past.

One final twist is possible in this complex thread, one derived from a theoretical approach to travel writing. Pratt coins the term 'autoethnographic texts'. By these she means texts generated in response to or in dialogue with metropolitan representations. They are not 'authentic' or autochthonous forms of self-representation but involve partial collaboration with and appropriation of the idioms of the conqueror.[97] For Pratt contemporary travel and exploration writings are constituted in relation to the older imperialist rhetoric of conquest. Such an assertion is consistent with the treatment of cargo above and most writing about the Pacific to this day. But Pratt goes on to suggest that 'autoethnographic texts are typically heterogeneous on the reception end as well, usually addressed both to metropolitan readers and to literate sectors of the speaker's own social group, and bound to be received very differently by each. Often such texts constitute a group's point of entry into metropolitan literate culture'.[98]

If the term 'performance' is substituted for 'literary text' in the context of Pacific tourism, the actors script their performances in relation to the prescribed tourist genre; the primitivist imperial perspective of the show ground is replaced by ecotourism, which has to be studied by performers in all its theological niceties in order to assure an appropriate production. But the novelty that Pratt introduces at this point, is that the audience for these texts or shows is no longer exclusively the metropolitan or the tourist. The literate and cosmopolitan indigène becomes a highly skilled expert in this repertoire, responsive to every nuance in the performance, reading not only the 'text' of the performance but how it can be differentially approached. For this sophisticated audience the postmodern devices suggested at the introduction to this chapter become a stock in trade. Indigenous performance, like indigenous curation, becomes a complex equation with the power to define at the heart of contestation. This new audience for ethnographic performance is poised not only to become a knowledgeable critic but a new script writer.

The question that remains at the end of the day is, who will come to own the script? There remains a tension between all parties involved in negotiating ethnographic spectacles in the Pacific, and especially in the context of cultural centres

[96] F. Hughes-Freeland 'Packaging dreams: Javanese perceptions of tourism and performance', 154.

[97] M. L. Pratt *Imperial Eyes*, 7.

[98] Pratt, 7–8

where agendas are brokered. Indigenous curation does not offer neat or easy solutions in locally sponsored venues. Kastom introduces a new dimension into the discussion of ownership of performance, but it does not determine the outcome of the negotiations. The same considerations that affect the Asian parks discussed earlier are of importance here. National and international interests operate as significantly in the micro states of the Pacific as in the mega states of Asia. The most significant difference between the two in the development of a global paradigm is that in the Pacific the players often have the opportunity to get nearer to the locus of decision making. Needless to say, this is not to suggest that the negotiations are even-handed or always transparent.

**4**

# Beyond the modern paradigm: from culture centres to interpretation centres in contemporary Europe

## Modes of representation

Both of the previous two chapters have suggested that actors in a variety of settings can become exponents of performance in order to demonstrate through visual means significant elements of culture. The problem that lies behind such a formulation is that the forms of representation are not isomorphic or even similar in their construction. In displays like Taman Mini Indonesia or China Folk Culture Villages the indigènes are players in the management scripts. The architects of forms of indigenous curation and the constructors of cultural centres, whilst they attempt to appeal to custom and notions of tradition, they yet remain caught in a double referent, needing, on the one hand, to find a 'springboard' from which to leap back into the past whilst simultaneously keeping a firm eye on the future in terms of the tourist potential to be derived from treating culture as a commodity.

What both examples ignore is the fact that these representations are variants or an interpretation of an underlying reality, and that, of necessity, such representations offer a simulation or version of what they are modelled on. Representations can never aspire to become 'true', the most they can seek is to be useful, suggestive or convincing: 'a good representation is one that works'.[1] There remains in even the most captivating enactment an indissoluble distance between the reality and its 'double'. As David Brett has noted, the element of simulation involved in creating re-enactment is worth careful consideration because simulations introduce questions of style. 'A sense of style is much more important than it may seem at first because the presence of style reveals the artifice and the play element in the display.'[2] This chapter considers some stylistic issues in representation in the theatre of North West Europe, and specifically in Ireland and Wales where two quite different projects have attempted self-consciously to reconnect contemporary life and culture with ethnographic displays of the nearly past. The nearly past consists of a way of life that is almost lost. The enactment involves actors with a foot in the ethnographic past who provide a link between that past and the present. Such individuals provide not only a bridge between the two but a sense of unbroken continuity.[3]

The linkage between the Pacific and Europe is stronger than might at first appear. The cultural centre movement in the Pacific is related to developments elsewhere in the world. Dwellers in the region are not unique in their desire to do away with the tyranny of classical museums. The oral history programmes both in Vanuatu and in Solomon Islands draw inspiration from UNESCO programmes in

[1] The point is made by Johannes Fabian in his 'Presence and representation; the other in anthropological writing, *Critical Inquiry* 16:4 1990, 754.

[2] D. Brett *The Construction of Heritage*, Cork University Press, 1996, 164.

[3] 'The appeal of heritage to a population undergoing yet another bout of the modernisation process (as is the case in both Ireland and Great Britain) is also clear; it offers the possibility (not entirely illusory) of maintaining contact with a vanished 'habitus' and keeping some sense of social continuity and valued difference consciously alive.' Brett, 158.

the Pacific in the late 1970s which in turn are constructed on the intellectual foundations of the ecomuseum programme generated by UNESCO and associated with the work of Georges-Henri Rivière.[4] For Rivière there were four defining features of an ecomuseum:

- Remembrance (the inventory of surrounding cultural and material resources);
- Understanding [*la connaissance*] (promoting a deeper awareness of the environment through research and education);
- The joint management and development of the locale by the inhabitants and a team of scientists (resulting in museum installations, exhibitions, publications and documentation);
- Artistic creation (artists' retreats; creative arts projects linked to local industry and technology).[5]

Each of these features contributed to the pan-Pacific cultural centre movement. Oral history, performance, recording, publication and the renaissance of craft traditions were all stimulated by these ideas which were enthusiastically promoted by expatriate-led education and development programmes.

But the ecomuseum was to have another agenda: 'the old task of salvaging and recording has been replaced by the business of discovering and interpreting culture'.[6] The cultural centres in the Pacific were designed to engage, educate and persuade their audiences which remained unambiguously the local and the indigenous. It is perhaps not surprising that the impact of the cultural centre/ecomuseum should be felt not only in the Pacific but within Europe itself. Interestingly, most of the inherent tensions encountered in the Pacific resurface in Europe. The lessons of kastom, in particular, have especially interesting ramifications in this new setting.

The two cases presented in this chapter are contemporary. The first is The Blasket Centre, opened in 1994 at Dún Chaoin (Dunquin)[7] in Co. Kerry, Ireland. The Centre is a singular and distinctive creation of the state's Office of Public Works and is one of some forty or more heritage centres that have sprung up in the country over the past decade or less, all under the aegis of heritage and tourist development with considerable assistance from the European Union Structural Fund.[8] The thinking involved is, therefore, in some ways analogous to that operating in the South Pacific under the aegis of the European Union. The Blasket Centre is, as will be shown beneath, certainly a cultural centre in the sense of the term as used so far. The linkage to the past is generated through a form of anthropology,

[4] see D. Poulot's 'Identity and self-discovery' for a discussion of Rivière' and the ecomuseum movement.

[5] Poulot 'Identity and self-discovery', 72.

[6] D. Poulot 'Identity and self-discovery', 78.

[7] For both cases when introducing bilingual expressions I give the term in full on the first occasion and only the English version subsequently. I recognise that this may be considered an unsatisfactory resolution to this important issue. Certainly, means of expression bring with them associated issues of power and access. I offer the lame excuse that I am unversed in translation. By providing dual versions on one occasion I alert the reader to the issue that I skirt subsequently. However, I use name forms in the language that they appear in most texts. So O'Crohan is given as Ó Criomhthain and O'Sullivan is rendered as Ó Súilleabháin.

[8] S. Browne 'Heritage in Ireland's Tourism recovery' 20. The current (1997) Heritage Island Touring Guide lists 59 major heritage centres. Over £IR100 Mhas been devoted to the OPW from the European Structural Fund 1994–9. J Blye, personal communication.

albeit a highly distinctive one that privileges language and literature through visual representation.

The second case provides a more direct experience of cultural enactment for the visitor. The Big Pit/ Pwll Mawr ceased to be a working pit in 1980 and reopened as a visitor centre in 1983. At the time of closure there were forty working mines in the South Wales area. Fifteen years later there were none left. The Big Pit therefore provides the only opportunity to visit and descend into a 'working mine' in Wales. The Big Pit is maintained in a state of readiness as though to restart tomorrow but there is a sense in which it is as near to cultural as well as physical redundancy as The Blasket Centre which marks the abandonment by the community of its island home in 1953. Both live in the future perfect, just touching the past by finger tip before it slips away. This is, of course, the material that heritage is constructed from.

The central focus of this chapter is the similarity between the two examples as well as their difference from other forms of spectacularized ethnography. The question to be posed is whether contemporary forms of heritage display behave like other types of cultural representation in other parts of the world. Do The Blasket Centre and The Big Pit transfer or translate issues of cultural copyright, indigenous curation, architectural reconstruction and pageants in a recognisable form, or is the context so far removed from those considered so far as to make such analogies or correlations too far fetched to be worth making? The intention in the following sections is to suggest that postulating such relationships may be fruitful and may indeed reveal how elements of visual anthropology may be recombined to similar effect in what appear initially unrelated contexts.

A further issue needs to be addressed before proceeding, namely, the connection between the two examples. Whilst both may demonstrate affinities with previous examples it may not be immediately obvious how they relate to each other. Both The Blasket Centre and The Big Pit share a number of assertions. Firstly, and most significantly, they both maintain that the passing elements of a formerly notable culture can be kept alive through the erection of memorials. The difference between Dunquin and Santa Ana is that in Kerry there remains an unbroken link both in architecture as well as performance in a Gaelic historic culture as lived within current memory, whereas the Melanesian custom house whether on site in Santa Ana or in the Cultural Centre in Honiara has had to be reconstructed. Similarly, the record of working practices can be kept alive by ex-miners who retain a culture shaped by the technology and specific nature of their former work. Both of the cases examined here suggest something more than salvage ethnography; the link with historic practice is mediated by the events that have made them both obsolete.

Another distinctive quality that unites both examples is a recognition that each 'deserved' in some manner to die. The remoteness of the Blasket islands added to their allure for early twentieth century visitors. They offered the location for the 'memory' that formed the basis for the new Irish writing both in English and Irish from Synge to Yeats and even to Joyce. The literary inheritance, however, was to appear as a bequest rather than a living tradition. This distancing was replicated in the history of the abandonment of the Blaskets. Dangerous currents and treacherous weather often cut the islanders off from vital services. But as the community declined the ability to muster a crew to row to the mainland became more difficult. A young man died on The Great Blasket in 1952 because medical attention could not be provided in bad weather.[9] This death symbolised the failure of the community to provide the basis for an adequate life in modern times. Within a year The Great Blasket was evacuated and has not since been inhabited. Hardship and danger were aspects of Blasket life that were seldom mourned. Similarly, coal mining wherever it is conducted, is constantly attended by immediate and long term perils, from the danger of injury and death at work, and the more insidious and equally debilitating consequences of pneumoconiosis. Former miners are seldom tempted to romanticise the conditions of their employment. There is, in both contemporary examples offered here, an ambiguous relationship to the inhospitable and dangerous aspects of life previously experienced by the actors. Both the islanders and miners share an uncertainty and equivocalness about their former lives. For both the transformations are irreversible; there is no return to either past hardship nor cherished forms of tradition. Nevertheless, for both groups there remains a distinct 'after-life' of memory of their previous existence with its different structures. For the Blasket islanders social life had quite different parameters to that lived on the mainland; 'the 150 people lived close together without police or priest. The control was through language and especially humour which enabled hard things to be said in coded form'.[10]

It could also be claimed with some justice that these examples are not only potentially anti-romantic but also postmodern in their refusal to close or privilege a particular account. Both also offer a form of 'historic revenge' in that they offer unexpected vistas on contemporary life. The Blasket Centre surprises the visitor by documenting photographically how the community has survived and

[9] Repeating similar previous experiences. Paddy Kearney wrote: 'My brother was very ill, it was Christmas 1947. We were cut off in the island because of storms for over two weeks. We could get neither doctor nor priest into the island. The sea was too rough. My brother died of meningitis. Eventually the lifeboat came in from Dingle to take his body out of the island.' P Kearney 'Leaving the Island' in A Haughey *The Edge of Europe*, 5.

[10] Pat Cooke, personal communication.

been transformed by the very activity it defied, emigration, showing the diaspora community in Springfield Massachusetts which has throughout this century contained the largest concentration of people from The Blaskets.[11] At The Big Pit, in contrast to the oft-emphasised solidarity of mining communities, there is frequent reference to the hierarchical nature of job specialisms and their differentiation which cross-cut an overall sense of class solidarity.

The Blasket Centre and The Big Pit make a claim on behalf of other similar expositions to provide a responsible spectacularization of culture. The implicit argument underlying their display is that it is through visible means that memory is preserved and revivified through a combination of social and historical documentation with topographic and architectural representation. Representation involves, as Brett reminds us, narration, visualisation and simulation.[12] These features are as significant in architectural representation as in any other form. Re-enactment is made possible through the combination of original settings, restored architecture and simulated conditions. In this way two innovations are achieved. Firstly, these expositions face up to one of the major issues evaded by the exemplars discussed in the previous two chapters, namely, the treatment of history. The parks in Indonesia and China are set in a continuous anthropological present tense where the changing interrelationship between different groups and movements in habitation are ignored, whilst those in Taiwan fail to incorporate satisfactorily their debt to Japanese ethnography; the cultural centres in Melanesia have yet to grapple with how the past becomes the property of the currently politically powerful. But, for The Big Pit as well as for The Blasket Centre, the treatment of history is a key issue to be constantly addressed.

These new forms of exposition also tackle a major problem confronting visualisation, particularly in heritage displays. Urry discusses the problem thus:

> Heritage industry is distorted because of the predominant emphasis on visualisation, on presenting visitors with an array of artefacts, including buildings (either 'real' or 'manufactured'), and then trying to visualise the patterns of life that would have emerged around them. This is an essentially 'artefactual' history, in which a whole variety of social experiences are necessarily ignored or trivialized, such as war, exploitation, hunger, disease, the law and so on.[13]

[11]  Fintan O'Toole in A Haughey *The Edge of Europe*, 54.

[12]  Brett *The Construction of Heritage*, 163–4.

[13]  John Urry *The Tourist Gaze*, 112.

[14]  An excellent example of this revisionist approach is to be seen in the Famine Museum at Strokestown, Co. Roscommon. Mary Robinson's preface underlines the importance of historical enquiry: 'How important it is to make a record of a darker past as well. There are grim statistics and painful details here. They give an account of a terrible time; they illuminate the defenceless suffering of the Irish people at that time. But they serve another purpose as well: they invite us to look steadily at a past we can neither share nor change. With all its pain and disorder, the past has constructed us in the actual and literal ways of generation and inheritance.' in J S Campbell *The Great Irish Famine*, 7.

[15]  Brett *The Construction of Heritage*, 62–3.

[16]  Marc Augé *Non-Places: An Introduction to the Anthropology of Supermodernity*, 50.

It is precisely these lacunae, these distortions that the curators of these new forms of spectacle see as their primary duty to redress.[14] But they also rebut Urry's charge by insisting that visualisation is both a licit and an important activity for visitor and actor alike. These new manifestations smash the twin certainties of imperial expositions and World's Fairs: a simultaneous *morality* (where anthropology assisted in establishing a proper order of peoples and their relationship to viewers) and *promiscuity* (people were only worth showing to the extent that they were significantly 'other' and thus had the potential to generate in the viewer boundless and constantly changing pleasure). In their place a new class of self-conscious viewers emerges that is alive to the narrative and aesthetic strategies adopted in the display, and the implications of style involved. They fulfil the conditions that Brett outlines for such a new public: 'The gathering together of individuals as witnesses to the spectacles of representation . . . are formative of new social relations and these new social relations are themselves formative of new understandings not least of nationality and history'.[15]

Both The Blasket Centre and The Big Pit sit squarely in this tradition and are important not only in terms of their display strategies and accounts but also for their contribution to the development of historically pluralist visions concerned simultaneously with the creation of both local and national identity. Both also share a new attitude to the visitor/viewer. As with the programmes of cultural regeneration in the South Pacific, these exhibits are concerned not only with the status of what is shown but also about how it is seen and understood by different categories of viewer. These representations serve a range of audiences from the actors themselves, through the local communities (however constituted) to broader publics, regional, national and international. For both, the local and the international publics have particular significance as will become apparent.

## Dunquin: from antiquity to the postmodern

'The ideal, for an ethnologist wishing to characterise singular particularities, would be for each ethnic group to have its own island, possibly linked to others but different from any other; and for each islander to be an exact replica of his neighbours'.[16]

Dunquin illustrates such an anthropological vision admirably; indeed, it exemplifies a particular distillation of ethnicity aligned with nationality, seldom found in such singularly emblematic form. There are several reasons for studying the Blasket Centre in the context of ethnographic display. Firstly, it responds dimly but distinctly to the traditions of portraying 'Irishness' in the Imperial past. Secondly, it offers evidence of a unique example of a swift but sustained piece of salvage ethnography conducted in the first half of this century with the prompting of an international cast of researchers. Thirdly, the Centre celebrates a particular form of representation and visualisation, one provided by indigenous informants in a literary form, folk tales and reminiscences told and written in the Irish language, at a time when the community was suffering steep decline,. The Centre provides visual form to this literary achievement. Finally, the Blasket Centre provides in its own construction and strategy a determinedly modern framework to undermine the common picture of the demise of one of Europe's oldest linguistic groups in a pre-industrial island fastness.

The Blasket Islands, like the other islands off Ireland's Atlantic shore, retained the use of Irish as the language of everyday use. As the west of Ireland became depopulated after the Famine the use of Irish declined sharply throughout the region.[17] This served to make more prominent and distinctive those communities where the language was still employed. Irish language became increasingly a curiosity and a mark of distinction and difference. For some it represented a past characterised by servitude, poverty and isolation. For others it was a priceless cultural asset. The Blasket Islands offered evidence for both views. What made it – and other places like the Aran Isles – so intriguing to many was its simultaneous nearness and remoteness in so many dimensions. Language was only one element, topography was another; Ireland was seen as sublime. 'Like the Highlands of Scotland, like Brittany and the Alps and other regions, Ireland (especially its western coast) has stood for the primitive, the unspoilt, the wild and the natural'.[18]

It is not surprising that all of these elements were played upon whenever Ireland was called upon to represent itself from the Chicago World's Colombian Exposition of 1893 to today's 'It's A Small World' in Disneyland. On the Midway Plaisance in Chicago the Irish Village had to share space with a Japanese Bazaar, the Hagenbeck Animal Show, and the Javanese village, 'the Street of Cairo', a Dahomey Village as well as one from Germany.[19] Quite where Ireland figured in the pecking order is a matter of some conjecture.[20] But identity was fixed by two traditional means: architecture and performance. Antiquity furnished the first with half size reproductions of Donegal Castle, Cormac's Chapel, Muckross Friary and Blarney

[17] 'The famine was a major blow to the Irish language, since those who died and emigrated were disproportionately speakers of Irish' N. Ó. Ciosáin 'Hungry Grass: the new Famine Museum at Strokestown House' *Circa*, 1994, 67, 26.

[18] Brett *The Construction of Heritage*, 127.

[19] David F. Burg *Chicago's White City of 1893*, 218–9.

[20] Coombes argues that what differentiates depictions of Ireland and Scotland from African displays in exhibitions like the Franco–British Exhibition in London in 1908 is the attribution of an historic pedigree to the former and its denial to the latter. Annie E. Coombes *Reinventing Africa: Museums, Material Culture and Popular Imagination in Late Victorian and Edwardian England*, 207.

**The Great Blasket from Dunquin**

Castle together with a round tower.[21] Performance was skillfully angled to appeal to the American visitor and was provided by girls engaged in cottage industries like lace-making and crocheting beside a peat fire. Prominent among the actors was 'Maggie Dennehy, from Valencia Island, Co, Kerry, "who talks real Irish."'[22] Visitors to the Irish Village were, it was reported,

> 'Captivated by the sight of the rosy colleens, the sound of their musical brogue as they worked beside the turf fires in the cottages, dispensed buttermilk and butter in the model dairy, danced jigs and recited Irish verse in the village hall.'[23]

This combination became a regular feature of Irish exhibits from the St Louis Exposition of 1904 onwards and became 'stabilised' into a standard format at the Franco–British Exhibition of 1908 in a village with the fanciful title of 'Ballymaclinton'.[24] Greenhalgh has contrasted this depiction of a rural, handicraft and agricultural society and speaking a foreign language with the tendency in imperial discourse to 'emphasise rurality, backwardness and nature when discussing subject-nations and the city, industry and culture when discussing the imperial

[21] Burg *Chicago's White City*, p 218; Steve Nelson 'Walt Disney's EPCOT', 113; Jeanne Sheehy *The Rediscovery of Ireland's Past*, 131, 147.

[22] Sheehy, 147.

[23] Sheehy, 147.

[24] Brett The Construction of Heritage, 82–3; Coombes *Reinventing Africa*: 206–8; Paul Greenhalgh *Ephemeral Vistas*, 106; Sheehy, 134.

ones.'[25] He also makes the observation, important for the discussion of The Blasket Centre, that 'the vision created of the various periphery cultures by the core imperial one often became naturalised and accepted as a true reflection of the real cultural situation by the periphery itself'.[26] In this context, recent studies of the postcard output of the photographer John Hinde show how his postcards have since 1957 concentrated on rural and idyllic settings in which Irish girls and women are posed.[27] Such stereotyped vignettes were virtually all that was available until the late 1970s and beyond for visitors to send home as evidence of their adventures. Paradoxically, John Hinde received much of his 'ruralist' training in a study of the countryside of Southwest England.[28] His photographic studies in Ireland and Britain are interchangeable in their use of standard props, costume and scenery in slightly surreal colour shifts.

Whilst it is fanciful to think of The Blasket Centre as being constructed on the foundations of Imperial Expositions, these styles of representation have retained significance long after the theatrical events that gave rise to them. What these expositions did so effectively was to demonstrate that seemingly innocent enactments could have complex ramifications. In particular, Ballymaclinton and its like made the ready acceptance of a romantic vision of a backward looking society subsequently difficult to accept. Embracing the historic past implied a rejection of modernity and notions of progress. To attempt to reconcile both of these objectives was a major political consideration for the first fifty years of Irish government after independence. It can be argued that representations of Irish life have brought together in a serious way issues of culture and politics. Such representations come to have immense political significance, as Brett has demonstrated so convincingly in his analysis of heritage centres across Ireland.

But the major features celebrated at the Imperial expositions were also considered important in quite different contexts. Whilst one can have sympathy for Greenhalgh's sentiments about the deleterious effects of these cultural enactments on the visitors to imperial expositions, merely decrying these shows is not an adequate response.[29] It seems to me more useful to inquire into the conditions under which these representations were engineered and propagated, and with what consequences. I take it as axiomatic that the tendency to make representations is irrepressible, and that much as psychoanalysis considers mental constructions as evidence of mental processes, so cultural practices may be analogously inspected for elements which may be highly conflictful with each other. Whilst

[25] Greenhalgh *Ephemeral Vistas*, 107.

[26] Greenhalgh *Ephemeral Vistas*, 111.

[27] Luke Gibbon *Transformations in Irish Culture*, 38.

[28] see W. J. Turner *Exmoor Village*, Colour Photographs by John Hinde. This was the first of a series entitled 'British Ways of Life'. Both collaborated on a second volume 'British Circus Life'.

[29] 'One can only guess at the extent of the harm caused by these human show cases, but within the bounds of speculation it can be asserted that an immense amount of damage was caused, with little good coming out of them in social, moral or intellectual terms. Fifty years after their demise, the damage remains unrepaired. *Ephemeral Vistas*, 109.

people may be persuaded into visual and intellectual stereotypes by the 'illusioneers' who create ethnographic representations, they are not, of necessity imprisoned by them for all time. The reality is more complex. Ballymaclinton can be read simultaneously in contradictory ways.

A unique set of circumstances elevated the Blasket Islands to a pre-eminence in Irish self-consciousness and all of these were related to the Irish language. Precisely those aspects of linguistic difference that entertained visitors to the Midway Plaisance were the source of wonder and delight to those who sought to revive a sense of distinctive culture in Ireland. The remoteness of the Blasket Islands Group (The Great Blasket and five smaller satellites) both united and differentiated the population from the mainland. Thomson characterises the community thus:

> No money circulated in the island. They were bound to one another by close ties of blood and marriage, all residing within a stone's throw of each other, all engaged in the same occupations and faced with the same dangers at sea. They were a community of kinsfolk. They had their quarrels, of course, but seldom carried them beyond a war of words . . . They had little formal education and no political understanding, but were well versed in their own ancestral lore, which was perfectly adapted to their way of life. It was a narrow life, but their knowledge of it was profound. It was a simple culture, but free from the rapacity and vulgarity that is destroying our own.[30]

The contrast between the 'ancestral' life and its modern industrial counterpart is significant. Thomson was a British scholar and linguist who first visited The Blaskets in 1923 to acquire the language. He was following a tradition that had started earlier in the century. John Millington Synge, author of *In the Shadow of the Glen* (1903), *The Playboy of the Western World* (1907), visited The Great Blasket in 1905, took photographs of inhabitants and wrote an account of his visit paying particular attention to the islanders and their ways. He is also credited with alerting W B Yeats and James Joyce of the significance of the Blaskets to Gaelic culture and language.[31] It was to be linguists and folklorists that were to assist a remarkable literary flowering that Thomson later called 'The Blasket Island Library'.

Carl Marstrander, a Norwegian linguist, stayed on the Great Blasket for five months during the summer of 1907. He worked with the islanders whilst learning the language from Tomás Ó Criomhthain. Marstrander sent one of his students,

[30] George Thomson Island Home: *The Blasket Heritage*, 84–5.

[31] Muiris Mac Conghail *The Blaskets: People and Literature*, 134.

Robin Flower, a manuscript librarian at the British Museum, to the islands in 1910. Flower was to spend several periods on the islands studying with Tomás Ó Criomhthain. He published his *The Western Island* in 1944 which gave an account of island life and culture and collected stories by Ó Criomhthain which were published in Irish in 1956. Brian Ó Ceallaigh went to learn Irish with Ó Criomhthain in 1917. Ó Ceallaigh provided the impetus for Ó Criomhthain to embark on an altogether new undertaking, an autobiographical study spanning the period of his childhood in the 1860s up to the 1920s. Ó Ceallaigh read to Ó Criomhthain Gorky's *My Childhood* and Pierre Loti's *Pêcheur d'Islande*.[32] Loti (real name Louis-Marie-Julien Viauld) had published a popular sentimental tale of a sailor's adventures in a Pacific paradise, *Le Mariage de Loti*, in 1898. Ó Criomhthain's work appeared in Irish in 1929 and was translated as *The Islandman* in 1937.

The work was an exceptional accomplishment. As Mac Conghail reminds us, there was scant literary or other direction for writing in Irish. The majority of Irish speakers could neither write nor read the language. Those who could would be 'priests, teachers and academics, yes, but a fisherman living in a remote island off a remote mainland?'[33] What Ó Criomhthain initiated was very clearly a form of indigenous study, stylistically distinct but widely accessible in its use of the 'Homeric' tradition, the recording of winning a living against the vicissitudes of nature on the land and at sea.

Ó Criomhthain was joined by a man of a younger generation, Muiris Ó Súilleabháin, who wrote what was to be an equally significant work, *Twenty Years Agrowing*, which received international success when it was translated and published in English in 1933. Ó Súilleabháin's promoter was George Thomson, who had come to the islands through Robin Flower's recommendation. Similarly, Flowers sent Kenneth Jackson to learn Irish from Peig Sayers in 1932. He published a set of tales in Irish in 1938 entitled *Stories from the Blasket*. Sayers' autobiography (*Peig*) was published in 1936. Her son, Míchaél Ó Gaoithín, completed his own story in 1953 under the title *A Pity Youth does not Last*.

Thomson characterises their common accomplishment as the seamless transition from speech to writing:

> These authors were all versed to a greater of lesser degree in the art of storytelling. Their mode of speech and their outlook on life had been moulded by the traditional tales which they had inherited from past

[32] Thomson *Island Home*; 56; Mac Conghail *The Blaskets*, 140; P Snow and S Waine *The People of the Horizon*, 203.

[33] Mac Conghail *The Blaskets*, 145.

[34] Thomson *Island Home*, 32.

[35] Tomás O'Crohan (Ó Criomhthain) *The Islandman*, 238.

[36] Pádraig Ua Maoileoin *Na Blascaodaí/The Blaskets*, 11.

[37] Visitors coming in and going out of our house talking and talking and they on their holidays and they at home having comfortable homes and no worry during the winter or summer would never believe the misfortune on this island, no school nor comfort, no road to success, no fishing, not five hundred of mackerel was caught last summer when it cost £3 a hundred. Eibhlís Ní Shúilleabháin *Letters from the Great Blasket*.

generations. What they did, therefore, was to select from their own experience a number of episodes which they had already cultivated as fireside tales and arrange them as continuous narrative.[34]

What Ó Criomhthain, Ó Súilleabháin and Sayers had done (and there were other writers later alongside Ó Gaoithín) was to create a national and international interest in a small community in Ireland's most southerly and westerly quarter. Marstrander, Flowers and Thomson were only the first of a flood of visitors who came to see and experience for themselves people living what they took to be a traditional life. Ó Criomhthain commented on the impact they had on daily life: 'Many people have been coming to the Island for years in quest of Irish. Most of them spent a month here. I had to spend a time in the company of each one of them, and do my own work into the bargain'.[35] So regular a feature of summer life did these visitors become that the islanders took to planting more vegetables.[36] It seldom occurred to the guests that winter life might be an altogether different experience.[37] But these later visitors came with their perception already sharpened and directed by what they had read. This was to be a very literary form of ethnography,[38] one committed to the depiction of a community at the point of its disappearance. But the results of this effort were to have a far greater significance than their geographic isolation would suggest.

Thomson provided the intellectual justification for the Blasket Islands writers and placed them on the stage of world significance. The key term that he employed was 'Homeric'. By this he meant 'the use of ornamental epithets and set passages repeated without variation to describe recurrent situations, such as starting out on a journey, preparing for battle, partaking of a meal'.[39] In his later *Marxism and Poetry* Thomson wrote, 'The conversation of those ragged peasants . . . electrified me. It was as though Homer had come alive. Its vitality was inexhaustible, yet it was rhythmical, alliterative, formal, artificial, always on the point of bursting into poetry'.[40] The epithet 'Homeric' served two purposes; on the one hand, it suggested a pedigree and a direct line back to classical antiquity, and, on the other, it was to remind the modern reader, visitor and critic that here in this backwater was preserved life and virtue lost in the headlong rush to modernity. This was a very different construction to that offered at Ballymaclinton.[41]

The Blasket Island Library was to have a very wide educational impact. The texts rapidly became modern classics in the Irish language, partly because there

[38] Mac Conghail reports: 'Dublin Opinion, the 'national humorous magazine of Ireland', carried a cartoon on its cover in the June edition of 1933 showing an island with every conceivable form of writing activity in progress: manuscripts and typewriters strewn all over the island and the islanders themselves engaged in literary pursuits. The cartoon is entitled 'The Literary Wave Hits Ireland' *The Blaskets*, 161.

[39] Thomson *Island Home*, 39.

[40] cited by Tim Enright in 'George Thomson: A Memoir' in Thomson *Island Home*, 137.

[41] Thomson may also have had in mind Malinowski's metaphor that forms the backbone of *The Argonauts of the Western Pacific*, first published in 1922. Thomson's first visit to the Great Blasket was in 1923.

were few contemporary competitors but also because they were made into set texts for public examinations, and, in Ireland's system of matriculation, Irish language was a compulsory component in the Leaving Certificate. Peig Sayers' auto-biography, despite its complex structure, rapidly became a prescribed text.[42] So, for generations of Irish school children who were learning the language, the vehicle of instruction was the ethnography and folklore of the Blasket Islands. The Blaskets came to conflate and epitomise a whole sense of national identity, one barely tangible but somehow essential in its detail. The placing of a map of the islands on the £20 note in 1980 provided the final official seal of national recognition, analo-gous to the representation of the *nagol* (land jump) on Vanuatu's 5,000 vatu note.[43]

What has happened with the Blasket Island Library is that a spectaculariza-tion of culture is provided through verbal and literary means. The publication of Ó Súilleabháin in English in 1933 and Ó Criomhthain in 1937 further extended the audience for the Library from the student of Irish to any interested in the contin-uance of what Thomson called a medieval outlook[44] still extant in the twentieth century. The texts have become artefacts in their own right composed of congealed memories.

A further element contributes to the intensity of the Blasket Islands' impact on Ireland and the world outside, the photograph. From Synge onwards the islanders were subject to the most intensive and extensive photographic investiga-tion. To have a very detailed, extensive record of the topography, architecture, farm-ing and fishing, domestic interiors and a host of studies of the one hundred and fifty or so individual inhabitants[45] seen both in family and friendship groups, is to have quite a different relationship to these subjects than that normally available through standard ethnographies. As the literary record extends, the photographs come to supplement and augment it. It is as though the texts are being filled out in visual form. Many of the photographs subsequently published were taken by the scholar visitors. The first recorded photographs are by Synge (1905). Flower also took pictures as did another visitor with him on The Great Blasket, Thomas Mason. Carl von Sydow, a Swedish folklorist and ethnographer took a series of celebrated studies of the island community in 1924. George Thomson took von Sydow's picture as the latter was being rowed away from the island.[46] Thomson also made a number of studies of Ó Criomhthain and Ó Súilleabháin and their neighbours. Thomas Waddicor was photographing extensively at the same time as Thomson. Later in 1931 and again in 1938 George Chambers took a number of pictures, particularly

[42] Mac Conghail *The Blaskets*, 159.

[43] 'The design elements of the new £20 note reflect the renaissance of literature in Ireland in both Irish and English in the early part of this century . . . The design on the back of the note sets a group of the Blasket Islands, off the coast of Kerry, against the background of an excerpt from an early edition of Tómas Ó Criomhthain's classic An tOileánach.' Press release, Currency Centre, Central Bank of Ireland, February 1980. An earlier form of state commemoration was the issue of a set of postage stamps of Ó Criomhthain in 1957 twenty years after his death.

[44] Thomson *Island Home*, 61.

[45] The population hovered around this size from 1840 to around 1916 when it started its steady decline. Pádraig Ua Maoileoin *The Blaskets*, 7; Mac Conghail *The Blaskets*, 34.

[46] Thomson *Island Home*, 102.

of one subject, Eibhlís Ní Shúillibheáin. She wrote to him for twenty years and these letters were published in 1978 as *Letters from the Great Blasket*. Nevertheless, the Islanders obeyed Cohen's dictum – 'native people rarely represent themselves.'[47] There are no self-portraits in the published Blasket record.[48]

But photographs were important to the islanders. Studio protraits, in particular, provided the visual bridge between two different worlds, enabling the Islanders to cross imaginatively between the Islands and the new community in America. Ó Súilleabháin gives a vivid example of the significance of the photograph when he describes his sister's vision of Springfield, constructed through pictures hanging in her island home.[49] The image of family members the other side of the ocean kept, as it does for all mobile communities, an effective memorial and the promise of being reunited.

The photographs give a calm and ordered appearance to island life. All the images are composed and mannered. Very seldom is any action suggested. This gives to the islanders a dignity and a sense of pictorial control. This is in vivid contrast to Luke Gibbon's reaction to early film footage which Mac Conghail incorporates in his *Oileán Eile – Another Island* (1985). Gibbon writes:

> There is a startling sequence in Muiris Mac Conghail's documentary on the Blasket Islands, Oilean Eile, in which after a succession of images recalling the past in black and white photographs and archival footage, the islands are suddenly illuminated in colour. For a moment, we assume that we are back at reality, and that the camera has caught up with the present. But as the images unfold, however, the bedraggled clothes and unkempt thatched cottages bring home to us that this is also archival footage, perhaps some of the earliest colour film of Ireland. The strangeness comes from viewing the myth itself in colour.[50]

Whilst the advent of colour 'modernises' the scene I feel that the difference in response that Gibbon experiences between the photograph and the moving image may also be related to the sense of control that the posed subject of the still image can retain, but which evaporates when the composition is handed over to the director and the film camera operator. *Oileán Eile* like O'Flaherty's *Men of Aran* is a documentary in the standard accepted sense; it is about rather than by the subjects.

Given this unique ethnographic, literary and visual record it becomes easy to understand why the Irish government when planning a range of heritage sites

[47] See Chapter 1 footnote 8.

[48] The most extensive and useful published collection of Blasket photographs is provided by Muiris Mac Conghail in his *The Blaskets*, 58–124.

[49] 'Kate Peg was now constantly coming to the house now and she and Maura talking of nothing but America. They would run across to the wall where pictures from Springfield were hanging. 'Oh,' Kate would say, 'we will go into that big building, the first day, Maura.' Then the two of them would run out on the floor dancing for joy.' Maurice O'Sullivan *Twenty Years A-Growing*, 216.

[50] Luke Gibbon 'Back Projection', 18.

should chose the Blasket Islands for particular consideration and to designate it by statute as a National Historic Park. In recent years the Office of Public Works has undertaken a number of architecturally and museologically interesting interpretation centres. Some are concerned with archaeology like the Céide Fields Visitor Centre in Co. Mayo with its display of megalithic bog field systems and the Corlea Trackway Exhibition Centre in middle of the bogs in Co. Longford.[51] Others have dealt with other aspects of heritage like waterways and wildlife.[52] But none has attempted quite so self-consciously to display aspects of Irish ethnography nor to engage the subjects of such an ethnographic display in decisions about how it should look. It is for this reason, in conjunction with those already offered, that The Blasket Centre is singled out for special consideration as an anthropological display. One of the aspects that will be of particular concern in such an examination is whether in planning and mounting the display the designers have been able to make theoretical or representational advances on those considered in the previous chapters, and whether the subjects of representation can genuinely enter into the discussions and decisions surrounding construction and narrative.

It might seem initially surprising from what has been suggested so far that one should talk about 'the subjects' in the present tense. Yet the Blasket Island memory is not as ephemeral as implied by the phrase used earlier, 'just touching the past by the finger tips'. This is no modern form of Skansen. There are still those living on the mainland opposite the islands who themselves, or whose parents were born on the islands. Memories remain fresh, and the views of individuals do not necessarily coincide, nor do they naturally share in their account of the past or their place in it. In this the current generation replicates the actions of its predecessors. As Ua Maoileoin records 'The Blasket books generated controversy and debate on the Island. Writers were accused of misrepresentation – 'that is not how it happened'; 'all lies and invention.' Much of this criticism was inspired by envy.'[53] To create a heritage centre within a living community is to incite a debate about the nature of the record and the society that is documented.

The planning, construction and eventual display at the Blasket Centre are all of considerable interest for the development of the concept of indigenous curation. From the earliest days of the Centre's conception the local community was actively involved, particularly in the form of the Blasket Island Foundation. The Foundation was created in 1985 in reaction to plans to sell the Great Blasket in the United States. The Foundation raised £400,000 and petitioned the government to

[51] See Brett *Construction of Heritage*, 130–9 (on the Céide Fields); Nuala O'Faolain 'A genial trip through prehistory and landscape in a satisfying building' *The Irish Times* 15 August 1994 (on the Céide fields) and 'As if a spaceship had landed in the alien bog' *The Irish Times*, 28 August 1994 (on the Corlea Trackway).

[52] for example the Waterways Visitor Centre, Grand Canal Quay, Dublin; the Wexford Wildfowl Reserve, North Slob, Wexford.

[53] Ua Maoileoin *The Blaskets*, 35.

adopt the islands as a National Park. The necessary legislation was passed in 1989 with three objectives; to sustain the environment of the island (including renovation of properties); to improve access (rebuilding quays both on the mainland and on the island); and to create an interpretative centre at Dunquin.[54] Only the third objective has so far been tackled. The Basket Centre was built as a direct result of this legislation. The Centre has, therefore, the direct interest of the state involved in the activity of the Office of Public Works (OPW) to bring about this interpretative attraction in consultation with the community of West Kerry. This has ensured that, unlike other regional enterprises such as Wexford County Council's Irish National Heritage Park,[55] the Centre has a national as well as regional perspective.

The Blasket Island Foundation entered a formal agreement with OPW 'to prepare and carry out a joint development plan for the Blasket Centre and for the National Park.' Together, they agreed to commission 'a thorough research of the Islands history, folklore, literature, music and orality'.[56] A multidisciplinary team worked for nine months researching information locally.

**The Blasket Centre**

[54]  personal communication, Pat Cooke.

[55]  see M N Dillon in E Culleton *Guide to the Irish National Heritage Park, Ferrycarrig*, Wexford, 7.

[56]  Ciaran O'Connor 'The Blasket Centre' *Landscape Architecture News*, 3, 5.

**The Slí or central corridor, Blasket Centre**

A process of local consultation took place with forty public meetings between Easter 1989 and August 1993. Plans for the architecture and content were presented and agreed, although An Taisce (The National Trust) objected to the scale and appropriateness of the building planned.[57] But throughout the planning and execution of the centre the Blasket Island Foundation remained in broad sympathy with OPW's developments. Partly, this may have been due to the fact that some key members of the Foundation had had experience of working at the top of national organisations and therefore felt comfortable dealing with a bureaucratic structure like the OPW whilst having their own roots in the locality. There was, however, much to try the commitment of the Foundation to the enterprise.

[57] personal communication, Ciaran O'Connor.

**The Blasket Centre from the south**

Architecture was a key element. Firstly, the Centre was to be in the sightline of the Great Blasket. This meant that it would occupy a prominent position. Secondly, the building was to be modern. An architectural grammar was created which considered sound, smell, wind, soil, vegetation and the placing of car parking as well as the narrative topology of pedestrian flows. The architect O'Connor was resolutely opposed to the idea that an exhibition should be mounted within a 'black box' isolated from its physical environment. The locale was to form a key element of the display. The central spine is a corridor running the length of the building dropping downward as it faces a plate glass window framing the Great Blasket in the middle distance. This passage is also an architectural metaphor, providing an equivalent of the field stone wall pattern or *Slí*, following the contours of the land. It also provides, as it changes level, opportunity for individual spaces to be strung off to left and right, cutting the straight line at angles in a way self-consciously copying the shape of ancient ogham writing.[58] A question raised by O'Faolain is worth considering here.[59] How important is it that visitors should grasp the architectural metaphors? I suspect that O'Connor's response would be to emphasise how

[58]  O'Connor 'The Blasket Centre', 4.

[59]  N. O'Faolain 'A bulky thing like a day hospital' *The Irish Times* 16 August 1994.

complex meaning is, and that variety in individual interpretations and response represents a strength rather than a weakness.

The building has provoked mixed responses. 'Many detest the look and describe it as a hospital, a cattle shed or a prison. Others maintain that with its green cladding it fits in with the landscape much better that the white-painted bungalows.'[60] But the arguments were not just about architectural appropriateness. They went to the heart of the question as to how culture and history are to be presented, which in turn raises the issue about the relationship of the present to the past. An Taisce's objection to the size of the construction is based on the premise that the landscape itself should be inviolable to further change. Cooke expresses the basic lines of cleavage succinctly:

> The Blasket Centre was a romantic state project which aroused strong emotional responses. Already in Dunquin forty per cent of the houses were holiday homes. The division in response was between, on the one hand, those who saw the building as an eyesore (the incomers), and those born in the area who saw the structure as a bringer of employment. A lot of people liked the look of the building because it was seen as modern rather than an anachronism: it validated them as part of living culture. For those opposed to the building it was seen as inappropriate in size, larger than a church hall, more like a Planter house (thus raising negative historic reference).[61]

The great majority of the population was firmly in favour of the architectural boldness and unapologetic presence of the centre. The building offered a clear declaration of its significance not only in the landscape but also, by implication, in its cultural importance.[62]

The exhibition within the building was entrusted to Pat Cooke who already had some of the greatest responsibility for curating and the interpretation of recent Irish history, being responsible for two museums of great significance for Irish nationalism, the Pearce Museum and Kilmainham Gaol.[63] The interior was to look distinctive without being overpowering. If the long *Slí* was designed to offer a range of mind sets and experiences for the visitor, the exhibition was similarly open in its aspirations. Cooke had a similarly open agenda, maintaining that 'an exhibition always offers a series of impressions which, hopefully, will strike the visitor at most three times in a visit, rather than driving a spectator through a didactic lesson.'[64]

[60] Personal communication, Jim Blye.

[61] Personal communication, P. Cooke.

[62] Predictably, perhaps, in her tour round OPW sites, Nuala O'Faolain reserved her special animosity for the Blasket Centre: 'Then we turned the corner. There was the valley dotted with little houses, sweeping down to the tucked-away, invisible harbour. And there, dominating the wide slope, was a bulky thing like a day hospital, maybe, or a small factory. I actually blushed as I assured the Belgians that that couldn't be the interpretative centre. Nobody – *nobody* – would have put it *there*. 'A bulky thing like a day hospital'.

[63] He has also been responsible for the complete redisplay and catalogue for the latter. See P Cooke A History of Kilmainham Gaol.

[64] Personal communication, P. Cooke.

As a result of sifting through the materials gathered by the OPW commissioned research Cooke decided to dedicate the display to two themes, the literary flowering earlier in the century and the Irish language. Copies of printed books, original and corrected manuscripts, together with correspondence were intercut with photographs. Cooke felt that photography sets up a special correlation between the text and imagery.

As a consequence Cooke commissioned Anthony Haughey to spend a year in West Kerry capturing the landscape in all its variety and provide a life of the Gaeltacht (the recognised geographic area where Irish speech is provided special privileges). A considerable collection of Haughey's photographs are exhibited at the Centre, providing a contemporary counterpoint to the historic ones made by the visitor scholars. Photographic endorsement has crucial significance. It is perhaps of more than casual interest that the Blasket Island Foundation overturned the designers' intention to incorporate images of the foreign scholars in a series of portraits planned to line the *Slí*. Their place would be taken by celebrated local musicians.

The photographic record completes the cycle of representation. If the Blasket authors achieved the heroic task of moving from the verbal to the written, then the written becomes extended into a new dimension creating a sense of immediate recognition which then feeds the reading of the text afresh. We see the upright and solemn looking image of Tomás Ó Criomhthain through the camera eye of Thomson or von Sydow as we read the text. Haughey's contemporary photographs demonstrate not only how the past persists in the present, but how it too has an historical, an archival aspect even as it is created.

Perhaps this is the most important issue that the Blasket Centre raises for contemporary forms of ethnographic display. The particularity of the Blaskets, its topography (all visible within a single glance), its size (sufficiently small for all its members to have known each other's affairs intimately), and its linguistic homogeneity, provide for a single vision of mythic proportions, one not dissimilar to that proposed of an ideal island and people by Augé and cited at the head of this section of the chapter. But, the Blasket display is subject in its very performative qualities to the same quandary facing any other. To be a record of the nearly past does not exempt the display from the dilemmas facing other contemporary shows elsewhere. In this respect it shares the same problems as other current attempts in Europe to align an archaeology and history with a political present.[65]

[65] In areas like the former Yugoslavia these considerations are matters of the deepest significance. see Julian Thomas 'The politics of constructing identities through archaeology'. Paper presented at British Association for the Advancement of Science: Anthropology/Archaeology Section, September 1997.

The Blasket Centre as an interpretation centre has, in addition to any local audience or community involvement, a clear obligation to entertain tourists from other parts of Ireland as well as from elsewhere in Europe. This is basis on which European Union Structural Fund grants are issued. Inevitably this brings all such interpretation centres within the ambit of tourist development and Ireland's commercial tourism spearheaded by the state body, Bord Fáilte. Early in the development of the Blasket Centre O'Connor and others from OPW were invited to join representatives from heritage towns and sites and international experts to discuss the potential of heritage development. It immediately became clear that there were deep philosophical differences between those in OPW who were keen to promote interpretative centres as complex experiences working at a number of levels and the heritage strategy of Bord Fáilte that dealt in 'products'. O'Connor was informed that his approach was far too sophisticated in marketing terms and that interpretation centres should cater unambiguously for the mind of a twelve year old.

The situation is reminiscent of that encountered with tourism in Vanuatu. In both cases there has to be, of sheer necessity, some negotiation on both sides. The indigènes always need visitors to finance the cultural activity and this involves promotion by international marketers. As with Vanuatu, so in Ireland, this can lead to cultural clashes. Those keen to promote cultural uniqueness and community integrity look to the needs of the community first, whereas international marketers seek ways of inserting this new market within the expectations of a well-defined and avowedly culturally conservative international clientele. As with Tanna, so with Ireland. The 'Traditional Village' in Irish Tourist Board heritage development 'would boast great charm, intimacy and character and would attend to every little detail of creating a satisfying holiday experience.'[66] The parallel with Tanna is uncanny. Browne, head of development planning within Bord Fáilte, displays the mind of international marketing: 'The fishing villages of the coast line are a hive of activity. They could be made most attractive to tourists if they were tidied up a little and cleansed of their eyesores.'[67]

But the real selling point for the Blasket islands is the Irish language. Ó Criomhthain recognised this clearly when he wrote: 'I hear many an idle fellow saying that there's no use in our native tongue; but that hasn't been my experience. Only for it I should have been begging for my bread!'[68] As Bord Fáilte recognises, 'the survival of Irish as the everyday life of the Gaeltacht is of great interest to visitors as a vital and a vibrant link with our past culture.'[69] The change of tense is perhaps unfortunate. It reinforces the sentiment that those who speak the language

[66] Sean Browne 'Heritage in Ireland's tourism recovery', 23.

[67] Browne 'Heritage in Ireland's tourism recovery' ibid.

[68] O'Crohan *The Islandman*, 241.

[69] Browne, 24.

are relics from the past, a view that the Department of the Gaeltacht has spent decades trying to counter. The Bord Fáilte policy for promoting the Gaeltacht hardly sounds inviting for those who continue to live there:

> The Gaeltacht traditions of literature, folklore, crafts, music, song and dance should be made more accessible to visitors. The many decaying cottages in the Gaeltacht should be refurbished as comfortable self-catering houses and evening entertainment could be staged in a traditional 'Teach Cheoil'. . . . It is comforting to realise that the heritage of our past is becoming such a potent force in creating a future for our present population.[70]

What such a commitment to heritage preservation (and tidying up) means is that a degree of slippage between the reality of daily life and the representation that is offered performatively becomes progressively more problematic. The danger is that interpretation centres, which should be subject to radical review, say, every ten years, become cultural sheet anchors providing resistance to modernising under any but marketing terms. It is easy to see how residents in the Gaeltacht might come to see themselves in a way similar to Victor Totu in Gaudalcanal, objects of scrutiny, defined as 'other' and archaic the moment they open their mouths.

Perhaps this is too gloomy a view and neglects the robustness and innovativeness of Gaeltacht dwellers. There is another aspect of marketing that celebrates what may be called 'cultural bricolage'. Jason Oakley describes what he terms 'neotraditionalism' as an Irish cultural development that integrates in postmodern terms a range of widely disparate elements. He illustrates the argument with an example from television advertising, one promoting Smithwicks beer. He describes the advertisement:

> It is composed of four simultaneous sequences of rapidly edited sound-and-video bites, presented in a split-screen format. In under a minute of information overload, the images range from celtic sites, thatched cottages and set dancers: to warehouse party ravers, suburban housing estates and the current unemployment figures. . . . Likewise on the soundtrack there is a couplet formed by the opening and closing audio samples: 'It's great to be back in mythical, mystical Ireland' . . . 'Maybe it's all just blarney'.[71]

137

[70] Browne, 24.

[71] Jason Oakley 'Get out of it' *Circa*, 67, 1994, 44.

Even if this 'neotraditional' future becomes viable for the nearly past it is doubtful whether its vibrancy will survive more than another generation. The problem with the future perfect as an interpretative tense is that it inevitably destined to be over-turned by the most finite of tenses, the pluperfect. This is the true tense of heritage where the links with living experience are utterly sundered. Interpretation centres like that at Dunquin provide a penumbra, but one of much greater longevity, vitality and interest than many promoters of heritage would have us believe. Furthermore, as one living link is broken another interpretative occasion presents itself for the succeeding generations. One of the enduring examples of such a shift has been the experience of emigration that is rightly stressed frequently at the Blasket Centre. The experience is different for each generation, yet there remains something actually continuous in the patterns of flow and counterflow, and which as Campbell notes, 'has been crucial for the formation of collective and uniform notions of Irish identity'.[72]

It seems to me important to study representations of ourselves and others that are, in a sense, in transit between daily life and the historic record. What

**The Big Pit, Blaenafon**

[72] J. S. Campbell *The Great Irish Famine*, 54.

institutions like the Blasket Centre offer us is case material through the examination of which we can discern the elements of selection, by whom the activity is undertaken, and how it is represented on the way to incorporation or rejection in the historic record. Such places have a real claim to be considered true 'living museums'.

## Representation in a post-industrial setting: miners as living exhibits

The rise of interpretation centres and museums in Britain devoted to mining in the last decade provides a parallel to those that have appeared in Ireland concerned with archaeology and history. The numbers are similar. There are more than thirty mining museums currently to visit, from reproduction coal faces in larger museums of science and industry to ones situated in recently closed mines.[73] Undoubtedly, some of the same motivation is at work: an attempt to capture the nearly past and to re-employ it in a redefinition of popular culture which is alive to the variety of interpretations from which the historical narrative is to be constructed. For purposes of illustration I will concentrate upon one such venue, The Big Pit Mining Museum at Blaenafon, Gwent. This has a particular claim for consideration as it is one of only two mines in Britain that invite the visitor to descend into the workings to experience the conditions in which mining took place in the company of an ex-miner as interpreter.[74] For this reason The Big Pit is offered as a 'living museum' and the miners as representing a form of 'living fossils'.

The Big Pit shares many intellectual features with the Blasket Centre. Both are concerned to represent aspects of a daily life that has been obliterated by major changes cutting off the possibility of return, and both are still bitter-sweet but vivid living memories. Both aspire to incorporate contributions from the communities represented and both come from the shock of recognising the finality of the change. For the Blaskets it was the demise of a pre-industrial community, for The Big Pit it was the disappearance of the industrial era demonstrated by the rapid decimation of the coal mining industry over a ten year period. Both seek to do more than provide salvage ethnography. They seek to take the visitor into the nearly past. Even the apparent differences, such as the degree of official sanction (there is no equivalent of the OPW to support mining museums) is likely to change as time progresses. By its very persistence The Big Pit becomes an ever more established authority in constituting the history of mining and miners. As long as the mine is staffed by ex-miners it can invoke the authority of the indigènes. In this way it is aligned with cultural centres in Melanesia as much as with the Blasket Centre in reintegrating the

[73] see R Shorland-Ball *Museums and Coalmining*, Museums and Galleries Commission, 1996.

[74] the other is the National Coal Mining Museum for England at Caphouse Colliery, Overton, near Wakefield.

**The pit head, the Big Pit**

past with the present and the future. Like these other two, The Big Pit has a revisionist agenda that it advances through enactment.[75]

Like the South Pacific, like Ireland, coal mining was seized upon by the architects of the Chicago World's Colombian Exposition as an exciting entertainment for the visitor. On the Midway Plaisance there was a subterranean theatre 'where one could experience the simulated sensation of descending over one thousand foot into the earth'.[76] This was a precursor of many similar contemporary developments that aim to provide 'authentic' representations without the inconvenience of visiting a mine. The solution adopted on the Midway Plaisance relied heavily on simulation, in a form that anticipated animatronics.

This formula has been eschewed at Blaenafon where a responsible spectacularization of culture has been attempted by addressing representation in a complex way, considering narrative topology, visualisation and simulation, to provide a form of indigenous curation. The Big Pit sets out squarely to offer strict realism:

[75] The authority that The Big Pit implicitly undermines is the official history of coal mining since nationalisation in the texts sanctioned by the National Coal Board.

[76] M. P. Handy (ed.) Official Guide to the Exhibitions on the Midway Plaisance, Group 176, cited by David F. Burg *Chicago's White City*, 230.

> Nothing is contrived or invented here – Big Pit is the real thing. It looks much as it did on that February day in 1980 when the last miners clocked off. There is the same clutter of buildings around the pit shaft, and the wheels of the winding gear still revolve every day. The difference today is that most of those who now make the descent to the pit bottom are not miners, but people who have never ventured underground before. They come in such numbers that the pit is more populous than ever. With former miners acting as guides, visitors learn something of what it was like to earn a living in one of the toughest working environments of all.[77]

There are a number of issues combined in this manifesto. Firstly, the location confirms the authority of the display. The pit is merely in suspended animation, 'as if it were frozen in time on a Sunday, with a skeleton force of maintenance men making sure everything is in order for another working week'.[78] Secondly, artefactual evidence supports the claim to veracity. They are the same props and tubs, the ventilation and communication systems that were used when the mine was working and, above all, the pit is still governed by the Coal Mines Act. In order to remain open as an underground display the mine is required to maintain the full safety system as a working mine. Managers, fitters, electricians, deputies and rescue teams have to be constantly in attendance and the winding gear and galleries are subject to regular visit by the Mines Inspectorate. This arrangement strengthens the claim for authenticity in the display, as will be detailed beneath. However, this argument that the mine is in 'suspended animation' and ready to restart production becomes more difficult to sustain as time passes. As the Manager states:

> In some areas, such as the winding engine house . . . it remains what it has always been, a fully functioning winder. In other areas, however, machinery and equipment that is no longer used and maintained on a daily basis soon comes to look abandoned and the personal ephemera, tools, etc. that formerly made the pit seem alive have to be reintroduced and the roadways themselves have to be repaired. Visitors undeniably experience a real coal mine, they are after all 300 feet underground and walking around old mine workings! but the 'reality' of what they see has to be constantly refreshed.[79]

77 *The Big Pit Story*, 2.

78 *The Big Pit Story*, 28.

79 Peter Walker, personal communication.

The chief attraction of The Big Pit is this invitation it offers the visitor to become, albeit for one hour only, a miner going on shift to the coal face. The narrative topology[80] is directed to introduce a range of themes that are encountered in sequence throughout the underground tour. All of these rely on the skill of the narrator to link the tableaux and to provide a sense of coherence to what otherwise would be a meaningless stumble through industrial detritus. A sense of engagement and adventure is provided at the pit head where visitors are stripped of cameras, watches and electronic car keys in accordance with the Mines Act and supplied with hard hats, heavy batteries and miners' lamps. The descent down the shaft provides a symbolic entry into a new world.

The guides in mining overalls produce a theatrical experience. The underlying motif is that of the sublime or the terrible, and the setting is laid out as a rational inferno. The heat, the dust, the noise and the conditions at the coal face are evoked by the guide and reinforced with stories from their own experience. A sense of disorientation occurs when the guide asks visitors to turn off their lights for a moment to experience the intensity of the dark. The life of the pit pony is told in the underground stalls, and is used to provide a metaphor for the life of the miner. As a guide pointed out on a recent tour: 'Horses worked for twenty years. We worked until we were sixty five until Maggie Thatcher had other plans'.[81] What these guides attempt is what Debord has called 'the communication of the incommunicable'.[82] In this case the visualisation that the guides suggest contrasts industrial rationality, exemplified by mining machinery in the advances in coal technology in the pursuit of ever greater productivity, with the unpredictability, constant danger and arduousness of the work.

It is initially surprising to discover that neither at The Big Pit nor at The National Coal Mining Museum for England at Caphouse are the guides formally trained in terms of script or topics to be covered. The reasons relate to the desire to offer authenticity. The guides do not share a single occupational background. Although the average mining experience of the guides is thirty years, they have had different jobs. As the manager explains:

> These men are miners, not historians, they don't know everything about mining. Each man's experiences are different, there are many different jobs underground and not every miner will have worked on a coal face, so although they may know the basics, they may not know the detail.

[80] 'Narrative topology is, briefly, the arrangement of spaces and the connections between them such that they set up, suggest or assert relationships between whatever is displayed in those spaces'. Brett *The Construction of Heritage*, p 88.

[81] Eric. September 1996.

[82] 'Spectacular consumption preserves the old culture in congealed form, going so far as to recuperate and redefine even its negative manifestations; in this way, the spectacle's cultural sector gives overt expression to what the spectacle is implicitly in its totality – the communication of the incommunicable' *Society of the Spectacle*, 136.

> If there is a technical question they can't answer, they'll say so, but there will usually be someone amongst the other men who will know. The tour is like being able to stand on Hadrian's Wall and actually talk to a Roman soldier. As if to prove these men are real miners, they each have different approaches to the tours and will express a variety of political views if questioned.[83]

Thus the heterogeneity of the different accounts lends support to underlying structural features of the presentation. Precisely because there is no script visitors are left to interpret and evaluate the accounts. As the manager states: 'We try not to preach to people. We don't try to make out that all mine owners were evil exploiters of the poor and that workers were angels. We try to state the facts and let people make up their own minds.[84] The accounts when taken together do, however, offer an oppositional history. Details are slipped in frequently to undermine the view that the National Coal Board had solved the miners' problems. Visitors are shocked by sober facts: life-preservers (gas masks) only made an appearance at the mine in 1971, whereas they had been standard issue in Germany over a decade earlier; dust suppression was only introduced at the coal face in 1981 and dust masks were not introduced into Welsh mines until 1988.

If the guides come with varied experience, the audience may be similarly differentiated. There is an easy assumption that miners and ex-miners from the locality form a substantial segment. As one writer has suggested:

> Ex-miners and their families will undoubtedly form a huge potential visitor constituency for museums with coal-mining displays. Their expectations with regard to coal-mining will be diverse. Those with specialist interests, such as lamp collectors, will look for full coverage of particular technical aspects; those who have worked in the industry will expect authenticity in its portrayal; and many will feel that museums should provide a monument to the industry, the engineering achievements and the workforce.[85]

However, this expectation is not born out in visitor numbers to The Big Pit. Local visitors are in a distinct minority. Only 25 per cent in 1994 came from Wales, compared with 27 per cent from France and 39 per cent from England. These puzzling figures may be accounted for by seeing the visitors divided into local and

[83] Peter Walker, personal communication, March 1997.

[84] ibid.

[85] Alison Gale *Fuel for Thought: The Status and Future of Coal-Mining Collections in North East Museums*, 70.

international, with the intermediate regional group largely absent. It may be that, unlike the local population in Dunquin, inhabitants around Blaenafon do not see the mine as anything special nor do they see it as providing an historical bridge.[86]

Two reasons suggest themselves to account for this failure to engage the surrounding area. Firstly, the decline in mining has been so rapid that its full impact has yet to be appreciated. When The Big Pit opened in 1983 there were 40 working deep mines in the immediate locality. There are now none left. Despite this fact there appears to be an ambiguity towards the museum. Local people both know about mining through their own experience or that of close relatives and they also remember many aspects of mining that they do not care to have revived, particularly the heavy toll of injury and death. The very realism of the museum, the pit, the baths, and the guides as living reminders of the past, all serve to underline the problematic aspects that cling to the nearly past which is as yet poorly recognised in former mining communities. Locals may resist the very performative aspects of representation that attracts the visitors from afar. It is still too near to home not only topically but symbolically. Representations are resisted by a sophisticated population unwilling to become engaged in re-enactment.

This does not mean, however, that there is no local interest in The Big Pit. Indeed, as Gale has suggested, there is a technically knowledgeable set of visitors who are insistent in their demand for accuracy in every detail. They share The Big Pit's commitment to realism and they also challenge Fabian's assertion that representations can never be true, only useful, suggestive or convincing. Both this category of visitors and the guides raise a new series of questions about the ethics of representation. They have, to develop their argument, another mining display near by, the Rhondda Heritage Park, constructed on the site of the Lewis Merthyr Colliery at Trehafod. This mining museum's promotional claims are subject to persistent criticism. The constructors of this museum are charged with dissimulation in the display and untruths in the guides' presentation. The visitor to Lewis Merthyr is invited to undertake a 'Shift in Time':

> Visitors take the journey of a lifetime to discover the hardship and joys of life in the Lewis Merthyr Colliery of the 1950's. In the Lamp Room your guide will show you what preparations are needed before going underground. Your party is supplied with safety helmets and, from the Trefor Pithead, you ride down in the cage to Pit Bottom. Transported

[86] 'Another factor which may be particular to south Wales is that people are more familiar with travelling down the valleys than up them. People living in the heads of the valleys region are more than happy to travel down to the coast at Cardiff or Newport to shop or to visit an attraction, but most people living in Cardiff think that North Wales starts at Caerphilly and are loath to risk their children in an expedition to remote places such as Merthyr or Blaenafon.' Peter Walker, personal communication.

back in time, you can explore the underground roadways and workings of the colliery and experience for yourself the sights, sounds and smells of Lewis Merthyr Colliery at work. Finally you take a mysterious and unforgettable thrill ride back to the colliery surface.[87]

The reality does not match this description. The lift cage travels in a series of jolts a mere 35 feet from the first floor to the ground floor of the building. The management of the museum appear to be nervous about the veracity of their claim. Elsewhere the promotional literature is slightly more cautious: 'with your helmet on you are ready to follow me to the Trefor Pithead and ride the cage to the "Pit Bottom" – just like a working miner'.

What upsets the critics of Lewis Merthyr is not so much the deception of the display but the way that this dissimulation implicates the guides. These, too, are ex-miners, and their scripts are carefully tailored to avoid revealing the truth of the display. The deception does not fool every visitor but all feel patronised and deceived. There is, so the critics would argue, nothing wrong in making reconstructions, and the more realistic the better. Indeed, good reconstructions can offer more than poor restorations.[88] There are considerable advantages to be gained, for example, by declaring the show to be a simulation. For many individuals, the prospect of going underground fills them with dread. But if they were told that the tour would not involve a real descent, they would be happy to join it. This potential sector of the market is far from negligible.

There are also ethical issues which can be treated as in some ways analogous to those of cultural copyright. Lewis Merthyr can be seen in this light as a retrogressive exhibition where the miners' accounts are adjuncts to a closely managed and professionally designed display. What is being lost is the self-determination of the miners to create their own script and performance. Interpretation is compromised by the ambiguous nature of the material to be worked with. In these circumstances the miners cease to be indigenous curators, they are actors in the normal theatrical sense. This distinction is a live one for visitors as well as for the guides at both locations. Visitors to The Big Pit who have already been to Lewis Merthyr are readily recognised by the suspicion they exhibit when confronted with the pit head. Their first question is whether this is a genuine pit and whether this is a real shaft that they are about to descend. This question itself is a warning that the visitor is

145

[87] 'A shift in Time – The Underground Tour' in *Rhondda Heritage Park: Lewis Merthyr Colliery* leaflet.

[88] the drift mine at Beamish, the restored Mahogany Drift, is criticised frequently for its poor and unconvincing display. It has also recently dispensed with miners as interpreters. See R. Shorland-Ball *Museums and Coalmining*, 39.

keenly aware of a number of issues surrounding representation and the first stirrings of a critique of what might be considered acceptable and what is trickery.

As with the Blasket Centre, so with the Welsh mining museums, local and other visitors have developed, even if they have not articulated it, a decided view on the nature of representation. Most of the questions asked of the guides in both mining museums concern not only technical issues but the very nature of the representation, how it has been achieved and what it is intended to state. Some of the most interesting conversations between visitor and guide are methodological, dealing, for example with how passageways have been relined and pit props re-installed in order to show conditions of previous eras. The visitors' comments are also frankly evaluative and often suggest how simulations could be improved.

## Coda

Both of the examples offered in this chapter provide a rebuttal of Fabian's thesis that representations are to be judged solely on the basis of their convincingness. It is precisely the distance of the double from the original that generates the tension which engages the viewer. The World's Colombia Exposition's Ballymaclinton and its subterranean theatre provide the foundation for a critique of unresponsible representation. The Blasket Centre provides in its interwoven themes the space for the visitor to form a more complex response to issues of emigration and the Irish language, and to escape the claustrophobia of ethnic stereotype to be found in the successors to the imperial expositions. Similarly, the representation of mining opens again a range of questions that might have been declared redundant with the closure of the last pit (though it should be remembered that although techniques have been transformed out of all recognition in the large private mines, there remain a considerable number of very small scale operations that are often almost pre-industrial in their technology, many in the Bleanafon valley).

Both the Blasket Centre and The Big Pit represent attempts to break free from straight narrative accounts. Neither could be realistically described as postmodern – there are too many historically linear strands to each display – but both create a plurality of accounts that provide the visitor with space to draw breath and to evaluate. For example the Blasket display provides complexity to the issue of emigration and suggests an antiphonal vision:

> As we mainland dwellers look out towards the island what strikes us most is its smallness set against the immensity of the ocean. But the islanders spent most of their lives with their backs to that ocean, facing the mainland. It is a perspective that called up feelings of both closeness and separation . . . Over the horizon and far away lay America, the idea of it tugging like the tide and the young Islanders' imagination with dreams of prosperity.[89]

Similarly, the tension between the official history of the National Coal Board ending almost simultaneously with the closure of The Big Pit, and the private and unofficial stories told by ex-miners offers a vivid contrast. In both examples visitors are invited to make an imaginative leap and place themselves within the tale recounted. In this way visitors are provided with a reverse transcription of the phenomenological journey that Natanson suggests we enter when we move from daily life to the historic record, or as Natanson put it, from little history to big history.[90] We are invited to inspect the historic record from within, and from multiple perspectives.

Both The Big Pit and the Blasket Centre sit firmly within the tradition of European folklore engineered by Rivière. They privilege the environment as the prime shaper of human culture. They involve local inhabitants with the equivalents of 'teams of scientists' ( in both cases museologists, designers and architects) in order to orchestrate remembrance. Above all, they attempt, following Rivière's model, to replace salvage with discovery and the interpretation of culture. Ecomuseums and ecotourism become elided in both these venues.

Yet the very engagement of these 'ecomuseums' with contemporary culture provides an ironic consequence; by their very closeness to the events that they interpret, they inevitably become themselves historic artefacts. But there is in both the venues discussed a ready sense that they inhabit what I have called the future perfect, in transition from anthropological present to the historic past. Tomas Ó Criomhthain's lament 'the like of us will never be again'[91] captures perfectly this sense of transition from the personal and lived to the historic voice. Ó Criomhthain becomes at the end of his narrative an outsider looking in on his own tale. So, too, inevitably, do the miners at Blaenafon. What interpretation centres suggest is that such phenomena have at most a limited life before they become museums where the ambiguity that is provided by living exhibits evaporates into the historic account.

147

[89] Blasket Centre. Gallery 2 'Perspectives'.

[90] Maurice Natanson *Literature, Philosophy and the Social Sciences*, 172–7.

[91] T. O'Crohan *The Islandman*, 244.

5

# The future of ethnographic display

## The tradition of melancholia

The optimism that ethnographic performance can be employed to positive effect is not widely shared, despite the examples that have been offered in the last two chapters. One of the best known figures in the field is profoundly pessimistic as to whether such enactments can ever be genuine or non-exploitative. Dean MacCannell's treatment of ethnographic performance[1] represents a distillation of revisionist orthodoxies, and makes a romantic and powerful case against the recolonizing of 'formerly primitive peoples' (a term he uses that is itself problematic) by global and white monoculture. MacCannell offers the reader the example of MCI Incorporated which obtained exclusive rights from the US Government to develop and market tourist experience in Yosemite National Park. For him this represents the advent of the sale of nature and the picturesque, that logically leads in turn to the marketing of 'savages', the inhabitants of such paradisal sites. For MacCannell this operation is already in full swing in every ethnographic performance; for the bringing together of 'primitive' costumes and the other attendant paraphernalia with rational planning and marketing does not produce a true hybrid. MacCannell argues that whilst such performances may appear to be less arduous than agricultural or industrial labour, they are, nevertheless, empty. The 'primitive' does not appear. All we are given is the image as a dead form. Furthermore, MacCannell argues, such a supposed combination of the 'primitive' with the modern is really only an abuse of the dead for financial motives. He concludes that: 'the image of the savage that emerges from these ex-primitive performances completes the postmodern fantasy of 'authentic alterity which is ideologically necessary in the promotion and development of global monoculture. The 'primitivistic' performance is our funerary marking of the passage of savagery.'[2]

MacCannell's vision is one that finds full confirmation in the imperial shows and World's Fairs as Benedict and others have demonstrated from the inspection of these shows' histories. It could likewise be argued that the nationalist successors have, in the very ideology that informs them, similar tendencies. But the establishment of programmes of cultural renewal in the South Pacific and elsewhere is predicated on the premise that a genuine bargain can be struck between tradition and not only modern but postmodern social organisation. MacCannell is not ignorant of such claims. Indeed, he suggests most appositely that the true 'primitive' is more likely to be a resistance fighter with the best contemporary military hardware.[3] Events in Afghanistan over the past decade give everyone considerable cause to ponder the relationship between tradition, modernity and power. But

[1] D. MacCannell *Empty Meeting Grounds*, Routledge, 1992, 18–20.

[2] D. MacCannell *Empty Meeting Grounds*, 19.

[3] 'There may still be a small number of real savages left. They would be found amongst those who took flashlights, carbines, chainsaws, kerosene, matches, and a few other portable amenities and retreated further into the forest or set up a defensible position on their reservations. They would not be found among those who dress in 'authentic' costumes and demonstrate the use of bows and arrows for tourists.' *Empty Meeting Grounds*, 69.

MacCannell's basic premise is that traditional forms are inevitably superseded or subverted by modern forms of monopolistic culture.

To sustain this claim MacCannell employs two key terms, 'savages' and 'primitives'. Whilst he always keeps the terms scrupulously within quotation marks, the irony becomes blunted. Even though he proclaims that there is no real difference between, on the one side, the modern, the tourist, and on the other, those who play the part of the primitives (both are after all involved in the same theatrical conspiracy), MacCannell's use of terms precludes his primitives becoming active agents in their own destiny. If we replace the word 'primitive' with one that does not suggest the same historical closure then the iron law that relegates traditional to the primitive is broken. It is for this reason that I have employed the term indigène. indigènes can be redundant coal miners or rural dwellers in a modern state. The difference between MacCannell's vision and the one proposed in this work is that for MacCannell, '"reconstructed" ethnicity' is a creation that emerges in response to the demands of 'White culture and tourism'. This work does not make such an assumption, preferring instead to enquire whether and under what conditions individuals and groups may sustain their sense of identity through performance in a postmodern world. MacCannell's thesis leaves him in danger of collapse into the thinking of that entity for which he has so much loathing, Disneyland in Orange County[4] where the manipulation of the tourist's sense of identity is achieved through ruthless stereotyping and the double refraction of cultural forms through cinematic cartoon imagery.

MacCannell's melancholia can be seen as a form of what Robertson calls 'wilful nostalgia'[5] which is the product of the globalization of culture. Put simply, the world economy no longer provides space for anything other than a singular system. Pluralism in culture is consigned to a prior period, perhaps towards the end of the nineteenth century. This thesis is incompatible with the argument offered here. The first major difference is to be found in the weight that MacCannell gives to semiological analysis throughout his work which is not replicated here. It does not seem, within the context of ethnographic representation and performance, easy to strike a clear correspondence between unambiguous signifiers and their signified. There seems to be considerable room for ambiguity, for fluidity in categories and, above all, for changes in significance over time. What is proposed here is something more like a genealogy, a history of strategies for ethnographic representation and display.

[4] See his 'Orange County, Yugoslavia' in *Empty Meeting Grounds*, 74–86.

[5] A term developed by Roland Robertson in his 'After nostalgia'.

In this context classical role analysis does not present a satisfactory framework. Instead, another subset of role theory has been preferred, the dramaturgic. Fabian's proposition is central to this: 'performances need actors and audiences, writers and readers. Therefore representations ought to draw their convincingness primarily from communication, rhetoric and persuasion, and only secondarily from systematic fits or logical proofs'.[6] If there is a discernible trend in the pattern of ethnographic representation it is not necessarily to be found in historic progression. While some forms of ethnographic representation are no longer considered licit in, say, a western metropolitan environment, this scrupulousness does not necessarily extend to representation of Africa, the South or North East Pacific by Chinese actors. It could be argued, in contrary fashion, that indigenous curators in the South Pacific dwell in an entirely new set of circumstances to which ethnographic performance contributes. It might also be argued, parenthetically, that some of the most retrogressive representations worldwide are to be found in the domain of cyberspace and computer games where simulated warfare pits caucasians against non-caucasians, sometimes under the cover of galactic enemies. The central point of the argument, however, is that there is no simple law of development. Some performances are remarkably aware of the traditions from which they draw (the Are Are Pipers may be a particular case in point here), others may differentiate their style and mode of representation. At Window of the World, for example, Japan is depicted with considerable tact and respect in all details, the 'Maori' dancers execute fairly authentic footsteps, whilst the script for 'Africans' seems purely fanciful. If there is an overall tendency, it has to be one of increased knowledge not necessarily of the content of other cultures but of the variety of display strategies that are available.

This relativistic and unprogrammatic approach is unlikely, on its own, to persuade those committed to a melancholic and nostalgic vision of ethnographic performance. Such critics would stress the ubiquity and hegemony of the modern western globalized culture and the sheer impossibility of escaping its crushing embrace. In the next section I propose one candidate as an example of just such an attempt to avoid this fate. The strategies adopted are complex but interconnected but all revolve around attempts to situate cultural traditions in the most contemporary forms of ethnographic display.

[6] J. Fabian 'Presence and representation', 757.

## Supping with the devil

The Kwakiutl[7] appear at first sight to perfectly fit the melancholic view of the fate of indigenous people in the modern world. Living around the northern end of Vancouver Island, off the west coast of British Columbia, they have experienced the devastation firstly of imported diseases like smallpox, the appropriation of territory, then the loss of their sacred potlatch regalia to ethnography museums, and more recently the visual and ecological disaster of commercial logging. Current land settlement agreements and reparations by the British Columbia provincial government hardly seem a proper restitution or compensation for the assault on the community by political, economic or educational agents. The latter may have ultimately been the most destructive in the imposition of native boarding schools. It could be argued that the Kwakiutl are famous for the extent of the documentation of their 'disappearance'. A large range of books and postcards published today show historic photographs that attest to the loss of a way of life, traditional architecture and costume. And yet, I argue, such a picture is fundamentally misleading. The history of the Kwakiutl, like that of many of their neighbours in the North East Pacific, can be depicted quite differently, as an example of persistence rather than disappearance, of innovation in the face of change, as winners in the war with museums over their property and, above all, in their retaining ownership of the means of representation into the electronic age both in the context of museums and in popular entertainment.

It would be disingenuous and wrong to pretend that the people of the North East Pacific remained in full control of events once Europeans arrived. But, equally, what is significant in the record is the degree of cultural authority that such peoples retained. Their perspicacity as traders demanding equality of exchange was recognised by European adventurers at once.[8] This engagement and active response to the world outside the Pacific littoral has remained. The Kwakiutl even provide a new perspective on the world of imperial expositions and World's Fairs. Burton Benedict goes as far as to suggest that we see the World's Fairs as variants on native structures: 'the towers of the various expositions can be compared to the totem poles built by the potlatching North West Coast Indians. These poles depicted various totem animals and spirits associated with particular clans. In a similar way large allegorical statues at World's Fairs depicted the spirit of a nation or an ideal.'[9] Whilst this imagery is perhaps fanciful, it nevertheless attests to the significance that the Kwakiutl and their neighbours were accorded in the displays.

[7]  As elsewhere in this work names and their forms are politically significant. I have used the most commonly employed form recognisable to the non-specialist reader. There are two contemporary versions in common use among the people themselves, Kwagiulth as used on Quadra Island and Kwakwaka'waka used in the possessive form at Alert Bay.

[8]  'From the start, Nootka Indians had proven themselves shrewd and assertive traders, refusing to accept the strings of beads that had proven popular among Indians of the California coast and elsewhere. Instead they sought metal goods that would be useful or decorative, and they accepted the European traders into their world of elaborate ritual and song.' Peter H. Wood 'North America in the era of Captain Cook', 500.

[9]  B. Benedict *The Anthropology of the World's Fairs*, 16.

It comes as something of a surprise to learn how intertwined academic anthropology and commercial displays could become. Precisely because the Kwakiutl had become so renowned they were accorded a place in the first anthropology building to be constructed at the World's Columbia Exposition of 1893. Franz Boas worked as second in command to Frederick Ward Putnam, curator of the Peabody Museum at Harvard University, for two years, collecting archaeological and anthropological material from all over North and Central America.[10] Boas arranged for his assistant, George Hunt, who was brought up in a Kwakiutl community, to collect a specimen house, a model of Fort Rupert Village and canoes, and items for religious ceremonies such as masks and rattles. Hunt and seventeen Kawkiutl women, men and children then spent the summer in the anthropological exhibition demonstrating their crafts and ceremonies. Interestingly, Boas used this opportunity to study Kwakiutl language and devise a system of orthography as well as to record songs on gramophone cylinders. At the end of the exposition Hunt's gathered material became part of the foundation collection of the Field Museum in Chicago.[11]

What is significant about the Kwakiutl exhibition at Chicago is that it was made by Hunt who has a firm claim to be considered an indigenous anthropologist. Not only did he assist Boas in making the exhibition, he orchestrated performances. He went on to document Kawkiutl life both collecting and making inventories of items of daily and religious use but he also took a large number of photographs. As a shaman, Hunt was particularly well placed to capture important occasions.[12] Hunt's activities placed him in an interestingly ambiguous position. He was highly conscious of the dichotomy between indigenous systems of value and those of his employers, the curators of the great ethnographic collections in North American museums. A number of other Kwakiutl became agents and collectors as museums across America sought to extend their collections. As a figure of importance in Kwakiutl life Hunt was in a position to explain the modalities of exchange to his kin and neighbours as well as to curators. The worth and significance of items of Kwakiutl culture to the colonizers was readily appreciated as Hunt noted.[13]

This self-confidence extended to performance as well. Macnair reports that at the St Louis World Fair of 1904 the Kwakiutl and Nootka performers staged a hamatsa (cannibal dance) for the fairgoers. At one performance the principal actor, Bob Harris, appeared to kill a member of another troupe and then eat the victim. The verisimilitude was, reportedly, so great that the remaining members of the

[10] C. M. Hinsley 'The world as marketplace', 348.

[11] I. Jacknis 'George Hunt: collector of Indian specimens', 181–3; P. Macnair 'The Northwest Coast Collections', 4.

[12] I. Jacknis 'George Hunt, Kwakiutl photographer', 146.

[13] 'George Hunt wrote to Boas in 1904 about his efforts to buy things from the Friendly Cove Nootka: "I never seen any Body like these people for asking so a High Price for there things as this people, for they say they can go to seatle and tacoma and get High Price for What Ever they Bring there"' quoted by V. Dominguez 'The marketing of heritage', 551.

troupe attempted to spear the perpetrator of the outrage. The Kwakiutl performer then 'brought to life' the victim in an apparent piece of magic. Only later were the mechanics of this theatrical enactment explained. This performance was to have later echoes.

Performance was not something destined to degenerate into mere tourism. There was another side to Kwakiutl life and self-respect that put the communities in direct conflict with the national and provincial government, the potlatch. The *hamatsa* performed at St Louis was already banned in Canada alongside the potlatch. Potlatches are occasions when important and noble families invite guests to witness the status of the host. The event combines all the elements of a true cultural performance. Traditional songs are sung by both hosts and guests, *hamatsas* and other dances are performed with appropriate masks according to the story, orations are made attesting to the status of the host and relationship between the hosts and their guests, large quantities of food are ceremonially eaten, and, one of the most constitutive characteristics of the potlatch, presents are distributed according to rank and importance to every guest.

In 1885 the Canadian government proscribed the potlatch.[14] This proscription was in response to requests of British Columbia Indian agents and missionaries and enacted as a means of doing away with the conspicuous waste of both time (large portions of the winter months) and resources. Whilst the practice among the Haida and Tlingit peoples had virtually ceased by 1900, potlatching increased markedly among the Kwakiutl with the new financial opportunities provided by work in logging, fishing and canneries. Although the enforcement of the law against potlatching was only fitfully enforced, by 1913 the climate hardened and an active prosecution policy was enforced. The 'largest potlatch ever recorded on the central coast', one given by Dan Cranmer, brought prosecution in 1922. The defendants were offered a choice. They could avoid a custodial sentence if they voluntarily surrendered all their potlatch property. This they did and so '17 containers of masks, rattles, whistles and other dance paraphernalia were crated and shipped to the Victoria Memorial Museum in Ottawa'.[15]

This event brought the two world systems into collision. The Kwakiutl continued to potlatch but in secret, but their relationship to their expropriated property changed. Dominguez is correct in her statement that at the time of the museums' collection mania in the late nineteenth century: 'the interest in collecting those items for storage and display came not from the Indians themselves, but from

[14] My discussion of the potlatch draws heavily on Douglas Cole's 'The history of the Kwakiutl potlatch' in Ira Jacknis (ed.) *Chiefly Feasts*.

[15] Gloria Cranmer Webster 'The "R" Word', 43.

the Americans and Europeans. The objects collected had varied significance for the Indians, but ethnological significance for the collectors. The products were ethnological displays, not acts of Indian self-representation'.[16] But for the Kwakiutl the events of 1922 ensured that the potlatch collection became symbolically central to Kwakiutl cultural identity. The museum collection (or collections as they became when divided between Ottawa and Toronto) became a focus of 'Indian self-representation' and a means of direct access to 'the nearly past'. Potlatch celebrations provided occasions to grieve the loss of the masks and to refresh memories over the historic injustice done to forbears and the continued injury.

The Indian Act of 1951 deleted any reference to potlatching. Moves then began to reclaim the collections. After much negotiating the holdings at the Canadian Museum of Civilization and the Royal Ontario Museum were returned in 1979 and 1987 respectively to the Kwakiutl people on condition that museums be built to house the returned items. The Kwagiulth Museum was constructed at Cape Mudge and opened in 1979 and the U'mista Cultural Centre at Alert Bay was completed in 1980. Much has been made of the museological contrast between the two

**Kwagiulth Museum, Cape Mudge**

**U'mista Cultural Centre**

constructions, mostly concentrating on the way in which the displays have been mounted.[17] However, as Clifford notes, it is the similarities that are the most significant. Both collections are shown as part of the patrimony of the Kwakiutl people, especially those living in the village where they are exhibited. The objects are presented as emblems of cultural struggle and local, community history. At the Kwagiulth Museum, the masks and other treasures are displayed in glass cases and the family ownership is indicated for each item. At the U'mista Cultural Centre the visitor is offered a range of historic photographs of sites of Kwakiutl villages married to texts giving a range of creation stories, many of them adapted from Boas and Hunt *Kwakiutl Texts 1903–06*[18] (providing more than a casual parallel with the Blasket Centre in the intercut of literary narrative and historic imagery). These paired panels lead the visitor into a large chamber with massive roof beams formed from single tree trunks. This houses the returned potlatch collection which is displayed around the walls on a raised deep bench, not in cases but on metal plinths.

    The U'mista Cultural Centre has an inherent dynamic that has been frequently remarked. There are a number of sources. Firstly, and of great significance, this is a collection that demonstrates the persistence of culture in both material and symbolic form in greatly altered circumstances. The collection has until

[16] V. Dominguez 'The marketing of heritage' p 550.

[17] in particular James Clifford 'On collecting art and culture', 248 and his 'Four northwest coast museums', Marie Mauzé 'Exhibiting one's culture: two case studies'; Heather Norris Nicholson 'Cultural centres or trading posts?'; Gloria Cranmer Webster 'The "R" word'.

[18] Clifford 'Four northwest coast museums', 236.

recently been managed by Gloria Cranmer Webster, the great-granddaughter of George Hunt and daughter of Dan Cranmer, the holder of the fateful 1921 potlatch. She is a trained anthropologist and museum curator of national and international significance.[19] She thus brings together the traditions of her family and people along with an understanding of both the agenda and the shortcomings of a museo-logical approach to representing culture. The display in the big-house at first looks ethnographic; the items are displayed in relation to their place in the choreography and narrative of the potlatch. But here the resemblance stops, for the large panels that are placed in front of the masks do not relate to the objects adjacent. Instead, they reproduce comments from contemporaries who lived at the time of the potlatch, excerpts from written reports of the Indian Agent, W. M. Halliday who expropriated and exiled the collection, juxtaposed with recent memories of older members of the community at Alert Bay. The effect, as Clifford notes, is to open a space between the maker, the exhibitor and the viewer and to implicate the audience in such a dramatic story.

Cranmer Webster explains the exhibit in terms of the conditions obtaining at the time of its construction:

> The Potlatch Collection exhibit at the U'mista Cultural Centre turned out the way it did, because the only exhibit designer I wanted to work with became quite ill and was unable to help us. We also knew that the names attached to individual objects in the collection were mostly inaccurate and our decision was not to use them. As is said in our film, 'Box of Treasures', we also decided not to place the objects in cases, because they had been locked up in a strange place for a long time and we didn't want them locked up anymore. I had trouble working out a story line and the Board of Directors, mostly fishermen, said, 'We don't know anything about storylines – you worked in a museum, you figure it out.' The idea to use text from the Potlatch Files came about when I realised that I couldn't tell the story any better than the people who had actually experienced the banning of the potlatch and those who worked hard to enforce the law'.[20]

The issue of audience is equally important. The Cultural Centre has, as the title implies, a primary orientation towards the local community from which it springs and which it serves. The U'mista Cultural Centre 'is not a memorial to the past but a

[19] She was, for example, a member of the Task Force on Museums and First Peoples set up in 1990 bringing together representatives from the Assembly of First Nations and the Canadian Museums Association. She also was a member of the curatorial team for the major 1991 exhibition *Chiefly Feasts* mounted by the American Museum of Natural History.

[20] Gloria Cranmer Webster, personal communication.

**Bill Cranmer outside entrance to U'mista Cultural Centre**

centre of strength for now',[21] and relates to contemporary issues facing the community. This approach is one endorsed in North American Native Studies. W. Richard West Jr expresses the concept well:

> What I want to see are life experiences, all those aspects that constitute Indian culture. That may involve the arts of dance, drama and literature as well as painting and sculpture. Second, this 'living museum' must reflect the full chronology of Indian culture, not settle on one frozen chapter of an often romanticized historical past. We have to bring our exhibitions forward in time to see what they mean in the context of contemporary life. and to do that we need live bodies – not static dioramas'.[22]

[21] Bill Cranmer, personal communication.

[22] W. Richard West Jr. cited by Ruth B. Phillips 'Why not tourist art', 119 footnote 4.

The 'living bodies' are the people that the Cultural Centre draws into its life, the members of the community.

The potlatch collection provides a primary source for training and also for enactment. Bill Cranmer (Gloria Cranmer Webster's brother and Chairman of the Centre) recognised that these priorities could sometimes conflict. At one point the U'mista Cultural Centre was going to build another big-house to provide a theatre where performances could be put on for tourists. But they decided, instead, that it was more important to catalogue their history and culture. The result has been the production of language texts for those of school age for, as Cranmer states, 'we have about two or three generations within which Kwakwala will be spoken unless we do something about it. Unless we teach all subjects up to Grade 8, unless our administration is conducted in our language, then we will lose it. You need to know your past if you want your future'. In order to extend cultural awareness and competence the Centre also teaches young people to learn songs, stories and dances.

Performance and enactment is not restricted to the education of Kwakiutl youth. There is a re-established tradition of Kwakiutl performance for others under modern conditions. Jimmy Sewid founded the Kwakwala Art Society which had contracts with tour ships to hold performances at Alert Bay,[23] and in the mid 1970s Larry Russell, one of Doug Cranmer's carving students, visited the Polynesian Cultural Center and returned enthusiastic to emulate the experience.[24] Unfortunately the logistics were not favourable. Alert Bay is isolated and distant from major tourist destinations. Whilst Russian tour ships were forbidden to stop in US ports in the 1980's they called in at Alert Bay for a forty minute dance and a barbecue fish lunch, but these visits ceased as soon as the Russians were allowed into US waters. Now, tour ships on their way through the inner passage from Seattle to Alaska pass close by but they have to travel in convoy with a fixed schedule. As a consequence they can stop but at an inconvenient time and with unsuitable numbers of passengers (who would care to entertain 700 people after breakfast on a Sunday morning? How would tourists respond?). Educational tours, using smaller boats carrying 100 or so students, only call three times a year.[25]

The rhythm of contemporary life has exerted pressures on performance and the duration of the potlatch itself. As Cranmer Webster notes, the traditional potlatch would last for up to a week. But the distance that family members live apart, the importance of being available for fishing trips, and the pattern of weekend leisure have all helped to compress the potlatch into an event of no more than

[23] Peter Macnair, personal communication, April 1995.

[24] Doug Cranmer (brother of Bill Cranmer and Gloria Cranmer Webster) personal communication, April 1995.

[25] Macnair, personal communication, April 1995.

twenty four hours.[26] The chief casualties have been the formally composed orations.[27] But there have been some spin-off benefits from this telescoping of performance. If there are not many tourists with the stamina to reach the north of Vancouver Island there are several ways that Kwakiutl enterprise has found of reaching out. The tradition of showmanship, begun at the 1893 Chicago Exposition, continues in a new format with a range of shows such as the joint performances with other indigenous artists at song and dance programmes with the American Indian Dance Theater.[28] But the U'mista Cultural Centre has also made films, most notably *Box of Treasures* (1983), in collaboration with the Field Museum, Chicago and has maintained a high profile in World Fairs. For Expo '86 in Toronto Kwakiutl carvers created a thunderbird sculpture for Canada Place as might have been anticipated. What was less predictable was the involvement of the U'mista Centre in one of the largest commercial pavilions, that of General Motors. The U'mista Cultural Centre explained the collaboration thus:

> Last year [1985 – NS] we had been approached by Bob Rogers about working with him on a show for EXPO '86. Our initial reaction to the idea of working with an American producer on a show for a car companys' pavilion was one of scepticism. We soon realised that Bob Rogers was determined to produce a quality show with an indigenous theme and he decided that we were the people to help him. Our collaboration resulted in 'Spirit Lodge', the most popular show at EXPO. Although the show was only nine minutes long, people waited in line for up to three hours to see it. In addition to our consultant's fee, through Bob Rogers' generosity, the Centre also received all revenues from the sale of books, posters and pins from 'Spirit Lodge'. Working with Bob and his crew was an enjoyable and satisfying experience, one that we would be more than happy to repeat anytime.[29]

What was it that the public queued up to see? Ley and Olds situate the exhibit in the context of the public questioning of the taken-for-granted assumption that technology is an alloyed good:

> Most interesting of all was the ambivalent view of technology included in two of the corporate pavilions. The Canadian Pacific exhibit had two imaginative shows presenting social impacts of new technology and user

26  G Cranmer Webster 'The contemporary potlatch' in A Jonaitis *Chiefly Feasts*, 229.

27  Macnair, personal communication.

28  B Cranmer 'Chairman's report', U'mista Cultural Centre Newsletter, Spring 1994 n.p; The American Indian Dance Theater have been licensed to perform Kwakiutl dances for a five year period at the end of which the masks used for performances have to be returned to the Kwakiutl. Doug Cranmer, personal communication.

29  U'mista Cultural Centre 1980–90, 2.

conflicts. Equally unpredictable was General Motors' 'Spirit Lodge', a reflection on the meaning of new technology. In a pavilion that included an automobile display, the narrator of 'Spirit Lodge', an old Indian, challenged the claims of new technology and offered his own standard: 'are our machines making us more like humans? Or are they making us more like machines'.[30]

The descriptions contain more than a hint of irony. What captivated the audience of 'Spirit Lodge' was the ultra-sophistication of electronic imagery, though employed to tell a romantic tale with Kwakiutl acting as illustrations for bygone simple life and values.

The U'mista Cultural Centre was to have another opportunity to collaborate with Bob Rogers. This time the context was an ethnographic part of Knott's Berry Farm, Disneyland's chief competitor and near neighbour in Buena Vista, Southern California. This large theme park created a section in 1990, or in World's Fairs language, a village, called Native America. It obeys the standard format for such displays. Indigenous architecture is recreated in long houses, tepees and totem poles. There are, of course, performers: 'artisans at work include canoe makers, totem-pole and ceremonial-mask carvers, leatherwork artists, face painters, and silversmiths . . . created specially for youngsters, Children's Camp lets them assist in handcrafting traditional honor bonnets, beadwork and sand paintings. They can listen as storytellers recount living history and have their faces painted in tribal fashion'.[31] But Native America has not proven a great success. This may, in part, be due to the lack of active performance available. Watching craftspeople at work is not always a gripping experience. To liven up the Indian Trails the management looked to Bob Rogers and 'Spirit Lodge'. The result has been a collaborative venture between BRC Imagination Arts of Los Angeles (Bob Rogers) and the Cranmers to produce a successor to 'Spirit Lodge' entitled 'Mystery Lodge' which opened in its own theatre in October 1994.

'Mystery Lodge' is a cunning piece of showmanship combining holograms (usually consisting of swirling and changing shapes of smoke that congeal into a succession of animal forms from Kwakiutl lore, such as owls, ravens, sea otters, and killer whales) with a living performer wearing a Kwakiutl mask and acting as a narrator. The swift changes provide an ingenious combination of the traditions of the Kwakiutl transformation mask, which may change a raven into a killer whale

[30] D. Ley and K. Olds 'World's Fairs and the culture of heroic consumption', 203–4.

[31] J. Wade et al. *Disneyland and Beyond*, p 91; Knott's Berry Farm is also discussed by Eco *Travels in Hyper-reality*, 41–2.

by the manipulation of rigging,[32] together with the new forms of illusion created by computer-generated images. The text has only a surface dependence on Kwakiutl culture and stories. It is really a paean to the virtues of family life and the joy to be had by parents caring for their children and for their own parents in a non-specific cultural form. A clever trick has the narrator gradually disappearing like a Cheshire cat (right down to the smile) leaving an authentic walking stick on which he has been leaning, remaining on stage after he has vanished. The walking stick then finally crashes to the ground and so announces the end of the performance. Members of the Cranmer family provide the voice-over that the narrator mimes. Whilst the technology of 'Mystery Lodge' may have advanced, the performance falls into the same repertoire of illusion employed by Bob Harris at the St Louis World's Fair.

The question that remains is whether this latest form of performance, enacted, as it happens, by non-Kwakiutl actors at Knott's Berry Farm, seals a modern bargain between indigènes and contemporary amusement. Have the Kwakiutl made a Faustian bargain in the name of contemporary public education or have they supped with the Devil and successfully lived to tell the tale? Will Bill Cranmer's aspiration to use the five million visitor throughput at Knott's Berry Farm as a platform for the promotion of the U'mista Cultural Centre be realised?[33] Will the audience be persuaded to make the pilgrimage to Alert Bay? These are not casual questions but raise issues about the significance of indigenous performance in its many manifestations. Despite the technology involved here there remains the persistent worry, articulated by MacCannell, about 'primitives' being consigned to the past. It could be argued that 'Mystery Lodge' like its predecessor, 'Spirit Lodge' only inserts a view of vanished life into a contemporary medium, and sacrifices detailed account for generalised pieties. It could further be asked how the performance puts the audience/viewer in a more receptive state to seek to explore the U'mista agenda. This question is reinforced by another exhibition. The Smithsonian's Museum of Natural History has at its entrance a continuous video of Potlatch, yet apart from the list of swiftly scrolled credits there is little sense of what function the video performs, how it relates to the museum experience the visitor is about to enjoy, or how it provides worthwhile publicity for the U'mista Cultural Centre or the Kwakiutl people more generally.

The drift of the argument in the last two chapters has been that in the Pacific and in Northwest Europe one can discern aspects of what Spivak has described as 'subaltern studies or consciousness'.[34] The subaltern agenda stresses

163

[32] 'Typically, a dancer entered the house with the mask sitting high on his head in a closed position. The dancer then manipulated the mask's rigging underneath a blanket to hide mechanisms from the audience. He did this while lowering his head, so that when he lifted his head the audience would briefly see the transformed image. The dancer again brought his face down to change back to the outside form' Stacy Alyn Marcus in A Jonaitis *Chiefly Feasts*, 212.

[33] 'About five million visitors go through Knott's Berry Farm every year and "Mystery Lodge" will no doubt become the main attraction. Again the objective is to work with other organisations to educate other people about our history and culture. In addition the U'mista will receive a fee for the work and this helps us to keep the doors of the U'mista Cultural Centre open'. U'mista Cultural Centre Newsletter Spring 1994, 1.

[34] G. C. Spivak 'Subaltern studies: deconstructing historiography' in her *In Other Worlds*, 197–221; N. Thomas *Colonialism's Culture*, 46–57.

that indigenous anti-colonial perspectives turn the world upside down, and it is a proposition that Spivak finds wanting. There is a fundamental problem faced by those who would wish to intellectualise or describe the life of the underclass or subject people, namely that such descriptions need to be expressed through the language of intellectual discourse which is itself implicated in dominant culture. What the highly self-conscious and market-oriented approach described immediately above risks is a two-fold tendency. On the one hand, as has been hinted, the desire to promote knowledge of Kwakiutl life to a non-Kwakiutl general public necessarily involves the streamlining and simplification or abstraction of performance. Secondly, as the performance becomes commodified it may become congealed and resistant to change. Whilst it remains conceivable that 'dub performance' could develop in Kwakiutl settlements where a keen interest in music outside the community exists, it is doubtful whether such a development could become part of a ceremonial or public repertoire. But if any form of performance has the right to call itself subaltern, dub poetry and music have a prime claim.

Sielu Avea, the Samoan coconut husker at the Polynesian Cultural Center also has a subaltern attitude which is both subversive and constantly innovative in his attempt to find new ways to discomfort visitors without utterly enraging them. The Are Are Pipers evoke a similar discomfort. So, indeed, does the text at the U'mista Cultural Centre that implicates the non-Kwakiutl viewer in its tale. What gives particular power to this display is that the viewer confronts two contradictory frames of reference; that of the Government Agent whose account is juxtaposed with those whose ceremonial property was expropriated. This tension drains away in 'Mystery Lodge' where the Kwakiutl sense of identity dissolves into mystic and obscure romantic abstraction. New technology, it might appear, ensnares as readily as it empowers.[35]

One of the most significant problems that new means of dissemination present is the paradoxical conservatism that it engenders in both the viewer and the ethnographic performer. Precisely because excerpts from historic imagery can be reinserted in new format, it can become a recognised trope of authenticity. This has certainly happened in the case of the Blasket Centre video. Because all that we have as an image of Blasket life is restricted to Mac Conghail's clip from early in this century we, as viewers, and those that would be performers, approach the spectacle of contemporary performance reduced to the narrow slice preserved in the film. New forms of media enable us to reproduce and splice this in fresh ways, but these very

[35] But Cranmer Webster refutes this thesis maintaining 'there is a clear distinction that we make: Mystery Lodge is for white people, U'mista is for us. So comparing the two doesn't make a lot of sense to me'. Personal communication.

[36] though often the performance is neither near the home of the indigène nor the visitor but in a vacation resort, as in the Polynesian Cultural Center, or Orchid Island, Fiji. Martin Parr provides a visually interesting study of such venues in his *Small World*.

media ensure that it is the same image that gets reproduced over and over again. Digital media complete the work begun, as Benjamin asserted, by the camera.

But there is more to this conservatism than the technology implies. Not only are we all, performer and viewer alike, presented with an historically partial picture, but one that comes through the eyes of the holders of particular views of this vision and its significance. In the case of the Kwakiutl, the lineage of George Hunt has had an unrivalled access to means of representation to the outside world and, of course, to the community itself. I am not implying that such a representation or account is necessarily coercive or inherently conservative in a political sense, but I do maintain that forms of representation that are not subject to contestation, in electronic as well as face to face performance, risk becoming marooned. It is for this reason that I have raised the prospect of dub music and poetry which is constantly possessed of a thoroughgoing critical approach. Perhaps Sielu Avea or Vercoe's 'couple in the cage' are the ethnographic equivalent.

## Postmodern ethnographic display: the consumers' revenge

The conservative bias built of necessity into ethnographic display and performance makes parody or ironic inflection a singularly dangerous adventure. There are too many interests to fall foul of. For the owners of customary rights, playing about with tradition is not merely blasphemous, it is bad for business; for, if there is a conservatism built into ethnographic display, this conservatism is, at least in part, a reflection of that of the audience. Audiences come to expect a recognisable repertoire as much in ethnographic performance as in the circus. Audiences may have a surprising investment in engagement with the ethnographic other, but may exact some very steep terms.

The chief requirement that audiences have constantly imposed on ethnographic subjects is movement, the movement of the performer to a metropolitan venue.[36] All of the parks discussed in this study obey this dictum: each sets up an enclave which both the indigènes and their audience pretend is a transposed little piece of home. But audiences can have their own specific agendas. Hendry has documented some to be found in Japan where topographic/ethnographic theme parks have taken firm root.[37] Tobu World Square, a Japanese original for Window of the World, although smaller and less disrespectful, with 102 world-famous buildings all at a scale of $\frac{1}{25}$ enables the Japanese (and Hendry maintains that this park is only for Japanese with little accommodation to foreign languages) to introduce the rest

[37] I am indebted to Joy Hendry for three studies of Japanese theme parks; 'Who is representing whom? Gardens, theme parks and the anthropologist in Japan'; 'Old Gods, new pilgrimages? A whistlestop tour of Japanese international theme parks; 'Nature tamed: gardens as a microcosm of Japan's view of the world'.

of the world for local consumption.[38] This is a more serious example of the domestication that is attempted at the Formosan Aboriginal Culture Village where Europe is brought to Taiwan at the same time as the Taiwanese are introduced to 'their own' aboriginal people.[39]

Ethnographic representation can have quite different consequences and can even be used to subvert both history and cultural identity. The most singular case of such a development is also to be found in Japan at Huis ten Bosch, developed from an original site called Hollanda Mura, near Nagasaki. Here a Dutch park has been built by Dutch architects close to the Dutch settlement of Deshima which was an enclave during the 200 year period when Japan was closed to foreigners. In the park Dutch students learn Japanese in a replica of Huis ten Bosch (the royal palace in the Hague). The same costume change such as is practised at the Folk Culture Villages can be enjoyed here; Dutch costumes are for hire but, more significantly the pageant can become much more realistic as the site is not merely an ethnographic visitor park, it is also a piece of real estate. Huis ten Bosch has apartments and even Dutch houses for sale.[40] Indeed, there are plans to develop the site into a themed Dutch town.

Huis ten Bosch may offer a culturally accented future secure in an image of the past. If this is so then the dwellers will have to elaborate a lifestyle that embraces Dutchness to ensure its thematic security. Quite what this entails remains something of an enigma. Alternatively, the site may demonstrate an example of postmodern consumerist ethnography, and the development of an elective ethnicity. As Japan has so many different nationally themed parks, there is adequate scope for a range of housing developments associated with each of them that purchasers may move between as their mood or taste changes. Such fickleness will not dilute ethnographic realism. On the contrary, one of the most marketable aspects of these developments will be their insistence on the most minutely authentic detail in both performance and costume as well as in architecture. They will ensure that the 'ethnographic moment' is constantly sustained.

Such developments are not necessarily confined to Japan. Architecture remains the most welcoming host to utopian sentiment. Having failed to deliver futurology at EPCOT the Disney imagineers are busy combining interactive technology with 'themed living' beside Walt Disney World at Celebration in Osceola County. The name of the town development itself suggests a grim jollity. Here, in the best traditions of 1930's town planning, purchasers can chose the style of their

[38] J. Hendry 'Who is representing whom?', 12.

[39] Japan also has its own 'aboriginal people', the Ainu of Hokkaido, whose dance was declared by the Japanese government a 'national living treasure' in 1984. The term 'a living treasure' appears to be conceptually similar to what I have called 'the nearly past'.

[40] I am grateful to Marc Treib for these details.

house; Classical, Victorian, Colonial Revival, Coastal, Mediterranean and French. 'Landscaping has to be appropriate not just to the local climate but to the style of the house – no palm trees in front of the French house'.[41] As with all true fantastic topia the world is turned upside down, at least in the imagination. The hospital will not only treat disease but will promote 'wellness'. As the promoters declare, health means feeling good mentally and spiritually. When people feel good they are better because they can promote their own health. Similarly, Celebration School will look to the Disney Corporation to develop new learning skills. Citizens are keen to sign up to a detailed book of Disney designated rules of living that might be considered restrictive or coercive elsewhere, because the wager looks so behaviourally attractive.

What Celebration offers, as will doubtless its many successors,[42] is a form of 'Skansen imaginaire'. It suggests that the theatrical space between an original and its copy can not only be crossed, it can be lived in. This further implies that the status of indigène and visitor can also be collapsed. But to sustain this theatrical stasis, policing is required. Order in a themed world requires the same detailed social engineering as in Bacon's New Atlantis to ensure that the fairytale existence is not threatened. The ethnographic magic is similar to that provided by Legoland where mundane Legobricks combined with modern engineering design create Tatiana's Palace. This palace is not merely a structure but the receptacle and mnemonic for an out-of-this world experience. The difference at Celebration is that one does not have to go home at the end of the day, the effect lingers on.

Whether Celebration, or for that matter, Huis ten Bosch, develops into more than a visual parody or a clever piece of real estate marketing is not of major concern here. What is of more significance is the kind of thinking that lies behind the phenomenon. At the heart of the enterprise is an assertion, concocted by Disney realtors and readily conspired in by the citizens of Celebration, that life can be other than generally lived, free of normal constraints (which may include visually indecorous neighbourhoods and neighbours). An ethnographically-tinted location provides the opportunity for residents to take as much of the exotic as is palatable and to graft it into a new domesticity. On the way, naturally, exotica (both locations, people and customs) become commodified and thus interchangeable, although not all exotics are necessarily equally valued. 'French' may in the context of Florida represent something solid and respectable; 'Mediterranean' on the other hand may not include Hispanic (which is a taken-for granted every-day reality in Florida)

[41] S. Hayman 'Two-dimensional living', 16.

[42] Such was the consumer demand that the first 571 houses were allocated by lottery.

though it is likely to incorporate Italianate. The pedigree for Celebration is undoubtedly to be found in Disney World's 'World Showcase' at EPCOT. The difference is that at Celebration the imagineers have left the theme park and made their way into daily life, inculcating an ethnographic perspective into the everyday.

## Theses on representation

As has already been suggested, it is an unprofitable pursuit to seek a strict genealogy for ethnographic theme parks. There are landmarks that cannot be ignored from the Columbian World Exposition and Skansen to the Polynesian Cultural Center, but these are never reproduced by their imitators or successors, they are quoted, as much for the incidentals of their organisation as for their philosophy of display. What has happened is that the rhetoric of display and discourse has decomposed. The strict cultural quarantine between colonial performers and imperial audiences practised in 1893 can no longer be maintained, even if there were a desire to do so. The traces of ethnic absolutism are no longer hitched to the chariot of imperial display. In even the most serious examples of ethnic instruction such as Taman Mini and China Folk Culture Villages the actors recognise the theatrical nature of their performances.

It could be argued that political changes will make both of these parks obsolete. The Chinese Government's current ethnic minority peoples policy is clearly reflected in FCV whilst Taman Mini explicitly enacts the philosophy of Indonesia's New Order Pancasila. When the present governments are replaced their cultural symbols, like official statues, may be torn down. But, events may work out differently. Each of these parks has evolved a display rationale that is potentially independent of its origins. Because of the theatrical nature of the events at each park, the actors become involved in the development of plot, treatment and choreography. This, of course, is recognised by management which often attempts to police performances and to extirpate unsanctioned novel elements. But there is no return to a previous state; there are no more ethnographically innocent performers, if ever such a category existed. Even in the fastness of kastom at Yakel, there is a ready appreciation of the theatrical nature of performative transactions and the irony that this involves.

One of the major issues that confronts performer and visitor alike is the nature of the spectacle. Is it to be judged in terms of *performance* or *representation*? This is probably the most significant question that one might ask of ethnographic enactment. If representation is considered to be of primary importance then a range of further questions flow from this judgement. As Dyer has noted, 'how a group is represented, presented over and over again in cultural forms, how an image of a member of a group is taken as representative of that group, how that group is repre-sented in the sense of spoken for and on behalf of (whether they represent, speak for themselves or not), these all have to do with how members of groups see themselves and others like themselves, how they see their place in society.' Dyer concludes that 'how we are seen determines in part how we are treated; how we treat others is based on how we see them; such seeing comes from representation'.[43] What Dyer's formulation serves to emphasise is the importance of the power to define the situation, combined with a further suggestion that those who represent others have an obligation not to defame or misrepresent those who possess cultural copyright. Representation by non-owners can all too readily be a form of appropriation.[44] The problem that such a requirement might impose is similar to that faced by MacCannell, namely that it fails to integrate ideas of cultural innovation and borrowing. Said offers a partial solution to the dilemma when he argues:

> If we no longer think of the relationship between cultures and
> their adherents as perfectly contiguous, totally synchronous, wholly
> correspondent, and if we think of cultures as permeable and, on
> the whole, defensive boundaries between polities, a more promising
> situation appears. Thus to see others not as ontologically given but
> as historically constituted would be to erode the exclusivist biases we
> so often ascribe to cultures, our own not least. Cultures may then be
> represented as zones of control or of abandonment, or of sharing,
> all taking place in the global history that is our element.[45]

Said's definition works well until the last clause which postulates a taken-for-granted universalism that the very notion of cultural contention cannot concede. It is precisely this problematic aspect of representation that so worries critics of ethnographic performance. Those who share MacCannell's melancholia would be reluctant to treat 'zones of control or abandonment' so casually.

However, if, instead of representation, performance is considered of primary importance, the picture can look quite different. Dening chooses a deliberately provocative term to develop an approach that privileges performance. The word he uses is 'claptrap'. This he describes as 'the moment of theatricality in any

[43] R. Dyer *The Matter of Images*, 1.

[44] A theme developed by Hendry 'Who is representing whom?', 5–6 and 19.

[45] E. Said 'Representing the colonized: anthropology's interlocuters', 225.

representation, the space created by the performance consciousness of the representer in which the audience – or the reader or the viewer – participates in the creative process of representing'.[46] Such an approach places the actor centre-stage. In Dening's view ethnographic transactions can only take place when a genuine rapport is created, and by implication, this requires the actor to have charge of the event and for the audience to willingly suspend disbelief, if only for an instant. For Dening theatricality is not a shortcoming, it is the very basis for realism. As he puts it, 'the sense of artefactuality in representing does not necessarily detract from its realism. It is the key to realism. And realism is what ethnography and observing are about. The theatricality of observing and being observed is that guarantee of their being faction rather than fiction'.[47]

How are we to reconcile these opposing perspectives? It would be simple to suggest that both obtain simultaneously, but such a conclusion lacks dynamic sense as these frameworks contradict each other. Perhaps it would be useful here to consider Debord's thesis that 'the spectacle is not a collection of images; rather it is a social relationship between people that is mediated by images'.[48] The relationship itself may be variable and involve the inspection of strategies adopted by each party to the transaction and the degree to which each makes reference to the 'moment of theatricality'. One way to explore this variable relationship is to draw up a polar typology which has at one end the performer as subservient to the audience; this may described as the operation of 'politeness'. At the other end lies its opposite, 'embarrassment' where the audience is in thrall of the performer

All of the enactments considered within the framework of ethnographic display operate between the polarities marked out by these terms. One the one hand, successful actors need to be able to 'read the mind' of the audience and establish intersubjective rapport with them; they have to be able to understand how the representations and enactments that they are about to execute will be received and evaluated by members of the current audience, and how it fits into their field of experience and imagination. Ethnographic actors become highly sensitive to indicators which help situate their audiences. Dress can be a shorthand indicator that marks accurately from considerable distance a whole bundle of behavioural attributes, whether they be course differences attributed to national character, or more refined ones that relate to psychological dispositions. This prudential know ledge is of vital importance in considering how to treat members of an audience. Politeness dictates that the performer will respect what s/he anticipates might be

---

[46] G. Dening 'Europe "discovers" the "Pacific" ', 459.

[47] Dening, 459.

[48] G. Debord *The Society of the Spectacle*, 12.

core values for members of the audience. As a consequence, actors will be careful in discussing issues of religion, politics or international relations for fear of offending sensibilities. So actors often resort to a series of well-rehearsed cultural stereotypes that have wide currency and are unlikely to surprise audience members.[49] Face-threatening behaviour is risky because it is likely to evoke overt hostility in the audience, and actors seek to gain early rapport to make the performance smoother and more successful, enjoyable to both parties.[50] Politeness also comes in other forms. Gamelan orchestras performing in hotel lobbies in Jakarta only play quiet, short and light pieces in order not to interfere with the conversations of international visitors sitting nearby. Similarly, 'palace dancing' and barong dance dramas have been adapted to meet the taste of tourists.[51]

But this functionalist explanation misses the heart of the true spectacle. The gamelan pieces described above hardly constitute full performances. What they lack is audience engagement, which is only achieved by the actor's taking a theatrical risk (the 'claptrap' described by Dening above) challenging the expectations of the audience and ambushing its members by making observations that redescribe their behaviour and beliefs in an alternative and unflattering light. This provokes embarrassment but as Kuentz has noted, embarrassment can be a form of pleasure when taken-for-granted cultural assumptions are contradicted from below.[52] It is when the tables are turned on members of the audience and they become part of the spectacle, that a new form of engagement takes place. The haole joke at the PCC derives its force from the serious comment that it makes about white American culture, and it is the plausibility of the characterisation that makes this April Fool joke so potentially embarrassing for those who are forced to see themselves implicated in the image, and as ethnographic subjects.

A first thesis may be generated from this discussion about the nature of the ethnographic spectacle. It can be asserted that ethnographic enactment has remained constrained historically by issues of power. Whenever performance has been oblivious or careless to questions of authentic representation it has been because notions of cultural copyright have not been considered important, the views of the actors being accorded little if any significance. In such a setting performance is not informed by considerations of representativeness. However, once the notion of ethnographic representation becomes central, there is a stress on authenticity in all aspects of enactment. This does not, however, mean that performance becomes less important. On the contrary, demands for ethnographic authenticity

[49] However sophisticated actors may be in intercultural settings, where understanding is problematic because of language barriers, they are likely to find, often to their utter consternation, that they come to resort to performing stereotypically to fill both the vacuum left by incomprehension and the horror of prolonged silence.

[50] Brown and Levinson distinguish two modes of politeness, positive and negative. In the first mode the actor makes minimal demands upon the other, defers and is indirect for fear of being seen to impose. In positive politeness the actor emphasises the common characteristics that unite the actor and the other and, to demonstrate closeness often resorts to joking to underline the common values that both share. P. Brown and S. Levinson *Politeness: Some Universals in Language Use*, 102, 131. Politeness theory, disguised as etiquette, operates continuously in ethnographic theme parks. Indeed, their operation could well be seen as the ultimate laboratory for research and development of the theory.

[51] F. Hughes-Freeland 'Packaging dreams'; M. Hitchcock et al 'Introduction', both in M J Hitchcock et al *Tourism in south-East Asia*, 143, 11.

[52] J. Kuentz 'Working at the Rat' in Project on Disney *Work and Play at Disney World*, 236.

open up a range of opportunities not available to the traditional performer. It might be possible to state this schematically thus: *ethnographic performance in a contemporary setting involves a strategic judgement by the performer about the expectations of the audience and the extent to which this performance may be used to offer a critique of the audience's values.* As with all the subsequent theses discussed here, there is a conscious attempt to distinguish what I call ethnographic seriousness from the caricature that I maintain epitomises the entertainment offered by the Disney Corporation. So, for example, what distinguishes EPCOT from the PCC is the orientation of the enactment. I choose the PCC as an example here because it appears in its marketing philosophy closer to Disney than other ethnographic parks but it is still, in its ethnographic orientation (however slickly orchestrated) quite different in character to the world of the illusioneers.

A second thesis may be drawn from this distinction, namely that the ethnographic vision implies the development of self-consciousness in audience as well as actors. One of the most significant changes that successful performances make in their audience is the enforced abandonment of pre-encoded, stereotypical conservative response. What I call the ethnographic imagination is based on the flowering in the audience of a sense of 'wonder'. This term is one that Greenblatt employs to describe an orientation to exhibitions in general. 'By wonder', Greenblatt states, 'I mean the power of the displayed object to stop the viewer in his or her tracks, to convey an arresting sense of uniqueness, to evoke an exalted attention.'[53] This seems a particularly appropriate way to consider the ethnographic imagination which involves the development of an aesthetic approach to cultural difference, revelling in the detail and the variety of cultural forms for their own sake. The thesis might be put in this way: *ethnographic imagination develops as members of an audience become discriminating judges of cultural enactments which are enjoyed for the style and conviction that these presentations contain.* In this respect the enjoyment of the audience is not restricted by considerations of strict veracity but it does not tolerate 'whimsification' which in its romantic childishness is antithetical to realistic treatment. The earlier question 'is this presentation authentic?' is no longer adequate for this aesthetically engaged audience. The ethnographically self-conscious audience comes to weigh the particular claims for authenticity made by a particular performance against other similar or alternative enactments. It is the adequacy, the conviction and the novelty of the representation that becomes the object of aesthetic scrutiny, much as would be the case in theatrical or cinematic performances.

[53]  S. Greenblatt 'Resonance and wonder' p 42.

A further consequence may follow from the idea of an ethnographic aesthetic based on wonder, namely, that performances that attempt to involve the audience breach the conditions necessary for aesthetic contemplation. The very tension suggested in the title of this work emphasises the distance that has to exist between performer and audience in order for wonder to develop. What is important is the way in which the ethnographic performer represents something foreign to the viewer. This provides material for the development of a third thesis relating to what I call alterity. As actors in the ethnographic park have to embrace both performance and representation, politeness and embarrassment, so they have to appear both different but recognisable. Two related counter-examples help extend this point. The reason that the Small American Homes Exhibition at the New York World's Fair of 1939 is a missing footnote to the history of ethnographic representation is because it did not obey this principle of alterity: the couples looked too similar to those who were inspecting them to be of ethnographic interest. On the other hand, the mythical Amerindian couple in the cage, produced as a piece of performance art by Vercoe, serve to demonstrate on what shaky foundations we construct our sense of otherness. The lesson to be drawn from this cautionary example is that this sense of alterity is almost entirely based on the spectacularization of the visual. The thesis that may be derived from this proposition is that *ethnographic performances take as axiomatic that there are specific ways in which the performer is marked as different from members of the audience, and that such alterity is almost exclusively to be found in visual form.* This is why Totu objects so vociferously (see p 000) to cultural centres in the Pacific basing their exhibitions and performances on the alterity of South Pacific life rather than its normalcy for those who dwell there. But miners, fishing folk, aboriginals in America and Asia, are all immediately recognisable by the distinctiveness of their appearance and before they open their mouths. They fulfil a visual expectation.

A further distinctive quality of ethnographic performance relates to tense. As I have argued earlier, ethnographic spectacles exist in a particular penumbra, in transit, as it were, between the quotidian and the historic, in what might be described it as the 'historic continuous', or, to use a term I have employed in this work, 'the nearly past'. The nearly past links previous experience to contemporary life but does so in a way that is crucially different from that proposed by salvage ethnography. Salvage in its original context refers to the physical demolition of a building and the subsequent picking over the spoils to locate items which the finder selects as attractive relics. The image is entirely visual. Combing building sites and beaches is a visually charged activity and one that operates with serendipity: items glisten in the debris and 'deserve' to be reborn in a new existence. Salvage ethnography imports the same conception in its metaphoric extension, and suggests that all that can be done at this eleventh hour is to rescue cultural items and to preserve them from the ruin from which they have been plucked. For salvage ethnography the culture described is treated in the pluperfect tense; it has finally ceased to operate. The nearly past, on the other hand, is in the future perfect. From this might be deduced a fourth thesis: *ethnographic representations occur in the nearly past, in a frame that encompasses the living memory of the oldest performer or viewer but stops short of the historic.* As such it is a continuously moving frame. But this is one of the constitutive features of the nearly past in ethnographic performance; the frame moves over time. As a consequence of this thesis all the performances described in this study have a circumscribed life-span. As cultures develop, their enactments will likewise change. I would claim that Skansen and much of the World's Fairs traditions have now moved into the historic mode. We no longer have personal access to the issues of ethnicity and folklore that motivated Hazelius's collecting passion in Sweden in the early twentieth century. Shortly, despite the cultural and political desires embodied in the Blasket Centre, it too will become an historic setting. The nearly new acts as a brake on the development of the historic moment but is not equipped to halt it.

Despite the assertion at the head of this section that historical investigation into the pedigree of ethnographic theme parks is likely to be a disappointing exercise this does not mean that there is an unchangeable quality that marks all such parks. There is, as the order of examples and types discussed in this work suggests, a gradual accretion of new elements and treatments. The future of these parks relies upon the ethnographic imagination remaining an important quality valued by audience and constantly elaborated on by performers. One of the most significant dangers facing these forms of entertainment is that the genre will become too successful, that the rapid growth in the numbers of such outlets will overstretch the conceptual frame that currently unites such a disparity of venues. As the market expands new types of conflict will become more prominent. One of these is clearly becoming increasingly apparent in the development of tourist performances in the South Pacific. As one critic has noted

All Melanesian states, on becoming independent, acquire all the colonial apparatus of power and 'constitutionalise' most former colonial acts or omissions. Traditional institutions and norms are swept beneath the carpets of power or neglected to an idyllic future when 'custom' or 'tradition' will be incorporated into state practices and law. Whilst state power increases, implying an increase of power for the 'law men' and a limited number of 'law women', the power of the villages, the clans and the people withers.[54]

Tourism, cultural centres and rights to perform become of economic significance to governments with a narrow economic base and where commodity prices for goods produced is so low that they cannot sustain official expenditure. Apart from grant aid few other sources of potential income are so attractive to many Pacific nations, or to many other national governments elsewhere. Under these conditions there is an inexorable pressure (paradoxically strengthened by green politics and economics) to expand sites and forms of cultural tourism based on ethnographic displays.

But economic pressure does not come solely from government sources. Debord argues that spectacles takes place in a world of the commodity ruling over lived experience.[55] So, for Debord, there is an economic imperative in generating the spectacle. Nothing is excused an appearance, every cultural manifestation can and will be subjected to spectacular commodification. In Debord's extravagant terms the spectacle expresses 'the communication of the incommunicable'.[56] The question that immediately arises from this formulation is whether such a tendency must indeed be universal. Are there no cultural forms that can be spared this spectacularization? This has become a live issue.

The inherent centrifugal tendency in representation is not only driven by economic imperatives. One of the most troublesome questions confronting ethnographic spectacularization is how to deal with enactments that are *not* focused on celebration. All of the examples discussed above have elements of tragedy buried in their past but each insists that a future emerges, albeit in different form, to provide a positive point of reference. But the Famine Museum, discussed by Brett, does not fit this scenario. Here, memorialisation replaces celebration. But the Famine Museum represents events securely in the pluperfect.

Other historic enactments cannot be so readily treated entirely in the past tense. In Colonial Williamsburg, a preserved eighteenth century town in Virginia,

[54]  B. Narokobi cited by B. Rudkin and C M Hall 'Unable to see the forest for the trees', 206.

[55]  G. Debord The Society of the Spectacle, 26.

[56]  Debord, 136; see also U. Eco *Travels in Hyper-reality*, 293–4.

black actors were hired in 1979 to role play slave characters. This caused them considerable distress and demoralisation, feeling that they had become adjuncts to a slave owner account. Their response was, in this context instructive: 'they began introducing the characters in the third person, role-playing them in first-person, and then breaking out of role to discuss the issues with the audience'.[57]

However, the recent creation of Holocaust museums[58] stretch both the limits of representation and the tolerance of the nearly past in a way that highlights dramatically the ethical issues that lurk beneath the surface in any form of cultural enactment. Bernstein suggests that the Holocaust 'created a decisive breach in the fabric of the modern world'.[59] For Primo Levi the events of the concentration camps were indescribable as 'daily language is for the description of daily experience, but here is another world, here one would need a language "of this world," a language born here'.[60] There is no means of communicating experiences such as these.

For these reasons there are widespread objections raised against any form of spectacularization. The protest is against the evocation of theatrical performance of something that can only be described as the breakdown of humanity. Evocation inevitably conjures up the actors in the Shoah. On the one hand, this involves showing the perpetrators' planning, devising the means of murder and the carrying out of systematic genocide at both official level as well as in the day-to-day personal involvement of individuals. On the other hand, theatrical re-enactment of the victims of genocide bring in issues of suffering, brutalisation and murder, as well as the most difficult of subjects, how people could mitigate their fate by negotiation with their oppressors. Critics of the memorialisation of the Holocaust argue that, however good the motives of those wishing to memorialise and so help prevent the re-emergence of genocide, this activity is fundamentally misconceived as it is a study in death and not life. The whole focus, such critics would maintain, risks becoming a memorial to the perpetrators rather than the victims.

But this argument has not won the day. On the contrary, as cultural enactment becomes a dominant historic trope, there has developed a relentless pressure to attempt the imaginative feat, the communication of the incommunicable. This task is proposed from two different perspectives. The first is philosophical and is epitomised in Bauman's aphorism, 'the unimaginable ought to be imagined'.[61] This reinstates the enlightenment proposition that nothing is beyond the purview of the human intellect. This stance provides sustenance for the members of a second group, those involved in the nearly past. This orientation is nicely captured by one

[57] M. Simpson *Making Representations*, 24.

[58] Beside Yad Vashem, set up as Israel's Memorial Authority and museum in 1954, there are a range of monuments and displays in Eastern Europe (see J A. Young *Holocaust Museums in History*) and in Washington DC the United States Holocaust Memorial Museum opened in 1993. A Holocaust Museum is to be opened within the Imperial War Museum, London, in 1999.

[59] M. Bernstein 'The lasting injury', 3.

[60] P. Levi 'Revisiting the camps' in J. A. Young *The Art of Memory*, 185.

[61] Z. Bauman *Modernity and the Holocaust*, 85.

commentator. 'Time is running out. Memory will soon become history. Now we can talk together. Soon, even that luxury will be gone'.[62] One response to this intense desire to communicate has been the creation of museums of resonance, and the most significant and most controversial has been the United States Holocaust Memorial Museum (USHMM).

The USHMM brings together nearly all aspects of ethnographic representation with one glaring omission – the actors. The display solves this problem by demanding that the visitors come to identify and collaborate in bearing witness to their own inheritance of guilt. So the entry to the display is via an unadorned steel elevator designed to appear austere and even threatening. In this elevator the visitor is taken literally and symbolically from the everyday world into the other. To create a personal bond with the experience each visitor is provided with an identification card of a person of the same sex who was caught up in the Holocaust. This ID card is carried throughout the tightly controlled narrative topology and a full biography can be accessed via computer at the end of the tour. Another form of personification is generated through artefactual means. Recovered items with high symbolic charge from the major concentration camps, from cattle wagons to the uniforms worn by the prisoners and their personal possessions offer a powerful invitation to not only remember but to envisage camp life.[63] Still photographs and film sequences complete the record.

The USHMM in its very theatricality offends or worries some critics. It also tests the first and contradicts the second and third of my theses. The emotional charge of the experience tries the mental stamina of the audience with its relentless and overwhelming detail. The collapse of the sense of theatrical distance reinforces the impact of the experience on the moral imagination.[64] Ethnographic distance is eliminated and members of the audience become identified with the enactment. The chief problem that worries critics in this theatrical performance and representation is that it risks collapse into precisely what it sets out to defeat, a picture in the image of the oppressor. Whilst, on the one hand, the USHMM emphatically repudiates Urry's claim that artefactual history necessarily ignores such unpleasant issues as war, exploitation, hunger and disease,[65] these same artefacts 'also force us to recall the victims as the Germans have remembered them to us: in the collected debris of a destroyed civilisation'.[66] This problem may arise precisely because the sense of theatrical distance, the notion of aesthetic discrimination, and alterity are all breached in the display.

[62]  Stephen D. Smith 'Foreword' in P. Oppenheimer *From Belsen to Buckingham Palace*, 11.

[63]  having to pay a dealer for concentration camp uniforms provided the architect and director of Beth Shalom with a feeling of great distaste. Stephen D Smith, personal communication.

[64]  I am grateful to Pat Cooke for this observation. He states further: 'the ghosts of Auschwitz are not active appellants for their own case; they are passively present in a way that compels the audience into bearing witness to an unrepeatable crime. If this fails to challenge the audience's values in a subjective sense, it surely succeeds in challenging it *with* values'. Personal communication.

[65]  J. Urry *The Tourist Gaze*, 112.

[66]  J. A. Young *The Texture of Memory*, 132.

Nevertheless, ethnographic tourism in the nearly past, remains a growing phenomenon. The US educational tours of the 'March of the Living' that take in the concentration camps of Eastern Europe also stop at places like Kazimierz, the pre-war Jewish quarter of Krakow and now a UNESCO World Heritage Site with a Centre for Jewish Culture. Some of the results of the renewed interest in Jewish culture, religion and music have been paradoxical and provide a cautionary coda in cultural renewal. The concept of the indigène in Kazimierz is as highly problematic as in the Pacific. As Karpf notes, 'To many visitors, Kazimierz as it exists is virtually invisible. Yet when tourists do notice Jews it's almost worse: the residents feel gawped at like some anthropological specimens, the last Jews of Krakow'.[67]

A fifth and final thesis may be advanced in relation to the ubiquity of ethnographic representation. Kazimierz and Huis ten Bosch show two different aspects of the phenomenon, one positive and the other negative, but both attest to the power of ethnographic performance in creating heritage. Brett expresses this clearly when he states, 'constructing "heritage" is a form of structuring the present, albeit in a fantastic or displaced form'.[68] But something else also arises as a result of the universalising tendency to produce ethnographic representations through performances and this might be expressed thus: *Ethnographic performances in their ambition to provide the dominant form of cultural representation brook no opposition nor excuse any aspects of culture from being brought into the service of spectacularization.* From this it might be further deduced that any aspects or forms of culture that are not readily turned into visual form are not fully realised. It is the spectacle that provides the location for the representation of a particular culture by combining the emblematic elements in a typical display. Of course, what constitutes a typical display is at the heart of the discussion in this work. Successful ethnographic performances often disguise the controversial nature of the typification involved in persuasive and aesthetically pleasing ways. It is to the satisfaction that ethnographic performances provide, particularly in theme park settings, that the final section of this chapter is devoted.

## The pleasures of ethnographic theme parks

The chief enjoyment that such venues offer the visitor is what may be termed 'scopic power', that is a visual mastery of the setting. All of these venues provide visual challenges to the viewer. There are no elements in these landscapes that are unplanned; some of the architect's designs may not work in the way that they were envisaged, but none of the features is accidental or haphazard. The elements may be easy to read or complicated but they offer the viewer an opportunity to make personal sense of the ensemble. On the one hand, these parks are forms of a visual and cultural panoptikon. The display at first conceals and then discloses its logic of construction and modes of signification to the eye which takes in both topography and architecture from the viewing point at the top of the park (all of the parks have viewing points). Scopic pleasure is further enhanced by miniaturisation. Miniaturisation represents a form of mimesis, and makes the proposition that the representation is a wholly accurate simulacrum of its original. As Litzinger writes of Chinese parks, 'all the parks attempt a from of ethnographic realism which assumes a mimetic relationship between the image and the objective world'.[69] Miniaturisation also guarantees the viewer an exact reproduction of every detail to scale, and promises a grand tour in a minor key. Grand tours concentrated on landscape, art and architecture. Ethnographic theme parks, in contrast, employ these to provide a setting for cultures. That is why they add another ingredient and thereby change the whole character of the experience. As Kirshenblatt–Gimblett states, 'at their most mimetic, in-situ installations include live persons, preferably actual representatives of the cultures on display'.[70] Unlike the hermit in the gothic garden, the indigènes in the ethnographic theme park are the focus of display rather than decorative additions.

Visitors to these parks are probably seldom assailed by qualms over the authenticity of the display or the nature of the mimesis, though they are likely to have a well-honed sense of aesthetic judgement of the display and its attractiveness as well as an appreciation of how they are being involved in the spectacle. The essential difference between the World's Fair tradition and the contemporary ethnographic theme park is that one can no longer provide a straightforward answer to the series of questions that Cohen asks about touristic images of native people: 'who represents whom for whom, in what medium and under which socio-political circumstances and under which prevailing socio-political circumstances'?[71] The range of alternatives has become too wide for the sureties of MacCannell's vision to remain stable. As both these authors warn, the continued

[67] A. Karpf 'The last Jews of Krakow cringe', 27.

[68] D. Brett *The Construction of Heritage*, 157.

[69] R. Litzinger 'The work of culture and memory in contemporary China', 36.

[70] B. Kirshenblatt-Gimblett 'Objects of Ethnography', 389.

[71] E. Cohen 'The study of touristic images', 39.

exploitation of the weak by the powerful is not negated in the contemporary world, but the framework within which performers and audience meet has changed quite significantly.

On the one hand, the indigène can be found as much in an attitude or an orientation to the world as in material circumstances. Augé provides a term to describe this: 'indigenous fantasy'. By this he means that the indigène approaches culture in a closed way, as something just there from primeval times not requiring to be understood: 'all the inhabitants have to do is recognise themselves in it when the occasion arises'.[72] The indigenous perspective is quite capable of reconceptualizing ethnographic encounters in traditional terms. For example, the performers of the Pentecost land dive, the Sa, have a perfectly satisfactory account of tourism:

> To them, 'tradition' is an expression of strength or 'power' that comes from a sacred place. Tourism confirms this by attracting large numbers of spectators who are willing to exchange wealth to see the 'way' of kastom. Tradition is bound to Sa sense of cultural identity, place and social history. They look into the camera lens unimpressed by the 'floating ones'.[73]

But this perspective will only survive with difficulty the transportation to a theme park. Yet it can still be reached for in an elective fashion, 'when the occasion arises'. Both the Kwakiutl and the Blasket examples demonstrate the viability of a mixed genre approach to culture which becomes an invisible appurtenance of costume, to be donned as appropriate to the occasion. This argument is not ventured lightly nor is it to belittle the significance of this change in status. What it suggests is that performers, and all members of a culture under inspection, whether it be a troupe of folk dancers or a church choir, or, for that matter, indigenous experts in the South Pacific, have at least two options constantly before them: 'indigenous fantasy' or its alternative, the composite which recognises the performative and selective nature of all representations. In this new uncertainty, which arises paradoxically at precisely the moment that the term 'indigenous expert' has just come into favour,[74] the concept of cultural expertise becomes highly problematic because no longer does a single conceptualisation of culture remain adequate. That is why ethnographic performances are such contentious events; they constantly remind their audience what they have excised in their eagerness to appeal, and what other versions might have contained. In this scenario cultural centres have a crucial role

[72] M. Augé Non-places, 44.

[73] C. de Berlo 'Cultural resistance and ethnic tourism', 274.

[74] Lavine asks 'How can museums make space for the voices of indigenous experts, members of communities represented in exhibitions, and artists?' S. Lavine 'Museum practices' in I Karp and S. Lavine Exhibiting Cultures, 151.

as laboratories for the dissection and recombination of both knowledge and performance for domestic consumption and for export (theme parks are export outlets in this context). It is in cultural centres that the alchemy is performed which transforms a huge variety of untidy and inconsequential material into a crafted story. By good fortune, it is in the nature of storytelling that one version inevitably incites its rival to offer either a different version, or a new picture. Innovative cultural centres, therefore, are liable to be lively places and to have short lives. The performers they train are also likely to be as interested in embarrassment as politeness.

If performers have changed, so have audiences. Self-consciousness has affected them as well. Augé offers us the vision of the visitor as 'his own spectacle',[75] the narcissistic participant in his own show. Augé argues that the geographic location of the spectacle is no longer of significance, only the personal experience, thus rendering the site one of the interchangeable components of regular tourism. But ethnographic performances still promise more, they offer the visitor a sense of alterity, of seeing some things that are immediately recognisable whilst simultaneously presenting others that are perplexing and strange. The mimesis of the performance provides sameness and difference. As Taussig remarks, 'pulling you this way and that, mimesis plays this trick of dancing between the very same and the very different'.[76] Even the most simple ethnographic performance plays on this instability and tension, and this is an achievement that is built on the foundation of the ethnographic imagination. What is most remarkable about the new forms of spectacularization of culture is their persistence, their ability to adapt to some remarkably new circumstances and to colonise both the worlds of pleasure and imagination. We see ourselves as we see the other, through the lens of ethnicity and ethnography. Far from having died at the end of the world of imperial expositions, this attitude is constantly refreshed through current forms of ethnographic spectacle, and it embraces us all.

McCannell's proposition that 'the primitivistic performance is our funerary marking the passage of savagery' no longer works in a world where all performances have become self-conscious and are selected from a range of different variants in the repertory of 'being ourselves for each other'. We may be troubled at the apparent collapse of the categoric division between actors and spectators to be seen in Huis ten Bosch or Celebration. But if we consider these examples more carefully we will note that they represent impossible forms of utopianism. A Japanese

[75] M. Augé Non-places, 86.

[76] M. Taussig Mimesis and Alterity, 129.

city based on a Dutch model is destined to become either an anachronism or a new syncretic form.[77]

What MacCannel's vision lacks is a sense of what I have termed 'distance'. Distance is precisely the quality necessary to sustain ethnographic performance. Distance involves a range of significant dimensions. The first of these is aesthetic. Audiences recognise in the performance a quality of acting that is engrossing to the extent that disbelief is suspended. Even when the actor demonstrates the artifice of the performance the spell is not broken. Husking a coconut hardly seems a performative high point, but it is surprisingly difficult: there is an aesthetic to coconut husking.

Distance is maintained by performers by means of both politeness and embarrassment (both controlling mechanisms employed to keep audiences attentive and respectful). Only occasionally does this break down, as in the Formosan Aboriginal Cultural Village when the village women turn their backs on the inattentive audience. Performers normally evolve strategies to educate their audience into appropriate behaviour, or as in the Polynesian Cultural Center, they graciously excuse their behaviour as a feature of ignorance and poor socialisation.

But distance is most importantly to be seen in economic terms. Kastom is a term that now has currency not only in the South Pacific, but can be employed by extension wherever the right to performance and cultural knowledge is treated as a scarce commodity. It is this distance that provides the necessary condition for the performance constructed on the basis of alterity. This is a substantial change from the earlier styles of performance that were based on similarities which united all forms of early ethnographic performance. As Nora has written: 'a process of interior decolonization has affected ethnic minorities, families and groups that until now have possessed reserves of memory but little or no historical capital'.[78] This is the decisive shift that has taken place in ethnographic enactment. The nearly past provides for a wide range of groups material that can be employed in the construction of performance both for internal and external consumption. Heritage is now to be seen as a by-product of ethnographic self-interest and enactment for others. Both elements are now symbiotic. There is no ethnographic self divorced from the other. We become ourselves in our performances for each other.

Ethnographic theme parks do not simply exemplify novelty or changes of style in popular entertainment. They challenge some assumptions that are currently held in cultural theory. Firstly, they are not a postmodern synthesis of

[77] The developers see Huis ten Bosch as a new model design for living for Asia. see J. Robertson (1997) 'Internationalization and Nostalgia: A Critical Interpretation' in S. Vlastos *Mirror of Modernity: Invented Traditions in Modern Japan,* Berkeley, University of California Press. I am indebted to Joy Hendry for this reference.

[78] P. Nora 'Between memory and history', 7.

advertizing, marketing and public relations. Few are effectively marketed, most have a poor sense of the visitor as customer and all are suffused with a sincerity which contradicts the knowingness and ambiguity in postmodern identity. These are not forms of entertainment in the Disney mold, nor are they properly to be seen in Eco's notion of hyper-reality where reality is created in the absolute fake. No visitors in ethnographic theme parks imagine have become blurred with the performers.

More significantly, these parks question the widespread usage of the term 'hybridity'. Hybridity is a postmodern term that implies a fluidity to categories and proclaims that individual identity is negotiable and malleable according to setting and desire. But it is in the stability of performances in these parks that a pact is made between actor and audience. Undoubtedly, as I have suggested above, both parties are keenly aware of the theatricality of the occasion, but, as with other forms of the aesthetic, performances take place within an agreed framework. To transgress this is to violate the conditions of performance. Ethnographic representation comes not only to fix cultural forms but it also privileges the symbolic. Dress, song, and performance refer audience back to another reality to be found in the authentic homeland. At the back of the symbolic enactment there is a commitment to realism that is alien to both notions of hybridity and postmodern identity. Such representations also repudiate the 'invention of tradition' thesis by their insistence that there is, indeed, a genuine and respectable linkage between performance in the park with that at home. They are that exception that Hobsbawm and Ranger concede can exist, 'human natural sanctuaries for isolated corners of archaic life',[79] but in modern form.

These parks make a range of cultural and political claims, all achieved through visual means. Never is there a written text to direct the viewer. Instead there are a range of assertions in visual form about the nature of the relations between the groups represented and the state in which they reside. This is achieved principally through narrative topology where time is converted into space, the historic into the visual. What is significant about these manifestations is that the indigènes are shown not as archaic, but as a contemporary critique and alternative to urban industrial life.

Nations that are culturally diverse are often keen to find means of understanding and representing to themselves the shape of this complexity. There are several ways they go about this task, charting physical, geographic, linguistic and

[79]  E. Hobsbawm and T Ranger
*The Invention of Tradition*, 8.

183

cultural differences and displaying these in map form. It is also commonplace to represent the exuberance of cultural diversity in visual shorthand. Working in visual form is quite as engrossing and complex as linguistic analysis, genetic mapping or the study of kinship networks. Ethnographic theme parks unite all of these agendas and offer them to the visitor under the guise of a naturalistic representation. In such environments the picturesque survives in contemporary form.

This study has addressed the consequence of giving privilege to the visual. In turn this raises the further question as to whether visualisation is necessarily regressive, and whether we are all condemned to resort to primitive and unreformed stereotypes. It has been the argument of this work that the typifications of the imperial era can, albeit with difficulty, be surmounted by new forms of spectacle. These may, as cultural centres in the Pacific, and in Europe, assert new forms of cultural ownership and the possibility in turn of creating reformed versions of spectacle. There remains, however, in these new versions, a persisting dichotomy which is contained in the title; performances require both self and other. It is for this reason that ethnographic display and performance raises the perennial problem of who are the partners in 'being ourselves for you'. This work has depicted the changes that have become possible in the reformulation of ethnographic spectacle but suggests that the very core of the ethnographic enterprise, looking at and representing alterity, remains the vital element in the contemporary ethnographic theme park which continues to make them both attractive to visitors, and of considerable value to an understanding of current representations of culture as well as the theories that lie beneath the visual appearance.

# Bibliography

Abram, Simone; Macleod, Don; Waldren, Jacqueline (eds.) (1997) *Tourists and Tourism: Constructing and Deconstructing Identity*, Oxford, Berg

Acciaioli, Greg (1985) 'Culture as art: from practice to spectacle in Indonesia', *Canberra Anthropology*, 8:1 and 2, 148–72

Ames, Michael M. (1992) *Cannibal Tours and Glass Boxes: the Anthropology of Museums*, Vancouver, UBC Press

Anderson, Benedict (1973) 'Notes on contemporary Indonesian political communication', *Indonesia*, 16, 38–80

Anderson, Benedict (1991) *Imagined Communities: Reflections on the Origin and Spread of Nationalism*, London, Verso

Anagnost, Ann (1993) 'The nationscape: movement in the field of vision', *Positions: East Asia Cultures Critique*, 1:3, 585–606

Ariyoshi, Rita (1987) *The Polynesian Cultural Center*, Lai'e, Polynesian Cultural Center

Ariyoshi, Rita (1995) *Polynesian Cultural Center: All the Spirit of the Islands*, Lai'e, Polynesian Cultural Center [text as 1987 edition with new illustrations and captions]

Asmat Progress and Development Foundation (n.d. 1990) *Asmat*, Jakarta

Augé, Marc (1995) *Non-Places: Introduction to an Anthropology of Supermodernity* (translated by John Howe), London, Verso

Banks, Marcus; Morphy, Howard (eds.) (1997) *Rethinking Visual Anthropology*, New Haven, Yale University Press


Bhabha, Homi K. (1983) 'The other question . . .', *Screen*, 24:6, 18–36

Banham, Mary; Hillier, Bevis (1976) *A Tonic to the Nation: The Festival of Britain 1951*, London, Thames and Hudson

Bardgett, Suzanne L. (1995) 'The Holocaust: A New Museum within the Imperial War Museum', London, The Imperial War Museum

Bauman, Zygmunt (1991) *Modernity and the Holocaust*, Cambridge, Polity Press, Revised Paperback Edition

Benedict, Burton (1983) *The Anthropology of the World's Fairs: San Francisco's Panama Pacific International Exposition of 1915*, London and Berkeley, The Lowie Museum of Anthropology in association with Scolar Press

Berenbaum, Michael (1993) *The World Must Know: The History of the Holocaust as Told in the United States Holocaust Memorial Museum*, Boston, Little Brown and Company

Bernstein, Michael André (1997) 'The last injury: competing interpretations of the Nazi genocide and the passionate insistence on its uniqueness', *Times Literary Supplement*, 7 March, 3–4

Big Pit/Pwll Mawr (1992) *The Big Pit Story: A Look at Coalmining in South Wales*, Blaenafon, Big Pit Mining Museum

Birnbaum, S (1990) *Walt Disney World: The Official Guide*, New York, Disney Corporation

Bolton, Lissant (1993) 'Dancing in Mats: Extending Kastom to Women in Vanuatu', PhD Thesis, University of Manchester

Bolton, Lissant (1994) 'The Vanuatu Cultural Centre and its own community', *Journal of Museum Ethnography*, 6, 67–78

Bolton, Lissant (1996) 'An itinerant museum', *Art Asia Pacific*, 3:3, 25–6

Bonnemaison, Joël (1994) *The Tree and the Canoe: History and Ethnogeography of Tanna*, translated and adapted by Josée Pénot-Demetry, Honolulu, University of Hawai'i Press

Bonnemaison, Joël; Kaufmann, Christian; Huffman, Kirk; Tryon, Darrell (1996) *Arts of Vanuatu*, Bathurst, Crawford House Publishing

Bracken, Christopher (1996) *The Potlatch Papers: A Colonial Case History*, Chicago, Chicago University Press

Brett, David (1996) *The Construction of Heritage*, Cork, Cork University Press

Bronner, Simon J. (ed.) (1989) *Consuming Visions: Accumulation and Display of Goods in America 1880–1920*, New York, W. W. Norton & Co.

Brown, Penelope; Levinsin, Stephen C. (1987) *Politeness: Some Universals in Language Usage*, Cambridge, Cambridge University Press

Browne, Sean (1994) 'Heritage in Ireland's tourism recovery' in J. M. Fladmark (ed.) *Cultural Tourism*, 12–25

Bukatman, Scott (1991) 'There's always tomorrowland: Disney and the hypercinematic experience', *October*, 57, 55–78

Burg, David F. (1976) *Chicago's White City of 1893*, Lexington, University Press of Kentucky

Butler, Richard; Hinch, Tom (eds.) (1996) *Tourism and Indigenous Peoples*, London, International Thomson Business Press

Campbell Stephen J. (1994) *The Great Irish Famine: Words and Images from the Famine Museum*, Strokestown Park, County Roscommon, Strokestown, The Famine Museum,

Carrier, James G. (ed.) (1995) *Occidentalism: Images of the West*, Oxford, Clarendon Press

Clifford, James (1988) *The Predicament of Culture: Twentieth-Century Ethnography, Literature and Art*, Cambridge, Harvard University Press,

Clifford, James (1991) 'Four Northwest Coast museums: travel reflections' in I. Karp and S. Lavine (eds.) *Exhibiting Cultures*, 212–54

Clifford, James (1997) *Routes: Travel and Translation in the Late Twentieth Century*, Cambridge, Massachusetts, Harvard University Press

Cohen, Eric (1993) 'The study of touristic images of native peoples: mitigating the sterotype of a stereotype' in Douglas G. Pearce and Richard W, Butler *Tourism Research: Critiques and Challenges*, 36–69

Conan, Michel (1996) 'The Fiddler's indecorous nostalgia', paper delivered at Dumbarton Oaks Studies in Landscape Architecture 1996 Symposium, Washington DC

Cook, James (1777) *A Voyage Towards the South Pole and Round the World Performed in His Majesty's Ships The Resolution and Adventure in the Years 1772, 1773, 1774 and 1775*, London, W. Strahan & T. Cadell (in 2 volumes)

Cooke, Pat (1991) 'The real thing: archaeology and popular culture', *Circa*, 56, 24–9

Cooke, Pat (1992) 'A modern disease: art and heritage management', *Circa*, 61, 30–3

Cooke, Pat (1992) 'Imline de Mholtai do Thaispeántas d'Ionad An Blascaoid Mhóir' (Outline for an Exhibition at the Blasket Island Centre), Dublin, Office of Public Works

Cooke, Pat (1995) *A History of Kilmainham Goal 1796–1924*, Oifig na nOibreacha Poiblí/The Office of Public Works, The Stationery Office, Dublin

Cooke, Pat (1997) 'Image, Drama, History', *Circa*, 80, 42–3

Coombes, Annie E. (1994) 'The distance between two points: global culture and the liberal dilemma' in G. Robertson, M. Marsh et al *Travellers' Tales*, 177–86

Coombes, Annie E. (1994) *Reinventing Africa: Museums, Material Culture and Popular Imagination in Late Victorian and Edwardian England*, New Haven, Yale University Press

Cranmer Webster, Gloria (1988) 'The "R" Word: Repatriation', *Muse*, 6:3, 43–4

Cranmer Webster, Gloria (1991) 'The contemporary potlatch' in A. Jonaitis (ed.) *Chiefly Feasts*, 227–48

Crawford, Margaret (1992) 'The world in a shopping mall' in M. Sorkin *Variations on a Theme Park*, 3–30

Crocombe, Ron (1994) 'Cultural Policies in the Pacific Islands' in L. Lindstrom and G. M. White *Culture – Kastom – Tradition*, 21–54

Culleton, Edward (1990) *Guide to the Irish National Heritage Park, Ferrycarrig, Wexford*, Wexford Heritage Trust Ltd


Davis, Susan G. (1996) 'The theme park: global industry and cultural form', *Media, Culture and Society*, 18: 399–422

Debord, Guy (1994) *The Society of the Spectacle*, New York, Zone Books

de Burlo, Chuck (1996) 'Cultural resistance and ethnic tourism on South Pentecost, Vanuatu' in R. Butler and T. Hinch *Tourism and Indigenous Peoples*, 255–76

Dening, Greg (1994) 'The theatricality of observing and being observed: eighteenth century Europe "discovers" the eighteenth century "Pacific"' in S. Schwartz (ed.) *Implicit Understandings*, 451–83

Dikötter, Frank (1992) *The Discourse of Race in Modern China*, London, Hurst and Company

Dodd, Luke (1992) 'The Famine Museum at Strokestown Park', *Museum Ireland*, 2, 13–18

Dominguez, Virginia R. (1986) 'The marketing of heritage', *American Ethnologist*, 13, 546–55

Dyer, Richard (1993) *The Matter of Images: Essays on Representation*, London, Routledge

Eber, Shirley (ed.) (1992) *Beyond the Green Horizon: Principles for Sustainable Tourism*, Godalming, Worldwide Fund for Nature

Eco, Umberto (1986) *Travels in Hyperreality*, London, Picador

Edenheim, Ralph; Larsson, Lars-Erik; Westberg, Christina (1991) *Skansen*, Stockholm, Informationsgruppen AB

Edwards, Elizabeth (ed.) (1992) *Anthropology and Photography 1860–1920*, New Haven, Yale University Press,

Edwards, Elizabeth (1996) 'Postcards: greetings from another world' in Tom Selwyn (ed.) *The Tourist Image*, 197–221

Elfström, Gunnar (n.d. 1994) *Old Linköping*, Friluftsmuseut Gamla Linköping, Linköping

Eoe, Soroi Marepo; Swadling, Pamela (eds.) (1991) *Museums and Cultural Centres in the Pacific*, Papua New Guinea National Museum, Port Moresby

Errington, Frederick; Gewertz, Deborah (1989) 'Tourism and anthropology in a post-modern world', *Oceania*, 60, 37–54

Fabian, Johannes (1983) *Time and the Other: How Anthropology Makes Its Object*, Columbia University Press, New York

Fabian, Johannes (1990) 'Presence and representation: the other and anthropological writing', *Critical Inquiry*, 16:4, 753–72

Fagence, Michael (1995) 'Ecotourism and Pacific Island nations: towards a realistic interpretation of feasibility', *Studies and Reports*, series B, vol 19, Aix-en-Provence, Centre International de Recherches et d'Etudes Touristiques

Fladmark, J. M. (ed.) (1994) *Cultural Tourism*, Aberdeen, Donhead

Foanaota, Lawrence (1991) 'The Solomon Islands National Museum' in S. M. Eoe and P. Swadling *Museums and Cultural Centres in the Pacific*, 107–12

Foanaota, Lawrence (1996) 'Educating public taste: the National Museum's role in the development of contemporary art in the Solomon Islands', *Artlink*, 16:4, 50–1

Ford, Clellan S. (1971) *Smoke From Their Fires: The Life of a Kwakiutl Chief*, Hamden, Connecticut, Archon Books (unaltered edition of 1941 edition from Yale University Press)


Gale, Alison (1994) *Fuel For Thought: the Status and Future of Coal-Mining Collections in North East Museums*, Newcastle-Upon-Tyne, North of England Museums Service

Gerwertz, Deborah B.; Errington, Frederick K. (1995) 'Duelling currencies in East New Britain: The construction of shell money as national cultural property' in James G. Carrier *Occidentalism: Images of the West*, 161–91

Gibbons, Luke (1996) *Transformations in Irish Culture*, Cork, Cork University Press

Gladney, Dru C. (1994) 'Representing nationality in China: refiguring majority/minority identities', *Journal of Asian Studies*, 53:1, 92–123

Greenblatt, Stephen (1991) 'Resonance and wonder' in I. Karp and S. Lavine (eds.) *Exhibiting Cultures*, 42–56

Greenhalgh, Paul (1988) *Ephemeral Vistas: the Expositions Universelles, Great Exhibitions, and World's Fairs 1851–1939*, Manchester, Manchester University Press


Harvey, Penelope (1996) *Hybrids of Modernity: Anthropology, the Nation State and the Universal Exhibition*, London, Routledge

Haughey, Anthony (1996) *Imeall na h Eorpa/The Edge of Europe*, (téacs/text: Fintan O'Toole), Dublin, An Roinn Ealaíon, Cultúir agus Gaeltachta/Department of Arts, Culture and the Gaeltacht, in association with the Gallery of Photography

Hay, John E. (ed.) (1992) *Ecotourism in the Pacific: Promoting a Sustainable Experience*, Conference Proceedings, University of Auckland

Hayman, Sheila (1989) 'Two-dimensional living', *Independent on Sunday*, 30 June, 15–17

Heberer, Thomas (1989) *China and its National Minorities: Autonomy or Assimilation?*, Armonk, New York, M. E. Sharpe, Inc.

Hendry, Joy (1997) 'Nature Tamed: Gardens as a Microcosm of Japan's View of the World' in Pamela Asquith and Arne Kalland (eds.) *Japanese Images of Nature: Cultural Perspectives*, Richmond, Curzon Press

Hendry, Joy (1997) 'Pine, ponds and pebbles: gardens and visual culture' in M. Banks and H. Morphy (eds.) *Rethinking Visual Anthropology*, 240–55

Hendry, Joy (1997) 'Who is representing whom? Gardens, theme-parks and the anthropologist in Japan' in Allison James, Jennifer Hockey and Andrew Dawson (eds.) *After Writing Culture: Epistemology and praxis in contemporary anthropology*, London, Routledge

Hewison, Robert (1987) *The Heritage Industry: Britain in a Climate of Decline*, London, Methuen

Hinsley, Curtis M. (1991) 'The World as marketplace: commodification of the exotic at the World's Columbian Exposition, Chicago, 1893' in I. Karp and S. Lavine *Exhibiting Cultures*, 344–65

Hitchcock, Michael (1986) 'Images of an ethnic minority in Indonesia: photography and education', *Anthropology Today*, 1, 1, 1–4

Hitchcock, Michael (1995) 'The Indonesian Cultural Village Museum and its Forbears', *Journal of Museum Ethnography*, 7, 17–24

Hitchcock, Michael; King, Victor T.; Parnwell, Michael J. G. (eds.) (1993) *Tourism in South-East Asia*, London, Routledge

Hitchcock, Michael; Norris, Lucy (1995) *Bali: The Imaginary Museum; The Photographs of Walter Spies and Beryl de Zoete*, Kuala Lumpur, Oxford University Press with the co-operation of the Horniman Museum and Gardens

Hitchcock, Michael; Siu, King Chung; Stanley, Nick (1997) 'The Southeast Asian "Living Museum" and its antecedents' in Simone Abram, Don Macleod and Jacqueline Waldren (eds.) *Tourists and Tourism*

Hoggart, Simon (1995) 'Man or mouse on Space Mountain', London, *The Guardian*, 14 June

Howe, K. R.; Kiste, Robert C.; Lal, Brij V. (eds.) (1994) *Tides of History: The Pacific Islands in the Twentieth Century*, Honolulu, University of Hawai'i Press

Hubinger, Václav (1992) 'The creation of Indonesian national identity', *Prague Occasional Papers on Ethnology*, 1

Hudson, Kenneth (1987) *Museums of Influence*, Cambridge, Cambridge University Press

Huffman, Kirk W. (1996) 'Trading, cultural exchange and copyright: important aspects of Vanuatu arts' in J. Bonnemaison et al *Arts of Vanuatu*, 182–94

Huffman, Kirk W. (1996) ' "Up and Over": the opening of the Vanuatu Cultural Centre 1996 Complex's new National Museum building', *Pacific Arts*. 13, 49–58

Hughes-Freeland, Felicia (1993) 'Packaging dreams: Javanese perceptions of tourism and performance' in M. J. Hitchcock et al *Tourism in South-East Asia*, 138–54

Jacknis, Ira (1991) 'George Hunt: collector of Indian specimens' in A. Jonaitis (ed.) *Chiefly Feasts*, 177–225

Jacknis, Ira (1992) 'George Hunt: Kwakiutl photographer' in E. Edwards (ed.) *Anthropology and Photography 1860–1920*, 143–51

Jolly, Margaret (1992) 'Custom and the way of the land: past and present in Vanuatu and Fiji', *Oceania*, 62:4, 330–54

Jolly, Margaret (1994) 'Kastom as commodity: the land dives as indigenous rite and tourist spectacle in Vanuatu' in L. Lindstrom and G. M. White *Culture – Kastom – Tradition*, 131–44

Jolly, Margaret (1996) 'European perceptions of the arts of Vanuatu: engendered colonial interests' in J. Bonnemaison et al *Arts of Vanuatu*, 264, 267–77

Jolly Margaret; Thomas, Nicholas (1992) 'The politics of tradition in the Pacific: introduction', *Oceania*, 62:4, 241–8

Jonaitis, Aldona (ed.) (1991) *Chiefly Feasts: The Enduring Kwakiutl Potlach*, New York and Vancouver, American Museum of Natural History, and Douglas & McIntyre

Jonassen, Jon (1991) *Cook Island Drums*, Rarotonga, Ministry of Cultural Development

Jonassen, Jon (1993) 'Politics and culture in the Pacific Islands', paper presented at Polynesian Cultural Center Alumni Reunion, Educational Conference, Lai'e, Hawai'i, July 13

Kaeppler, Adrienne L. (1996) 'Paradise Regained: the role of Pacific museums in forging national identity' in F. Kaplan *Museums and the Making of 'Ourselves'*, 19–43

Kaplan, Flora E. S. (1996) *Museums and the Making of 'Ourselves': The Role of Objects in National Identity*, London, Leicester University Press

Karim, Wazir Jahan (1996) 'Anthropology without tears: how a "local" sees the "local" and the global' in Henrietta L. Moore *The Future of Anthropological Knowledge*, London, Routledge, 115–38

Karp, Ivan; Lavine, Steven D. (1991) *Exhibiting Cultures: The Poetics and Politics of Museum Display*, Washington D.C., Smithsonian Institution Press

Karp, Ivan; Kraemer, Christine Muller; Lavine, Stephen D. (1992) *Museums and Communities: The Politics of Public Culture*, Smithsonian Institution Press

Karpf, Anne '(1995) The last Jews of Krakow cringe', London, *The Guardian*, October 28

Kasarherou, Emmanuel (195) 'Men of flesh and blood: the Jean-Marie Tijibaou Cultural Centre, Noumea', *Art and Asia Pacific*, 2:4, 90–5

Kasarherou, Emmanuel (1996) 'Kanak Portraits', *Art Asia Pacific*, vol 3:3, 28–9

Keswick, Maggie (1978) *The Chinese Garden: History, Art and Architecture*, London, Academy Editions

Kiberd, Declan (1996) *Inventing Ireland: The Literature of the Modern Nation*, London,

King, Margaret J. (1981) 'Disneyland and Walt Disney World: traditional values in futuristic form', *Journal of Popular Culture*, 15, 116–40

Kirshenblatt-Gimblett, Barbara (1991) 'Objects of ethnography' in I. Karp and S. Lavine *Exhibiting Cultures*, 386–443

Klein, Barbra; Wildbom, Mats (1994) *Swedish Folk Art: All Tradition is Change*, Stockholm, Harry N. Abrams in association with Kulturhuset

Kocher-Schmidt, Christin (1994) 'Cultural identity as a coping strategy towards modern political structures: the Nayudos case, Papua New Guinea', *Bijdragen Tod en Taal-, Land- en Volkenkunde*, 149:4, 781–801

Kou, Zhengling (1992) 'Kunming builds ethnic culture tourist zone'. *Beijing Review*, 35:14, 29

Kratz, Corinne A.; Karp, Ivan (1993) 'Wonder and worth: Disney museums in World Showcase', *Museum Anthropology*, 7:3, 32–42

Kuentz, Jane (1993) 'It's a small world after all: Disney and the pleasures of identification', *South Atlantic Quarterly*, 92:1, 63–88

Lewis, Peter (1991) 'The making of a museum' in *Beamish: The North of England Open Air Museum*, Beamish, Co. Durham

Lewis, Peter (1995) *Welcome to Beamish*, Beamish, Co. Durham, The North of England Open Air Museum

Ley, D.; Olds, K. (1988) 'Landscape as spectacle: world's fairs and the culture of heroic consumption', *Environment and Planning D: Space and Society*, 6, 191–212

Lindstrom, Lamont (1993) *Cargo Cult: Strange Stories of Desire from Melanesia and Beyond*, Honolulu, University of Hawai'i Press

Lindstrom, Lamont (1994) 'Traditional cultural policy in Melanesia (Kastom Polisi long Kastom)' in L. Lindstrom and G. M. White *Culture – Kastom – Tradition*, 67–81

Lindstrom, Lamont (1995) 'Cargoism and Occidentalism' in J. G. Carrier *Images of the West*, 33–60

Lindstrom, Lamont; White, Geoffrey M. (eds.) (1994) *Culture – Kastom – Tradition: Developing Cultural Policy in Melanesia*, Suva, University of the South Pacific

Linnekin, Jocelyn (1992) 'On the theory and politics of cultural construction in the Pacific', *Oceania*, 62:4, 249–63

The Little World Museum of Man (n.d.) *The Little World Museum of Man: the First Open-Air Museum of the Mankind of the World*, Aichi.

Litzinger, Ralph (1995) 'The work of culture and memory in contemporary China', *Working Papers in Asian/Pacific Studies*, Durham NC, Duke University

Lowenthal, David (1985) *The Past is a Foreign Country*, Cambridge, Cambridge University Press

Lowenthal, David (1997) *The Heritage Crusade and the Spoils of History*, London, Viking

Ma, Chi Man (1989) *Splendid China: Miniature Scenic Spot: Grand Opening Souvenir Catalogue*, Shenzhen, Splendid China Development Company

Mauzé, Marie (1992) 'Exhibiting one's culture: two case studies – The Kwagiulth Museum and the U'Mista Cultural Centre', *Native American Studies*, 6:1, 27–30

MacCannell, Dean (1973) 'Staged authenticity: arrangements of social space in tourist settings', *American Journal of Sociology*, 79:3, 589–603

MacCannell, Dean (1992) *Empty Meeting Grounds: The Tourist Paper*, London, Routledge

MacConghail, Muiris (1987) *The Blaskets: People and Literature*, Dublin, Country House

MacDonald, Sharon; Fyffe, Gordon (eds.) (1996) *Theorising Museums*, Oxford, Blackwell Publishers/Sociological Review

McGrevy, Noel L. (1975) 'The Polynesian Cultural Center: a model for cultural consensus' (mimeograph), Lai'e, Polynesian Cultural Center

Macnair, Peter L. (1982) 'The northwest coast collection: legacy of a living culture', *Field Museum of Natural History Bulletin*, 53:4, 3–9

Mead, Sidney Moko (1973) 'Folklore and place names in Santa Ana, Solomon Islands', *Oceania*, 43:3, 215–37

Mead, Sidney Moko (1983) 'Indigenous models of museums in Oceania', *Museum*, 138, 98–101

Middleton, Victor T. C. (1990) *Review of Museums and Cultural Centres in the South Pacific*, Suva, Tourism Council of the South Pacific

Mitchell, Timothy (1988) *Colonising Egypt*, Cambridge, Cambridge University Press

Mitchell, Timothy (1989) 'The world as exhibition', *Comparative Study of Society and History*, 3:2, 217–36

Natanson, Maurice (1968) *Literature, Philosophy and the Social Sciences: Essays in Existentialism and Phenomenology*, The Hague, Martinus Nijhoff

National Coal Mining Museum for England (n.d. 1996) *Go Down A Real Coal Mine* (Education Pack), Wakefield

National Museum of Tanzania (1966) *Maelezo Ya Kijiji Cha Makumbusho: Guide to Village Museum*, Dar Es Salaam

Nelson, Steve (1986) 'Walt Disney's EPCOT and the World's Fair Performance tradition', *Drama Review*, Winter, 106–46

Ní Shúilleabháin, Eibhlís (1978) *Letters from the Great Blasket*, Cork, Mercier Press

Nora, Pierre (1989) 'Between memory and history: les lieux de mémoire', *Representations*, 26, 7–25

Norris Nicholson, Heather (1992) 'Cultural Centres or Trading Posts?', *Museums Journal*, 92:8, 31–4


O'Brien, Robert (1983) *Hands Across the Water: The Story of the Polynesian Cultural Center*, Lai'e, Polynesian Cultural Center

Ó Ciosáin, Niall (1994) 'Hungry Grass: the new Famine Museum at Strokestown House', *Circa*, 67, 24–7

O'Connor, Ciaran (1992?) 'The Blasket Centre', *Landscape. Architecture News*, 3–6

O'Crohan, Seán (1992) *A Day in Our Life*, Oxford, Oxford University Press

O'Crohan, Tomás (1951) *The Islandman*, Oxford, Oxford University Press

O'Crohan, Tomás (1986) *Island Cross-Talk: Pages from a Blasket Island Diary*, Oxford, Oxford University Press

O'Guiheen, Micheál (1982) *A Pity Youth does Not Last: Reminiscences of the Last of the Great Blasket Island's Poets and Storytellers*, Oxford, Oxford University Press

O'Hanlon, Michael (1993) *Paradise: Portraying the New Guinea Highlands*, London, British Museum Press

O'Hanlon, Michael (1995) 'Medusa's Art: Interpreting Melanesian Shields' in A. Taverelli (ed.) *Protection, Power and Display*, 74–108

O'Sullivan, Maurice (1983) *Twenty Years A-Growing*, Oxford, Oxford University Press

Oppenheimer, Paul (1966) *From Belsen to Buckingham Palace*, Newark, Beth Shalom Ltd

Parr, Martin; Winchester, Simon (1995) *Small World: A Global Photographic Project 1987–1994*, Stockport, Dewi Lewis Publishing

Pearce, Douglas B.; Butler, Richard W. (1993) *Tourism Research: Critiques and Challenges*, London, Routledge

Pemberton, John (1994) *On the Subject of 'Java'*, Ithica, Cornell University Press

Pemberton, John (1994) 'Recollections from "Beautiful Indonesia" (somewhere beyond the postmodern)', *Public Culture*, 6, 241–62

Pere, Baden (1980) 'Commercializing culture or culturizing commerce?' in F. Rajotte and R. Crocrombe *Pacific Tourism as Islanders See It*, 139–45

Phillips, Ruth B. (1995) 'Why not tourist art? Significant silences in Native American museum representations' in G. Prakesh (ed.) *After Colonialism*, 98–125

Pinney, Christopher; Wright, Chris; Poignant, Roslyn (1995) 'The Impossible Science' in *The Impossible Science of Being: Dialogues between Anthropology and Photography*, London, The Photographers' Gallery

Polynesian Cultural Center (n.d. 1995?) *Mana: The Spirit of Our People*, Lai'e, Polynesian Cultural Center

Poulot, Dominique (1994) 'Identity as self-discovery: the Ecomuseum in France' in D. Sherman and I. Rogoff (eds.) *Museum Culture*, 66–84

Prakash, Gyan (ed.) (1995) *After Colonialism: Imperial Histories and Postcolonial Displacements*, Princeton, Princeton University Press

Pratt, Mary Louise (1992) *Imperial Eyes: Travel Writing and Transculturation*, London, Routledge,

Price, Richard; Price, Sally (1992) *Equatoria*, London, Routledge

Price, Richard; Price, Sally (1995) *Enigma Variations*, Cambridge and London, Harvard University Press

Project on Disney (1995) *Inside the Mouse: Work and Play at Disney World*, London, Rivers Oram Press,

Putnam, Tim; Newton, Charles (eds.) (1990) *Household Choices*, London, Futures Publications

Rajotte, Freda (1980) 'Tourism impact in the Pacific' in F. Rajotte and R. Crocrombe (eds.) *Pacific Tourism as Islanders See It*, 1–14

Rajotte, Freda; Crocrombe, Ron (1980) *Pacific Tourism as Islanders See It*, Suva, University of the South Pacific

Regenvanu, Ralph (1996) 'Spirit Blong Bubu I Kam Bak: Vanuatuans reunited with their Past', *Artlink*, 16:4, 37–9

Regenvanu, Ralph (1996) 'Transforming representations: a sketch of the contemporary-art scene in Vanuatu' in J. Bonnemaison et al *Arts of Vanuatu*, 309–17

Riegel, Henrietta (1996) 'Into the heart of irony: ethnographic exhibitions and the politics of difference' in S. MacDonald and G. Fyfe *Theorising Museums*, 83–104

Riggins, Stephen H. (ed.) (1994) *The Socialness of Things: Essays on the Socio-Semiotics of Objects*, Berlin, Mouton de Gruyter

Riley, Robert; Young, Terence (eds.) (1998) *The Landscapes of Theme Parks: Antecedents and Variations*, Studies in Landscape Architecture, Washington, DC, Harvard University Press

Robertson, George; Marsh, Melinda; Tickner, Lisa; Bird, Jon; Curtis, Barry; Putnam, Tim (1994) *Travellers' Tales: Narratives of Home and Displacement*, London, Routledge

Robertson, Roland (1990) 'After nostalgia? Wilfull nostalgia and the phases of globalization' in Bryan S. Turner (ed.) *Theories of Modernity and Postmodernity*, 45–61

Robinson, Ann-Marie (1991) 'The Polynesian Cultural Centre: A Study of Authenticity', MA Thesis, California State University, Chico

Ross, Andrew (1994) *The Chicago Gangster Theory of Life: Nature's Debt to Society*, London, Verso

Royal Anthropological Institute (1995) report on the RAI/ESRC Exploratory Workshop 'International NGO's and Complex Political Emergencies: Perspectives from Anthropology', London

Rudkin, Brenda; Hall, C. Michael (1996) 'Unable to see the forest for the trees: ecotourism development in Solomon Islands' in R. Butler and T. Hinch *Tourism and Indigenous Peoples*, 203–26

Rydell, Robert W. (1989) 'The culture of imperial abundance: World's Fairs in the making of American culture' in J. Bronner (ed.) *Consuming Visions*, 191–216

Said, Edward W. (1989) 'Representing the colonized: anthropology's interlocuters', *Critical Inquiry*, 15, 205–25

Sarawak Economic Development Corporation (1990) Kampung Budaya Sarawak: *Living Museum of Sarawak, A Window of Cultural Diversity*, Kuching

Sayers, Peig (1978) *An Old Woman's Reflections*, Oxford, Oxford University Press

Schneebaum, Tobias (1991) *The Asmat: Dynamics of Irian, Jakarta*, to accompany the Festival of Indonesia

Schneebaum, Tobias (1993) 'Touring Asmat', *Pacific Arts*, 7, 52–6

Schwartz, Stuart B. (ed.) (1994) *Implicit Understandings: Observing, Reporting and Reflecting on the Encounters between Europeans and Other Peoples in the Early Modern Era*, Cambridge, Cambridge University Press

Selwyn, Tom (ed.) (1996) *The Tourist Image: Myths and Myth Making in Tourism*, Chichester, John Wiley

Sheehy, Jean (1980) *The Rediscovery of Ireland's Past: The Celtic Revival 1830–1930*, London, Thames and Hudson

Shen, Ping; Chueng, Yuet Sim (eds.) *China Folk Culture Villages*, Shenzhen, Splendid China Development Company

Shenzhen Architectural Design Corporation (1990) 'The "Splendid China" Planning' in *Shenzhen Urban Planning and Design: A Compilation for the First Decade Celebration of Shenzhen Special Economic Zone*, Shenzhen, 95–8

Shenzhen World Miniature Co. Ltd. (1995) *Window Of The World*, Shenzhen, Splendid China Development Company,

Sherman, Daniel J.; Rogoff, Irit (eds.) (1994) *Museum Culture: Histories, Discourse, Spectacles*, London, Routledge

Shorland-Ball, Rob (1996) *Museums and Coalmining: A Study for the Museums and Galleries Commission of the Representation of Coalmining in Museums, Heritage Centres and Other Displays*, London, Museums and Galleries Commission

Simpson, Moira G. (1996) *Making Representations: Museums in the Post-Colonial Era*, London, Routledge

Smith, Valene L. (ed.) (1977) *Hosts and Guests: The Anthropology of Tourism*, Philadelphia, University of Pennsylvania Press

Snow, Philip; Waine, Stefanie (1979) *The People from the Horizon: An Illustrated History of Europeans among the South Sea Islanders*, London, Phaidon

Sofield, Trevor H. B. (1996) 'Anuha Island resort, Solomon Islands: a case study of failure' in R. Butler and T. Hinch *Tourism and Indigenous Peoples*, 176–202

Sorkin, Michael (1992) *Variations on a Theme Park: The New American City and the End of Public Space*, New York, Hill & Wang

South Pacific Forum (with the United Nations Development Programme), Suva, (1995) *Suva Declaration on Sustainable Human Development in the Pacific*

Speiser, Felix (1991) *Ethnology of Vanuatu: an Early Twentieth Century Study* (translated 1991 by D. Q. Stephenson), Bathurst, Crawford House Press

Spivak, Gayatri Chakravorty (1988) 'Subaltern studies: deconstructing historiography' in her *In Other Worlds: Essays in Cultural Politics*, New York & London, Routledge, 197–221

Splendid China (1990) *The World's Largest Miniature Scenic Spot*, Shenzhen, Splendid China Development Company

Stagles, Joan and Ray (1984) *The Blasket Islands: Next Parish America*, Dublin, O'Brien Press,

Stanley, Nick (1989) 'The unstable object: reviewing the status of ethnographic artefacts', *Journal of Design History*, 2, 2/3, 107–22

Stanley, Nick (1994) 'Melanesian artifacts as cultural markers: a micro-anthropological study' in Stephen H. Riggins (ed.) *The Socialness of Things*, 173–99

Stanley, Nick (1994) 'Recording island Melanesia: the significance of the Melanesian Mission in museum records', *Pacific Arts*, 9 and 10, 25–41

Stanley, Nick (1997) 'Old collections and new connections: innovations in the South Pacific' in K. Schofield (ed.) *Connections and Collections: Museums, Galleries and Education*, London, London University Institute of Education, 13–26

Stanley, Nick (1997) 'The new indigènes: Culture, Politics and Representation', *Journal of Art & Design Education*, 16:3, 341–6

Stanley, Nick (1998) 'Chinese theme parks and national identity' in R. Riley and T. Young (eds.) *The Landscapes of Theme Parks*

Stanley, Nick; Siu, King Chung (1995) 'Representing the past as the future: the Shenzhen Chinese Folk Culture Villages and the marketing of Chinese identity', *Journal of Museum Ethnography*, 7, 25–40

Stanton, Max (1977) 'The Polynesian Cultural Center: a multi-ethnic model of seven Pacific cultures' in V. L. Smith *Hosts and Guests*, 193–206

Suharno, Ignatius; Mitaart, Bernard (1977) *The Art of Woodcarving in Irian Jaya*, Jayapura, Regional Government of Irian Jaya

Swain, Margaret Byrne (1990) 'Commoditizing ethnicity in Southwest China', *Cultural Survival Quarterly*, 14:1, 26–9

Swain, Margaret Byrne (1995) 'Staging sites/sights of Yunnan China's Stone Forest; whether post-modern authenticity', paper delivered at 'Rewriting the Pacific: Culture, Frontiers, and the Migration of Metaphors Pacific Bridges Conference', October 19–22, University of California, Davis

Task Force on Museums and First Peoples (1994) *Turning the Page: Forging New Partnerships between Museums and First Peoples*, Ottawa, Assembly of First Nations and Canadian Museums Association, Third Edition

Taumoepeau, Afu (1994) 'How the Tonga National Center attempts to do it' in Pacific Museum Directors Workshop: Developing a Living Museum with Grassroots Support, UNESCO, Apia, 19–21

Taussig, Michael (1993) *Mimesis and Alterity: A Particular History of the Senses*, New York and London, Routledge,

Tavarelli, Andrew (ed.) (1995) *Protection, Power and Display: Shields of Island Southeast Asia and Melanesia*, Boston, Boston College Museum of Art

Theroux, Paul (1992) *The Happy Isles of Oceania: Paddling the Pacific*, London, Penguin Books

Thomas, Nicholas (1991) *Entangled Objects: Exchange, Material Culture, and Colonialism in the Pacific*, Cambridge Massachusetts, Harvard University Press,

Thomas, Nicholas (1994) *Colonialism's Culture: Anthropology, Travel and Government*, Oxford, Polity Press

Thomas, Nicholas (1994) 'Licensed curiosity': Cook's Pacific Voyages' in J. Elsner and R. Cardinal *The Cultures of Collecting*, London, Reaktion Books, 116–36

Thomas, Nicholas (1995) *Oceanic Art*, London, Thames and Hudson

Thomas, Nicholas (1996) 'Dance party', *Art Asia Pacific*, 3:3, 26–7

Thomson, George (1988) *Island Home: The Blasket Heritage*, Dingle, Brandon Book Publishers

Toren, Christina (1991) 'Leonardo's "Last Supper" in Fiji' in S. Hiller (ed.) *The Myth of Primitivism: Perspectives on Art*, London, Routledge, 261–79

Totu, Victor; Roe, David (1991) 'The Guadalcanal Cultural Centre, Solomon Islands: keeping kastom in the 1980's' in S. M. Eoe and P. Swadling *Museums and Cultural Centres in the Pacific*, 113–31

Tourism Council of the South Pacific (1988) *Tourism Awareness: A Manual for National Tourism Organizations*, Suva

Tourism Council of the South Pacific (1990) *Guidelines for the Integration of Tourism Development and Environmental Protection in the South Pacific*, Suva

Treib, Marc (1996) 'The case of Huis Ten Bosch (Japan): theme park; themed living', paper delivered at Dumbarton Oaks Studies in Landscape Architecture Symposium, Washington D.C.

Tsu, Frances Ya-Sing (1988) *Landscape Design in Chinese Gardens*, New York, McGraw Hill

Turner, Bryan S. (ed.) *Theories of Modernity and Postmodernity*, London, Sage Publications

Turner, W. J. (1947) *Exmoor Village: A General Account based on Factual Material from Mass-Observation*, with 29 Photographs in Colour and 22 Photographs in Black and White by John Hinde, London, George G. Harrap & Co.

Ua Maoileoin, Pádraig (1993) *Na Blascaodaí/The Blaskets*, Dublin, The Stationery Office,

Urry, John (1990) *The Tourist Gaze*, London, Sage

Urry, John (1995) *Consuming Places*, London, Routledge

Volkman, Toby Alice (1990) 'Vision and revisions: Toraja culture and the tourist gaze', *American Ethnologist*, 17:1, 91–110

Wade, July; Gillenwater, Sharon; Ritz, Stacy (1992) *Disneyland and Beyond: the Ultimate Family Guidebook*, Berkeley, Ulysses Press,

Wall, Geoffrey; Oswald, Barbara (1990) 'Cultural groups as tourist attractions', *Studies and Reports*, series E, vol. 7, Aix-en Provence, Centre International de Recherches et d'Etudes Touristiques

Webb, T. D. (1994) 'Highly structured tourist art: form and meaning of the Polynesian Cultural Center', *The Contemporary Pacific*, 6:1, 59–85

Weinberg, Jeshajahu; Elieli, Rina (1995) *The Holocaust Museum in Washington*, New York, Rizzoli International Publications

White, Geoffrey M. (1995) 'Remembering Guadalcanal: national identity and transitional memory-making', *Public Culture*, 7, 529–55

White, Geoffrey M. (1996) 'War remains: the culture of preservation in the Southwest Pacific', *Cultural Resource Management*, 19, 3, 52–6

Wood, Peter H. (1994) 'North America in the era of Captain Cook: three glimpses of Indian–European contact in the age of the American revolution' in S. Schwartz (ed.) *Implicit Understandings*, 484–501

Wright, Susan (1998) 'The politicization of 'culture', *Anthropology Today*, 14:1, 7–15

Wylson, Anthony and Patricia (1994) *Theme Parks, Leisure Centres, Zoos and Aquaria*, Harlow, Longman

Yao, Te-hsiung (ed.) (1990) *Formosan Aboriginal Culture Village*, Taichung, Yin-Shua Publishing Co., 3rd Edition,

Young, James A. (1993) *The Texture of Memory: Holocaust Memorials and Meanings*, New Haven, Yale University Press

Young, James A. (ed.) (1994) *The Art of Memory: Holocaust Museums in History*, Munich, Prestel Verlag

**Video tapes**

Splendid China Corporation (1992) *China Folk Culture Villages*

The Polynesian Cultural Center (1994) *Mana: The Spirit of Our People*

RTE Productions (1994) *Ôileán Eile*

International Video Network Ltd (1995) *The Pacific Islands Experience: Fiji, Vanuatu, Solomon Islands*

# Index

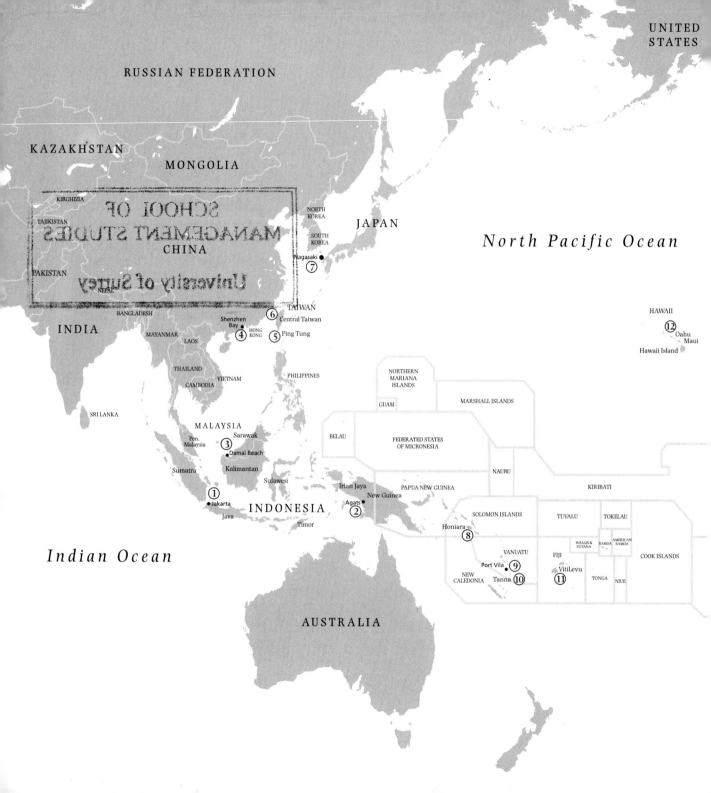